Introduction to International Politics

CONTEMPORARY POLITICAL STUDIES SERIES

Series Editor: John Benyon, *University of Leicester*

A series which provides authoritative and concise introductory accounts of key topics in contemporary political studies

Other titles in the series include:

Elections and Voting Behaviour in Britain
DAVID DENVER, *University of Lancaster*

Pressure Groups, Politics and Democracy in Britain
WYN GRANT, *University of Warwick*

UK Political Parties since 1945
Edited by ANTHONY SELDON, *Institute of Contemporary British History*

Politics and Policy Making in Northern Ireland
MICHAEL CONNOLLY, *University of Ulster*

British Political Ideologies
ROBERT LEACH, *Leeds Polytechnic*

Local Government and Politics in Britain
JOHN KINGDOM, *Sheffield Polytechnic*

British Government: The Central Executive Territory
PETER MADGWICK, Professor Emeritus, *Oxford Polytechnic*

Race and Politics in Britain
SHAMIT SAGGAR, *Queen Mary and Westfield College, University of London*

CONTEMPORARY POLITICAL STUDIES

Introduction to International Politics

DEREK HEATER AND G. R. BERRIDGE

New York London Toronto Sydney Tokyo Singapore

First published 1993 by
Harvester Wheatsheaf
Campus 400, Maylands Avenue
Hemel Hempstead
Hertfordshire, HP2 7EZ
A division of
Simon & Schuster International Group

Typeset in 10/12 pt Times
by Pentacor PLC

Printed and bound in Great Britain by Biddles Ltd,
Guildford and King's Lynn

British Library Cataloguing in Publication Data

A catalogue record for this book is available from the British Library

ISBN 0–7450–1090–3 (hbk)
ISBN 0–7450–1091–1 (pbk)

2 3 4 5 97 96 95 94

Contents

Preface

'International politics' is not a contradiction in terms despite the arguments of some political scientists. True, if we define politics as activity and thinking related to government, then there can be no international politics for the simple reason that there is no international government. But this is an unhelpfully narrow definition of politics. Relations between states clearly involve politics; they concern differences and tensions that require containment or resolution. Without such containment and resolution, wars – that is, the breakdown and negation of politics – would be even more endemic.

The study of international relations or politics emerged as an identifiable subject after the First World War. Since then the techniques of many disciplines (notably history, law, philosophy and economics) have been used to enhance our understanding of the relations between states. The underlying motive has almost always been the urge to comprehend and even to improve the methods states currently use to live in some kind of working relationship.

The present book is designed for those readers who wish to acquire a basic understanding. We presuppose no background knowledge beyond that which a lively interest in current world affairs and contemporary history provides. However, writing about these matters presents two problems.

First, because in reality international politics are a complicated network of interconnections, selecting and stranding out separate topics is difficult. We have chosen fifteen topics which we believe are the most crucial and we have clustered them under three headings: power, justice and order. These are surely three of the most central concepts underpinning any study of politics.

The second problem relates to the writing of any book that focuses on the present. Whatever is 'the present' at the time of writing is no longer 'the present' after the book is published. We have therefore adopted two devices. One is to write about issues and systems we judge will be of continuing interest and concern for many years yet; and we have provided illustrative detail mainly from recent times. Secondly, where we have referred to matters particularly close to the time of writing, we have indicated this in the text.

Part of the intellectual exercise involved in the study of international politics is, in fact, the constant necessity for the individual to relate new events and developments to a framework of understanding already firmly in place. We hope that this book will provide such a framework.

Derek Heater
G.R. Berridge
May 1992

Part I

Power

1

The Ending of the Cold War

The nature of the cold war

The states-system is an organic kaleidoscope. Historical forces of wealth, demography, military power, personal ambitions and ideology shake the pieces into constantly shifting patterns of alliances and enmity. But as we watch these changes occurring in the course of history we notice too that the component pieces of the picture alter in size. States grow, then shrivel; they rise and decline in power over the ages. And much of the fascination of the study of international relations lies in the attempt to understand how the various patterns work: whether a single state becomes so massively powerful as to be utterly dominant; whether several great powers, with minor allies perhaps, can be kept in balance with each other; whether rapid changes in relative power can be managed without the violence of war.

The era of the cold war produced a simple pattern. Two states, the United States and USSR, grew to such colossal strength as, between them, to dominate most of the planet. Like a giant bar magnet this international system led to a clustering of minor states round the two superpower poles. This bipolar world was rendered even simpler by two other factors. One was the ideological hatred which kept the two ends determinedly poles apart: capitalism and Communism were mutually repellent. The other factor was the possession by both superpowers of nuclear weapons. Any attempt by one superpower to neutralise the strength of the other would probably entail mutual annihilation. The simple dual balance of power was sustained by the balance of terror.

To discard our two analogies, we may say, alternatively, that the cold war was characterised by three major features: geopolitical relationships, ideological tensions and an arms race. It will be useful briefly to explain each of these.

The following quotation places the cold war in historical perspective:

> There are at the present time two great nations in the world. . . . I allude to the Russians and the Americans. . . .The Anglo-American relies upon personal interest to accomplish his ends, and gives free scope to the unguided strength and common sense of the people; the Russian centres all the authority of society in a single arm. The principal instrument of the former is freedom; of the latter, servitude. Their starting-point is different, and their courses are not the same; yet each of them seems marked out by the will of Heaven to sway the destinies of half the globe.
>
> (Tocqueville, 1956 edn, p. 142)

Those words, written by the French politician and scholar Alexis de Tocqueville, were published in 1835.

It was not, however, until after the Second World War that Tocqueville's forecast became reality and the two giant powers became bitter rivals. By about 1950 the two power blocs seemed solidly in place. The United States spawned military, naval and air bases across both the Pacific and Atlantic oceans. Spanning the Atlantic was the command system integrating the forces of North America and Western Europe – the North Atlantic Treaty Organisation (NATO). The Soviet Union, for her part, had substantial forces in place in the satellite Communist states of Eastern Europe, as well as fraternal Communist regimes in Asia, most notably China.

A non-aligned movement of primarily Afro-Asian states also grew up. Its object was to prevent the Third World from being attracted into the magnetic fields of either the American-dominated or the Soviet-dominated worlds. Even so, this did not stop the superpowers from trying to draw Third World countries into their spheres of influence – the United States operating mainly in Latin America, the Soviet Union, mainly in the Middle East and then Africa. One US Secretary of State, John Foster Dulles (1952–9), even went as far as to suggest that non-alignment was immoral. The cold war was a struggle between good and evil. The Americans were the righteous and should be supported.

The cold war was, therefore, not just a power political rivalry in the traditional sense – like that between Rome and Carthage in the third century BC or between France and Britain in the eighteenth century, for instance. It contained the intensifying element of ideology. On the one side was materialist Communism in its brutalised Stalinist form. On the other, Western capitalist democracy, sometimes expounded with Christian overtones.

The teachings of Karl Marx provided a secular creed as an alternative to spiritual religions. Heaven, paradise or nirvana was to be attained on this earth by means of radical economic and social changes. This promise or threat of revolution (depending on one's point of view) was a challenge to existing orders. When the revolution became reality in Russia in 1917 the hopes of the disadvantaged and the fears of the contented were stirred into agitated life. For some four decades after 1945 a growing number of countries tried the experiment. However, fears came increasingly to overwhelm hopes as, in so many countries which acquired Communist governments, revolution was succeeded by bloody terror and the iron discipline of the police state. Even the promised economic advantages failed to materialise to any evident degree.

As evidence accumulated of the apparent capacity of Communism to spread and of its tendency to adopt an authoritarian style, so the governments of the Western world became increasingly hostile to the ideology. Its atheism offended Christians; its authoritarianism worried those who appreciated the values of political and civil freedom; and its challenge to private wealth and the market economy frightened those who believed these conditions to be beneficial. In this last category we may count Western financial and commercial interests operating in underdeveloped countries where the appeal of Communism rendered their investments and profits vulnerable to nationalisation.

The Soviet leaders portrayed the West as decadent imperialists; American leaders portrayed Communist regimes as terrible autocracies. 'We will bury you,' declared the Soviet leader Khrushchev, boasting the superiority of the Communist system; US

President Reagan, a quarter of a century later, castigated the USSR as an 'evil empire'.

Insults are not lethal; nuclear weapons are. The 'cold war' (a term coined by the American Bernard Baruch in 1947) was 'cold' precisely because the principals did not engage in a 'hot' fighting war with each other. The conflict was prosecuted as a verbal confrontation or as localised wars in each of which only one superpower was directly involved – for example, the United States in Vietnam in the 1960s or the USSR in Afghanistan in the 1980s.

Nevertheless, both sides built up immense forces designed for use against each other. Initially these were equipped primarily with conventional weapons. As the years wore on huge stockpiles of nuclear weapons of ever-increasing variety and sophistication were amassed and came to be relied upon in tactical and strategic planning. Theoretically the purpose of these weapons of unthinkably awesome destructive power was to deter: that is, the threat of their use would inhibit any leader from either starting a war or crossing the nuclear threshold should war in fact break out. The matter of armaments is dealt with in Chapter 3. It is sufficient here to note that by the 1980s the two sides had between them some 50,000 nuclear warheads.

The taut superpower relations, caused by and expressed in these terms, could hardly fail to be a dominant influence in international relations generally during the cold war period, 1947–90. Yet relatively simple as the world scene was made by this tension, we must be wary of oversimplifying the picture. In the first place, some members of the superpowers' camps were at times less than wholly loyal or committed to the bipolar model of the world. For instance, President de Gaulle, sensitive of French pride and resentful of American influence, in 1966 withdrew French forces from NATO's integrated command. Even more dramatically on the Communist side of the cold war, Soviet forces intervened violently to suppress a popular uprising in Hungary in 1956, and a quarrel between the USSR and China became so aggravated that small-scale skirmishes broke out between contingents of their armies in the late 1960s.

Secondly, it would be wrong to assume from the above survey that relations between the United States and USSR were maintained at a constant sub-zero temperature. To change the metaphor, tension was occasionally wound up, sometimes almost to snapping point – for example, in the Berlin blockade in 1948, the Cuban missile crisis in 1962, and the Soviet invasion of Afghanistan in 1979.

Yet at other times relations were happier. After the death of Stalin in 1953 Khrushchev attempted a policy of 'thaw'. Two years later the American, Soviet, British and French leaders met in a summit conference at Geneva and posed for photographs wreathed in 'Geneva spirit' smiles. It is also true that at no time during the cold war were formal diplomatic relations severed. However, the Cuban missile crisis, which seemed to bring the world to the brink of nuclear war, was a fearful shock to that system. What the tense events of October 1962 revealed was the need for more rapid means of communication for crisis resolution, such as a 'hot-line' (see Chapter 3). The 1970s too, like the 1950s, was a period of relaxation, known as détente, when progress was made in two sets of Strategic Arms Limitation Talks (SALT).

The final thaw

Neither the 1950s thaw nor the 1970s détente were more than fleeting episodes. The change in the relationships between the superpowers and their blocs about 1990 was, however, of deeper significance. By that time most of the participants were willing to seize an opportunity to bring the cold war to a close if it were offered. Dramatic changes in the Soviet Union provided that opportunity.

In March 1985 Mikhail Gorbachev became the Soviet leader. He brought to the task of conducting his country's foreign policy a fresh and flexible mind. From 1985 to 1990 he worked in harmony with a like-minded Foreign Minister, Eduard Shevardnadze. Khrushchev had renounced the classical Leninist doctrine of the inevitability of war between Communism and capitalism in 1956. But his alternative of 'peaceful coexistence' had still posited inevitable rivalry, bitter indeed in its prosecution short of war. Gorbachev discarded even this belief in his 'New Thinking'. He wrote: 'The development of a new mode of thinking requires dialogue not only with people who hold the same views but also with those who think differently and represent a philosophical and political system that is different from ours' (Gorbachev, 1987, p. 152).

Gorbachev had two very compelling reasons for seeking more amicable relations with the West. One was the fearful state of the Soviet economy. Food production and distribution could not cope with the needs of the population; the quality of consumer goods was shoddy; and a massive proportion of the country's wealth was being absorbed by military expenditure. Though it is difficult to make accurate computations for the Soviet Union, it is likely that in 1985, proportionately, it was spending almost three times as much of its wealth on the armed forces as the United States (19 per cent compared with 6.7 per cent).

One drain, of skilled manpower as well as money, was the development of missiles and guidance systems for nuclear weapons. Gorbachev recognised that the nuclear arms race was not only costly but dangerous. In a key speech in 1986 he declared: 'nuclear weapons harbour a hurricane which is capable of sweeping the human race from the face of the earth.' Consequently, he announced the imperative need 'to terminate the material preparations for nuclear war' (Gorbachev, 1986, p. 80).

The Soviet leader rapidly translated his 'New Thinking' into effective action. He held summit conferences with the US Presidents – with Reagan at Reykjavik in 1986 and Washington in 1987 and with Bush on board ship in Maltese waters in 1989. At the Washington summit the two superpowers signed the Intermediate-range Nuclear Forces (INF) treaty – the first agreement actually to reduce stockpiles of nuclear weapons, namely, land-based medium-range missiles (see p. 19). Gorbachev also unilaterally started to withdraw some forces from the territories of the East European states (see p. 20). Soviet troops were also withdrawn from their bloody involvement in the Afghan civil war. In the United Nations Soviet delegates adopted a much more co-operative attitude, notably in supporting the United States in its initiative to condemn and then engage in war with Iraq over her seizure of Kuwait in 1990–1 (see Chapter 12).

The most startling events took place in Eastern Europe. Their outcome was materially affected by Gorbachev's policy of non-intervention. After the Second World War the presence of the Red Army ensured the establishment of Communist governments in the countries of Eastern Europe. Normal contact with the West was prevented by what Churchill called the 'Iron Curtain'. The chink in that barrier, namely, continued access between the eastern and western sectors of Berlin, was sealed by the construction of the Berlin Wall in 1961. Behind the Iron Curtain discontent periodically broke out in popular demonstrations, which were suppressed by force. In 1968 the Soviet leader justified this interference on the grounds that it was necessary to maintain 'socialism' in the region; this was known as the 'Brezhnev Doctrine'.

Even before the emergence of Gorbachev the system was starting to unravel in Poland. In 1980 popular riots forced the Party leader to resign; and the trade union 'Solidarity' was formed, free of any Communist Party control. Would Soviet forces move in as they had in Hungary in 1956 and Czechoslovakia in 1968? The ailing Brezhnev stayed his hand.

Then, from the summer of 1989 to the spring of 1990, exciting events rapidly followed each other. In Poland Solidarity, having turned into a political party, defeated the Communist Party in elections and the first non-Communist took office as prime minister in an East European state since the start of the cold war. Hungary opened its frontier with Austria, allowing (via Czechoslovakia) an exodus of discontented East Germans to West Germany. In East Germany the Berlin Wall was breached. In Czechoslovakia, the formerly imprisoned playwright Vaclav Havel became President, following a relatively peaceful 'velvet revolution'. In Romania, in contrast, a violent revolution was necessary to rid the country of the hated and mentally unbalanced dictator Ceauşescu.

By 1991 nothing was left of the former Soviet 'empire' in Eastern Europe. East Germany was merged into the Federal Republic with surprisingly little complaint from Gorbachev. Free elections placed non-Communist parties in power in much of the area. The Soviet-style secret police and command economy systems were being dismantled. The new governments conducted negotiations with the USSR for the removal of its remaining troops. Early in 1991 the Soviet-controlled military alliance, the Warsaw Pact, and economic grouping, Comecon, were disbanded.

The Americans and West Germans greeted these changes most happily. Reagan dropped his 'evil empire' style of rhetoric; while his successor, George Bush, emphasised his readiness to work co-operatively with both the Soviet Union and the countries of Eastern Europe, even to the extent of providing economic assistance for the restructuring of their economies. President Mitterrand of France and Chancellor Kohl of Germany also proffered the hand of friendship. Mrs Thatcher, the Prime Minister of Britain from 1979 to 1990, alone remained guarded, warning that the enthusiasm of 1989–90 might be misplaced if Gorbachev's hold on power proved more tenuous than appeared at that time.

The end of the cold war was formally recognised at a meeting in Paris in November 1990. The twenty-two heads of government or state of the NATO and Warsaw Pact alliances issued a Declaration, which stated: 'The signatories solemnly declare that, in the new era of European relations which is beginning, they are no longer adversaries, will build new partnerships and extend to each other the hand of friendship' (text reprinted, *NATO Review*, December 1990, pp. 26–7).

At the start of the century's final decade the international scene was confusing. The old cold war certainties lay in ruins. Yet its legacy could not be utterly ignored in the difficult task of constructing a new international system.

Aftermath of the cold war

Right-wing politicians and commentators, especially in the United States, were jubilant. The cold war was won. Western principles were the victors; Communism was vanquished.

The effect of the events of 1989–90 on members of Communist parties throughout Europe was traumatic. In the Soviet Union itself the CPSU was eventually abolished and outlawed in 1991. In Eastern Europe the remnants of the once dominant parties desperately sought new identities by changing their names and adopting more pragmatic programmes. The same reactions were to be discerned in Western Europe's largest Communist parties, the French and Italian. The collapse of Communist parties' power and authority with such rapidity suggested that the Marxist–Leninist philosophy upon which they were based was nothing but a hollow shell of ideas. In the 1950s disillusioned former Communists and sympathisers wrote essays with titles such as *The God That Failed* (ed. R.H.S. Crossman, 1950) and *The Naked God* (Howard Fast, 1958). The Marxist god was now shown to be not an unclothed failure, but a total myth. As the doctrinal light from Moscow faded, so Asian and African Communists waned in their commitment.

Only in Cuba and China were attempts seriously made to adhere to the dogma. But their regimes were, respectively, exhausted and discredited by savage repression of popular demonstrations. Castro was isolated; Deng Xiaoping despised by civilised international society for the massacre in Tiananmen Square in 1989.

The revolutionary fire of Communism had burnt itself out. It was the end of an era, inaugurated by the Russian Revolution, during which international relations were conducted with an eye on the revolutionary principles of Marx and Lenin: one could try to copy Communism or try to defeat it; one could try to contain it; but no foreign office of a major power could ignore it. International relations, it now seemed, could henceforth be conducted by pursuing either the classical pragmatic objectives of national self-interest and balance of power or the grander goal of a more stable and just order for the world as a whole.

Or were the events being witnessed not just the end of the era of ideology, but the end of history itself? This was the thesis propounded by the American Fukuyama. He argued that history has been a tussle for the acceptance of various social philosophies. The Western pluralist capitalist system has now proved itself to be superior to any other and has been accepted as such. All we shall now experience are happenings of superficial significance.

Such a philosophy of history, however, not only fails to give sufficient weight to the ideological power of religion in the contemporary world, especially of Islam. It also underestimates the role of power politics in the shaping of history. The Soviet–American duopoly of power had set the context and temper of international relations from about 1945 to 1990. Had the end of the cold war brought that duopoly to an end? And if so, what could replace it?

By about 1990 the term 'superpower' was no longer a very apt description of the USSR. Its power to act decisively and authoritatively on the world stage was emasculated by the most severe internal troubles: the economy, ethnic relations, constitutional structure and political leadership were all in crisis. Indeed, one of the criticisms levelled at Gorbachev by his political and military right-wing critics was the accusation that he had allowed the Soviet position in the world to slip so drastically. By 1992 the situation was clear. The USSR had disintegrated into its component states; and even the largest, the Russian Federation, could scarcely lay claim to the status of superpower.

In these circumstances George Bush saw the opportunity for a 'new world order', with the United States acting as a kind of global policeman under the auspices of the United Nations (UN). As the ancient world enjoyed a 'pax Romana', our own would benefit from a 'pax Americana'. It so happened that the shrinking of Soviet power coincided with America's effective mobilisation of world opinion against Saddam Hussein of Iraq and the targeting of the massive military might of the United States on that unhappy country. It was in September 1990, at the start of the Gulf crisis triggered by Saddam's seizure of Kuwait, that US Secretary of State James Baker outlined this new world scenario:

> America must lead, and our people must understand that. . . . Only American engagement can shape the peaceful world that our people so deeply desire. . . .We remain the one nation that has the necessary political, military and economic instruments at our disposal to catalyse a successful collective response by the international community.
>
> (quoted, *Guardian*, 6 September 1990)

On the other hand, America cannot necessarily sustain such an ambitious design. It can be argued that she has neither the moral authority nor the economic strength to undertake this exacting role.

Leadership implies a willingness on the part of others to follow. A number of states in the world are nevertheless too doubtful of American fitness and motives for wielding such authority to be willing followers. Her own social problems – for example, poverty, crime and drug-abuse – can scarcely qualify the United States as a model society. Left-wing, including Soviet, criticism of US policy in the recent past was by no means entirely vicious propaganda. The United States has been guilty of supporting obnoxious regimes for its own selfish purposes, notably in Latin America, the Middle East and South-East Asia. Trading and development activities by US business companies and banks have not always been in the best interests of poverty-stricken Third World countries. And in the notorious case of the mining of Nicaraguan waters, the United States categorically refused to abide by the ruling of the International Court of Justice – not the best of credentials for a nation destined to lead the world into conditions of justice and peace!

When we examine the state of the American economy doubts arise on this score too. Managing a new world order would be an expensive undertaking. Such a power would need to be ever-ready to shore up with economic aid tottering regimes whose poverty threatened local instability and to intervene with overwhelming military force to counteract any threat to local peace. There are very persuasive arguments to suggest that the United States is not in a condition to shoulder that kind of responsibility.

In 1988 the English historian Paul Kennedy caused a stir in the United States when he published *The Rise and Fall of the Great Powers*. In this work he showed that, over the centuries, various states have risen to a commanding position, overreached their strength, and by this debilitating arrogance, induced their own decline. The United States, he concluded, was but the most recent, current example of this rhythmical process. He revealed that the American national debt doubled from $914 billion to $1,823 billion in just half a decade, 1980–5 (Kennedy, p. 681). By the end of Reagan's presidency in 1989, it had risen still further, to $2,800 billion. The country was also running a massive payments deficit in its external trade. As the world's economic superpower it was being overtaken by Japan.

Not, of course, that Japan is or even aspires to be a superpower in a military sense. During the cold war era the most blatant badge of superpower status was a substantial armoury of nuclear weapons. By that criterion the United States and Russia (marginally) remain superpowers. A handful of other states possess such weapons but in numbers dwarfed by the American and Russian inventories.

Nor is there much likelihood that Washington and Moscow will dispense with these stocks altogether. There are three main reasons for this. The first is the continued general belief in their deterrent value. The second is that the future relations between the United States and Russia are unpredictable, especially in the light of the internal difficulties of the Commonwealth of Independent States. The third reason is that the number of states capable of producing nuclear weapons has been increasing. It is unrealistic to expect the United States or Russia to engage in total nuclear disarmament at a time when South Africa or Pakistan, for example, might be developing their own nuclear weapons.

None the less, negotiations to reduce the levels of their nuclear stockpiles and unilateral destruction of some weapons have been a feature of the relaxation of tension between the United States and the former Soviet Union. Another item on the post-cold war agenda is the continued management of this scaling down of the numbers of warheads. As the shorter-range devices particularly relate to the confrontation in Europe we shall deal with these in the next chapter. What concerns us here are the strategic weapons. These are the systems capable of striking at the enemy from great distances – Intercontinental Ballistic Missiles (ICBMs), Submarine-Launched Ballistic Missiles (SLBMs) and long-range bombers.

The three treaties signed in the 1970s (see p. 39) did not help to restrain the nuclear arms race very much. In the words of one authority: 'Neither SALT-I nor SALT-II committed either superpower to surrender any weapon that it really wished to keep' (Prins, 1983, p. 127). Yet a numerical reduction seemed sensible since both sides had a considerable 'overkill' capacity: that is, they were each capable of annihilating their opponent's population several times over.

Eventually, in 1982 Strategic Arms Reduction Talks (START) began in Geneva. The talks were interrupted and resumed, hopes were buoyed up and disappointed. In 1990 Presidents Bush and Gorbachev met in Washington and initialled an agreement to reduce their strategic nuclear forces by about a third. But translating a general agreement into a detailed treaty against the background of the confused conditions in the USSR proved difficult.

Yet the parlous condition of the Soviet economy suggested that a rapid diversion of resources to civilian purposes would be highly advantageous. Indeed, some American commentators even suggested that it was the punishing pace set by the United States in weapons research and development that finally broke the Soviet economy and led to her 'defeat' in the cold war. There is no real evidence to support this theory. In fact, by about 1990 both countries were looking for a respite in the arms race so that the consequent 'peace dividend' could be used to succour their ailing economies.

Such benefits to be derived from the end of the cold war were not, however, to be easily enjoyed. At the end of 1991 the situation was dramatically complicated by the break-up of the Soviet Union. Russia, by far the largest member of the new Commonwealth of Independent States (CIS), prepared to take control of the whole stockpile of 27,000 nuclear warheads distributed throughout Belarus, Ukraine and Kazakhstan as well as the Russian Federation itself. In both the United States and Russia suspicions remained. In each country there was, to use President Eisenhower's vivid term, a 'military–industrial complex' whose interests were bound up in high state expenditure on the armed forces. Rapid demobilisation of troops and the closing down of laboratories and factories devoted to the production of war *matériel* was starting to cause painful unemployment.

In the meantime in Europe rapid and deep cuts in forces were being achieved. These changes in turn raised awkward questions about the means of ensuring European security in the future.

2

European Security

NATO

The history of Europe had for centuries been a history of warfare. Then, after the Second World War, the most horrendous war of all, it seemed as though further conflict could be avoided only by the maintenance of the nerve-racking balance of terror between the two superpowers, the United States and the USSR. In military terms, the continent was flanked and overshadowed by these two extra-European states.

With the collapse of Communist authority in the revolutionary events of 1989–90, these cold war security arrangements were no longer relevant. In order to understand Europe's new security needs it will be useful to outline the existing institutions and agreements. These provide the necessary context for the evolution of systems more pertinent to the new age.

The foreign ministers of twelve nations met in Washington on 4 April 1949 to sign the North Atlantic Treaty. They committed themselves to the proposition that 'an armed attack against one or more of them in Europe or North America shall be considered an attack against them all' (Art. 5). The signatories were Belgium, Canada, Denmark, France, Iceland, Italy, Luxemburg, the Netherlands, Norway, Portugal, the United Kingdom and the United States. The treaty was a remarkable agreement for two reasons. In the first place, the members were committing themselves permanently in times of peace to the kind of military alliance that one normally associates with temporary wartime arrangements.

Secondly, the United States was surrendering its traditional isolationist policy and undertaking to involve itself in European affairs.

Both at the time and since, the creation of the North Atlantic Treaty Organisation (NATO) has been fraught with controversy. Was it a prudent precaution against a formidably armed Soviet Union whose forces were in occupation of the eastern portion of the continent and might readily conquer the rest? Or was the new alliance unnecessarily provocative to a frightened and exhausted former ally whose people had borne the brunt of the war against Hitler, suffering well over 20 million deaths in the process? Or was it just as concerned with countering Communist subversion internally in West European states with sizeable Communist parties and Communist–dominated trade unions? It is now fairly generally recognised at least that the Western propaganda in support of NATO exaggerated both the Soviet desire and ability to engage in an aggressive policy.

Be that as it may, the strength of NATO forces was steadily built up and placed under integrated commands. The European theatre was the most crucial and sensitive, for along the West German frontier with East Germany and Czechoslovakia the armed forces of the two sides in the cold war actually stood face to face poised for combat. The American commitment to Europe has been personified ever since, not only by the stationing of US troops on European soil, but by the appointment of an American general as the Supreme Allied Commander in Europe (SACEUR).

To the original members of NATO there were soon added Greece, Turkey and the Federal Republic of Germany and, more recently, Spain (see Figure 2.1); and in 1968 the Eurogroup was established to strengthen the co-operation amongst the European members (excluding France and Iceland). In 1955, following the accession of West Germany to NATO, the Soviet Union concluded the Warsaw Pact with her East European satellites.

With such a diverse membership it is scarcely surprising that tensions developed within NATO. We have already noticed (p. 6) that de Gaulle withdrew French forces from the integrated command structure while nevertheless remaining a member of the alliance. As a consequence, NATO headquarters were moved from Fontainebleau to Brussels. For many years relations between Greece and Turkey have been exceedingly strained because of the

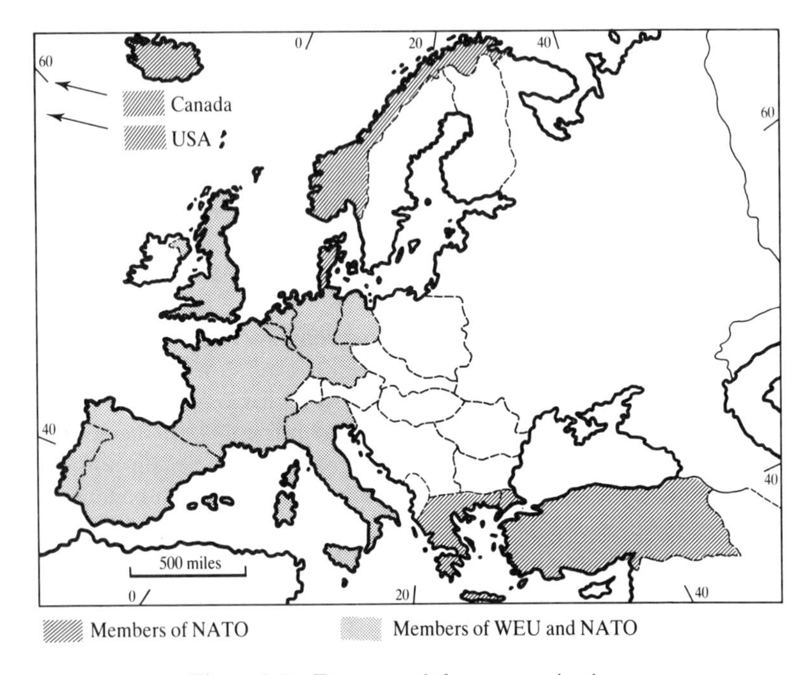

Figure **2.1** European defence organisations

tension between their respective ethnic communities in Cyprus. This quarrel has weakened the alliance in the eastern Mediterranean. A third internal dispute has been between the Americans and Europeans over the relative contributions to the alliance. For example, during the 1980s the United States allocated an average of 6.0 per cent of its gross domestic product (GDP) to defence expenditure, whereas the European members of NATO spent only 3.4 per cent of their GDP on defence (*NATO Review*, February 1991, p. 32). At the same time, however, the European Community (EC) and West Germany in particular were growing in economic strength and challenging the United States commercially.

Throughout its life NATO has suffered from basic geographical and financial problems with regard to European defence. During the cold war period planners had to face the fact that, in the event of a crisis, Soviet reserves had short, overland journeys to travel to the theatre of operations, whereas the Americans were a wide ocean away. The financial problem has lain in the expense of stationing US forces in Europe to bolster relatively weak West European armies.

As a result, NATO came to rely on nuclear weapons. In 1967 it adopted the policy of 'flexible response'. Central to this plan was the following proposition:

> An aggressor must be convinced of NATO's readiness to use nuclear weapons if necessary, but he must be uncertain regarding the timing or the circumstances in which they would be used. However, selective use of nuclear weapons could not be deferred until NATO's conventional forces were completely defeated.
>
> (NATO, 1981, p. 139)

This process of escalation was to include the use of American strategic nuclear forces against the Soviet Union. In other words, the defence of Western Europe rested, ultimately, on American willingness to risk retaliatory nuclear attacks on her own cities. This NATO reliance on nuclear weapons had two inherent weaknesses. One was the danger of escalation by misjudgment or accident in the inevitable confusion that arises once fighting begins. The second was the implausible scenario of an American President sacrificing his homeland cities for the sake of Europeans.

Yet the imbalance of conventional forces persisted. In 1990, on the continent of Europe, from the Atlantic to the Urals, NATO was still deploying only 25,500 tanks and 21,200 artillery pieces, for example, to the Warsaw Pact's 41,580 and 42,400 respectively. Not until 1992 were conventional and nuclear force reductions substantially under way in Russia.

Political and military agreements

The widespread recognition that tension and force-levels should be reduced was nevertheless already producing numerous discussions and agreements.

From 1987 to 1991 the military situation in Europe was transformed. In December 1987 the so-called Intermediate-range Nuclear Forces (INF) treaty was signed (see Chapter 3). This was an especially important agreement for Europe and indeed was designed to reverse the nuclear build-up there.

A year later Gorbachev made a startling speech at the UN General Assembly: 'In the next two years,' he declared, the strength of the Soviet armed forces 'will be reduced by 500,000 men, and substantial cuts will be made in conventional armaments. These cuts will be made unilaterally' (Freedman, 1990, p. 278). The key word was 'unilaterally'. Gorbachev was cutting through the haggling between the two sides and challenging the West to match his statesmanship.

For, at this time, discussions were under way to draft a CFE treaty: that is, an agreement between the two sides to reduce their Conventional Forces in Europe. This was in fact concluded in 1990. By providing the same ceilings for both NATO and the Warsaw Pact it required a substantial reduction of Soviet forces in Europe. For example, to take the categories mentioned on p. 19 above, the two sides were to be limited to 20,000 tanks and 20,000 artillery pieces each.

In practice, however, the treaty itself was not as important as the bald figures might suggest. In the first place, it covered only the European portions of the USSR. Much Soviet war *matériel* was therefore not destroyed, but redeployed east of the Urals. But in any case, and secondly, other events were fast overtaking the negotiators. For example, the Warsaw Pact was already disintegrating and in 1991 the East European states forced the Soviet authorities to agree to dates for the withdrawal of *all* Soviet forces from their territories. And most dramatically of all, a matter of weeks before the signature of the CFE treaty East Germany was merged into the Federal Republic and became part of NATO territory.

Meanwhile, a discussion of much broader scope relating to European security has been under way since 1975. This is the Conference on Security and Co-operation in Europe (CSCE). After the Soviet suppression of the 'Prague Spring' reform movement in Czechoslovakia in 1968, Brezhnev angled for a limited *rapprochement* with the West in the form of a mutual recognition of frontiers and spheres of influence. A meeting was eventually convened in Helsinki in 1973. It was attended by representatives of thirty-five states: the United States, Canada and all European states except the politically isolated Albania. The concluding document, known as the Final Act and signed in 1975, was divided into four sections, or 'baskets'. These dealt respectively with questions relating to security in Europe; co-operation in the fields of economics, of science and technology and of the environment; co-operation in humanitarian and other fields; and follow-up to the conference. The immediate outcome was to provide for increased contact between East and West Europe and a lowering of suspicion, including, most controversially, a reiteration of the signatories' commitment to human rights. The agreements on human rights stimulated liberal groups into life and most notably in the Soviet Union and Czechoslovakia. They afforded the West leverage for complaining about blatant persecution (see Chapter 7).

Since 1975 the 'Helsinki' process has been kept alive by periodic meetings in various venues. For example, in 1984–6 a meeting in Stockholm generated an agreement to strengthen the original provisions for giving advance notice of military exercises so that the purpose of troop movements by one side should not be misconstrued by the other. Such agreements are known as Confidence- and Security-Building Measures (CSBMs). Much important groundwork for disarmament was undertaken within the CSCE framework in the late 1980s. Even after the end of the cold war the CSBM process has continued to perform a valuable function. By increasing contacts mutual suspicions have been lessened. Furthermore, from 1992 CFE negotiations have been merged with the CSBM system.

In November 1990 a three-day CSCE summit meeting took place in Paris. (By this time membership was reduced to thirty-four because of the unification of Germany.) The planning of this great gathering was attended by great excitement: it was to be a splendid party to mark the end of the cold war and the opening of a new era in European history, an age of peace, security and justice. A number of agreements were signed. These included the CFE treaty and the joint Declaration by the twenty-two members of NATO and the Warsaw Pact (see p.10).

However, the most path-breaking document and the one which contained the signatories' most ambitious expectations was the Charter of Paris for a New Europe. In ringing opening paragraphs it pronounced that: 'The courage of men and women, the strength of the will of the peoples and the power of the ideas of the Helsinki Final Act have opened a new era of democracy, peace and unity in

Europe' (text reprinted, *NATO Review*, December 1990, pp. 327–31). The core of the charter described the wide range of issues which the CSCE members pledged themselves to tackle together.

The truly exciting potential of the charter lay in the final section, which formulated a programme for building new structures and institutions. These aimed at consolidating the CSCE as a permanent pan-European collaborative and trouble-shooting organisation. The main features of these strengthening mechanisms were as follows: the Foreign Ministers to meet annually as a Council, its work supported by a Committee of Senior Officials and a permanent secretariat in Prague; a Conflict Prevention Centre (CPC) to be established in Vienna; and a parliamentary assembly to be formed for meetings of Members of Parliament from all CSCE states.

Post-cold war issues

During the cold war Europe's security depended on the neither-war-nor-peace stability of the NATO v. Warsaw Pact rivalry. The cold war concluded, Europe's security was 'a great confusion' (Zielonka,1991).

For a fleeting moment, it is true, it looked as though cold war bipolar simplicity might be replaced by the new simplicity of Gorbachev's vision of 'a common European home'. Both domestically and internationally the states of Europe would share the agreed purposes of greater peace, prosperity and justice. These enhanced life-styles would be financed by the 'peace dividend' derived from the demobilisation of the now unnecessarily distended armed forces. But no sooner had this enticing vision been conjured up than it was shattered by the explosive force of new crises and problems.

Saddam Hussein's seizure of Kuwait diverted attention to the Gulf. Secessionist movements in some of the Soviet peripheral republics, notably the Baltics and Georgia, together with mounting economic problems, planted a large question mark over the internal stability of the USSR and consequently her ability to perform a stabilising role on the wider pan-European stage. The question remained worryingly unanswered as the USSR collapsed and gave way to the Commonwealth of Independent States in 1991. Further turmoil occurred in Eastern Europe with the violent break-up of

Yugoslavia. And lastly, the merger of the two Germanys proved to be a far trickier business than some optimists had blithely assumed. In other words, by the autumn of 1990 Europe's affairs were again proving the truth of Umberto Eco's wise aphorism that for every complex problem there is a simple answer – and it's wrong!

In order to discuss the possible security structures for Europe's new conditions we first need to understand how the continent's security might be threatened. There are five concerns.

1. The closest to the Western cold war nightmare is the scenario which depicts danger from the former USSR. The failure of Gorbachev and, after him, Yeltsin to effect a smooth passage for the policy of *perestroika* led to internal instability. No one can be quite sure whether another authoritarian form of government, civilian or military, might seize control. Such a regime would scarcely have the power or will to pose a military threat to the rest of Europe, it is true. On the other hand, it would at best be antipathetic to the style of liberal democratic government now almost universal throughout the continent; at worst, if faced with political disintegration, it could adopt violently repressive measures internally, which would provoke outraged protests from many other European governments and peoples. Moreover, as the centralised USSR was replaced by the virtually still-born CIS, new and therefore untried methods had to be devised for the control of the nuclear weapons based in four of the republics. Whatever European security structures might be devised must recognise that the role of the former Soviet Union could be somewhat uncertain. They may indeed need to span the area 'from Brest to Brest' (that is, from the French port to Brest-Litovsk near the Belarus border with Poland) and in some ways still be conceived as a protection against destabilising conditions in the Eurasian heartland.
2. It is possible also to conceive of renewed or continuing instability in Central and Eastern Europe – our second security problem. The Balkans present a particularly perilous set of ethnic problems, exacerbated by economic backwardness. The Yugoslav federation disintegrated in 1992; Romania has yet to recover from the horrendous Ceauşescu dictatorship and to resolve the fears of the Hungarian minority of

Transylvania; and Albania's poverty-stricken population is split between the interests of the rural and urban classes. No one is quite predicting another Sarajevo, the Balkan fuse which detonated the First World War; but few would dare to predict a period of calm. The economic prospects of the northern tier of former Communist states – Poland, Czechoslovakia and Hungary – might seem more favourable. Nevertheless, Poland is a poor and environmentally blighted country. Czechoslovakia has its own ethnic problem all the while the Slovaks feel they are second-class citizens. A European security structure needs to make provision for the damping down and containment of these tensions.

3. The third consideration is how to preserve European security against threats from the Third World. Clearly these dangers would not manifest themselves as military invasions. There are, however, plenty of reasons for quarrelling to occur between Europe and African or Asian states, which we shall consider below. The point to notice here is that some Afro-Asian states do have the capacity to provoke internal instability in Europe – through religious and demographic pressures – and a few might develop a nuclear potential which could be brandished to extract concessions. Security against these threats may therefore require greater efforts to ensure internal contentment and effective policing on the one hand and a credible nuclear deterrent on the other. The need to take into consideration dangers to Europe emanating from the Third World has already impinged upon NATO thinking. Within its councils advocates of extending its geographical responsibilities have for several years now recommended planning for 'out of area' tasks. Such considerations in no way presuppose any moral judgement on the rights and wrongs of European – Third World relations; they merely address practical security issues.
4. One may in truth respond to such a disclaimer by asserting that the distinction is a false one. It may well be that the best way to enhance European security against threats from the Third World is to treat these countries with greater economic justice and their cultures with more respect. It is a strategy that may also be relevant to our fourth problem, that of terrorism. The vulnerability of European citizens to terrorism

is by no means hypothetical. ETA in Spain, IRA in Britain, Red Brigades in Italy, Red Army Faction in Germany and Palestinian groups operating against airlines have seized the headlines on innumerable occasions with their slaughter. European security against these activities means improving collaborative human and technical intelligence and striking a delicate balance between more effective protection and less enjoyment of personal and civil liberties.

5. Finally, we need to notice the relatively recent acceptance of the broadening of the concept of security. From defence against full-scale military onslaught, it has come to embrace defence against the isolated actions of terrorist cells as well. In addition to worrying about the policies of states bent, or thought to be bent, on aggression, security planning now concerns itself with the internal instability that might be caused by economic or ethnic discontent in neighbouring states. And from the felt need to protect their fellow-citizens from weapons of war, security forces have extended their responsibilities to defences against such non-military threats as drug-trafficking, unwanted waves of immigrants or refugees and the attractions of unsettling religious or political doctrines. The migration of poor Muslims from the francophone states of the Maghreb (north-west Africa) to France is already causing cultural tension. This problem could be exacerbated if substantially more people of similar background arrived in Europe. Furthermore, the Single European Act (see p. 184) has removed frontier controls between states, rendering tight security at entry-points to the whole Community area that much more imperative.

Because the European security problem is so fluid and complex, it is obvious that planning to meet all the potential threats must be equally flexible and comprehensive. Again, we may produce a five-item list.

1. If the argument in favour of retaining the option of nuclear deterrence is accepted (and there is little evidence that it will be discarded), then a number of questions must be resolved. The deployment and targeting programmes as devised in the 1980s are now obsolete. New crisis scenarios need to be

constructed. These in turn will indicate the style of weapons required. And who is to provide these weapons? Will the United States be willing to continue to provide its nuclear umbrella – and at all levels, from strategic to battlefield systems? If not, how far and at what cost will the British and French nuclear armouries be able to cope?

2. When it comes to the disposition and combat-readiness of units of European armed forces, two questions (the second and third on our list) need to be resolved. One relates to their defensive posture in Europe itself. The NATO and Warsaw Pact doctrines of fighting in zones either side of the Iron Curtain are now quite evidently useless. NATO planners now refer to the 'currant-bun' formula – that is, units dotted about in readiness and adaptable for different uses. The immediate result of this rethinking appeared in 1991 with the production of plans for substantial force reductions and the creation of a corps-sized Rapid Reaction Force.
3. One kind of use would be for rapid redeployment outside Europe, in the way, for example, that British armoured units were shifted from Germany to Saudi Arabia for the Gulf War of 1991. This possible out-of-area employment of European men and equipment is the other contingency that must help shape planning with regard to force dispositions and readiness. An adequate supply of transport ships and aircraft may well prove a limiting factor to realistic schemes of this sort.
4. The fourth requirement concerns the personnel and equipment needs for internal security against the terrorist and non-military threats outlined above. Pooling of intelligence and co-ordination of security operations, which already occur across police and security forces, may need to be given higher priority above conventional military defence spending.
5. Finally, if security considerations must now encompass the mitigation of the destabilising effects of economic dislocation and poverty, then security must involve the redistribution of wealth. In Europe, massive sums were transferred from West to East Germany to ease, however partially, the pain of unification. Further transfers of funds as aid or investment to Eastern Europe and the CIS may be a legitimate form of security insurance.

How can the various key institutions be modified and states adapted to cater for these new security needs?

Has NATO now lost its *raison d'être*? It would like to think that it can adjust. The sixteen heads of state and government of its members met in London in 1990 and issued a declaration. This stated that the alliance must be:

> an agent of change. It can help build the structures of a more united continent, supporting security and stability. . . . We reaffirm that security and stablity do not lie solely in the military dimension. . . . We recognise that, in the new Europe, the security of every state is inseparably linked to the security of its neighbours.
>
> (reprinted, *NATO Review*, August 1990, p. 32).

The following year it demonstrated its flexibility by creating the North Atlantic Co-operation Council (NACC). This is a device for associating East European governments with NATO discussions on general security issues. By 1992 it embraced thirty-five states 'from Vancouver to Vladivostok'.

There has, however, been a growing feeling that the American-dominated NATO should give way to a system which provides for greater European self-reliance. This has led to speculation about the form of a new European 'security architecture'. There are four basic designs.

1. The first is an adaptation of NATO by strengthening the cohesion and autonomy of the Western European Union (WEU), the so-called European pillar of the alliance (see Figure 2.1, p. 18). This is a nine-nation body – Belgium, France, Germany, Italy, Luxemburg, the Netherlands, Portugal, Spain and the United Kingdom – which has lain dormant since its institutional crystallisation in 1954, following its conception as the European Union in the Brussels Treaty of 1948. If it were wakened to effective activity, it could reintegrate France into the NATO military structure and also relieve the United States of some of the burden of European defence.
2. The second possibility is to develop WEU as the security and defence organ of the EC. If political union is to be real (see Chapter 15), then the EC should have a means of ensuring its own security. All nine WEU states are members of the EC and

could act as a core around which other present and future members could cluster. Two difficulties arise, however. One revolves round Britain's nervousness that a realistic EC defence organisation would undermine the American-led North Atlantic alliance. The other relates to states who have adopted neutral stances in defence matters. Ireland has not wavered from that policy since she joined the EC, despite the fact that all other eleven fellow-Community states have been members of the North Atlantic alliance. In the event of equally convinced neutrals such as Austria and Sweden, even Switzerland, joining the EC, the development of a Community-wide defence and security structure could be even more difficult.

3. The third idea is that the CSCE should absorb all Europe's security arrangements. Although it has no military structure, it has the advantage of being geographically all-embracing. For example, the Baltic states of Estonia, Latvia and Lithuania immediately joined when they seceded from the Soviet Union, and the CIS republics followed suit, bringing the membership to fifty-one.
4. Perhaps the most likely 'architecture' will be a rococo edifice incorporating all of these elements. It would, of course, be important to ensure a careful allocation of functions to avoid too much duplication of effort. The relationship of WEU to NATO on the one hand and the EC on the other needs resolution, as does the relationship between NACC and CSCE.

However, a brand-new pan-European security system cannot be devised without a clear vision of the roles of certain key states. Are the successor-states to the Soviet Union to be incorporated or is a new system to be at least partially designed as a defence against them? Is the United States still to participate – in planning, intelligence, conventional and nuclear forces? Both US and European politicians and public opinion are confusingly ambivalent on this matter. Some Americans want to dispense with the cost but do not want to lose the influence; some Europeans want the assurance of US military power but not its interference in their affairs. And what of the role of Germany – demographically and economically the most powerful of European states? This is problematical because its army is by international treaty restricted to 370,000 troops and its constitution forbids their deployment outside its own territory. Finally, the more 'Westernised' of East European states – Czechoslovakia, Hungary and Poland – are desperately anxious to be incorporated in any revamped security arrangements outside CSCE. Could they become members of NATO?

In the age of the cold war defence planners gave the impression of knowing all the answers. We make no excuses for concluding this chapter with a series of questions. The answers are not yet to hand.

3

Arms: Purpose, Trade, Control

Purpose and proliferation

The development, manufacture, sale and use of weapons and munitions are huge businesses representing a large segment of the world's total economic activity. A few figures may help to illustrate the scale. In 1989 the United States spent $77 billion on military equipment; Britain, £4.7 billion. But the operation of this equipment in terms of wages, food, uniforms for the soldiers, sailors and airmen, fuel for the tanks, ships and aircraft and maintenance of the bases added to the total bills. These came to $304 billion for the United States and £21 billion for Britain, or 5.9 per cent and 4.2 per cent of those countries' GNPs respectively. There have been countries like the USSR, Israel and Iraq who have in recent years spent far higher proportions of their total wealth – even as much as a fifth of their GNP – on their armed forces.

In this section of the chapter we are primarily concerned with the manufacture and sale of armaments. But first we need to outline the various categories of arms we are discussing and the purposes for which they are designed.

Weapons are used by the three armed services, para-military and police forces in many states, and by 'irregular' guerrilla and terrorist groups. A broad distinction is often made between nuclear and conventional weapons. We deal with nuclear weapons specifically in the next section of this chapter. Because of the enormous destructive force of nuclear weapons, the potential for massive destruction and vast numbers of deaths by so-called conventional weapons is sometimes underestimated.

Chemical and biological weapons are particularly lethal. Chemical warfare in the form of poison gas was first used in the First World War. In 1925 the Geneva Protocol prohibited its use. This has not prevented the development of even more lethal nerve gases. Biological warfare is the spread of germs (by bacteria such as anthrax or viruses such as psittacosis). There have been no proven incidences of the use of biological weapons. The 1972 Biological Warfare Convention outlaws their very existence (and reiterates the ban on chemical weapons). The objections to both chemical and biological weapons is that their effects cannot be controlled. A shift in wind could blow a gas cloud in unforeseen directions. The release of biological warfare agents could lead to widespread epidemics.

In the meantime 'progress' (if that is the correct word) in the design and use of traditional incendiary and high-explosive weapons has increased in pace especially since the Vietnam War (1965–73). The Gulf War of 1991 demonstrated at least two important lessons. One was the ability of small weapons to inflict huge casualties. The other was the accuracy with which radar- and laser-directed weapons could pin-point their targets. One of the most devastating weapons used in this conflict was the Multiple Rocket Launch System (MRLS). Here is a description by one British authority:

> The launcher is a tracked vehicle carrying 12 missiles with a range of over 20 miles. The missiles can all be fired within a minute and can be aimed to spread out over a target area of 60 acres. As they detonate they release nearly 8,000 anti-personnel fragmentation grenades. During the closing stages of the war the US forces fired 10,000 MLRS missiles and the British another 2,500.
>
> (Rogers, 1991)

The sheer concentration of firepower and intensity of killing and wounding in the last days of the Gulf War led to the coining of the term 'hyperwar'.

It is obvious that the invention, development and production of sophisticated modern weapons requires the mobilisation of the efforts of an immense range of talent – scientists, mathematicians, engineers, industrial manufacturers, not to mention the highly trained soldiers, sailors and airmen who use them. This network of people is often referred to as the 'military-industrial complex', a term coined by President Eisenhower in his farewell address in 1961. He said:

> We have been compelled to create a permanent armaments industry of vast proportions: this conjunction of an immense military establishment and a large arms industry is new in the American experience. The total influence – economic, political, even spiritual – is felt in every city, every statehouse, every office of the federal government. . . . In the councils of government we must guard against the acquisition of unwarranted influence, whether sought or unsought, by the military – industrial complex. The potential for the disastrous rise of misplaced power exists and will persist.
>
> (quoted, Sampson, 1977, p. 102)

Two decades later the British scholar Mary Kaldor (1982) coined the term 'baroque arsenal'. Her argument is that because of military and industrial/commercial pressures weapons systems have become far more complex than is militarily necessary. Moreover, the expenditure of skilled manpower and money on this process is damaging to any country's economy that indulges in it.

Criticisms like these build up to a picture of a machinery for the production of armaments that has developed a momentum of its own. The exercise of effective political restraint is consequently difficult.

Weapons are designed to destroy and kill. Since 1945 it is estimated that there have been well over a hundred 'major' wars, defined as conflicts in which more than a thousand people have been killed in a year. Besides the people directly killed in war – some 20 million since 1945 – there are in addition those who die of disease and starvation because of the attendant dislocation .

The economic costs of arms manufacture are impossible to calculate. In addition to the destructiveness of the fighting in which they are employed, we must recognise the diversion of resources that could be used for civil purposes. For example, it has often been remarked that, in the relatively rich northern hemisphere, states like Germany and Japan that spend little on weapons development have enjoyed faster increases in their GNP than states like the United States and Britain that spend relatively lavishly in this way. And when we look at the Third World we see that, despite the poverty of many of these states, expenditure on the purchase of weapons has increased enormously. From 1965 to 1983 (the period of most obvious weapons build-up) the countries of the Third World increased their expenditure on major weapons six-fold (from the equivalent of $1,559 million to $9,557 million).

Governments, manufacturing companies and individual entrepreneurs sell billions of dollars' worth of arms every year. The exact figures cannot be known as some of the trade is clandestine. Furthermore, although it would be difficult to conceal the sale of a second-hand frigate, for instance, the trade in ammunition and small arms can by no means be fully recorded.

Not that trade of this kind is especially new. The modernisation of Japan and the rise in tension prior to the outbreak of the First World War stimulated arms deals substantially at the turn of the century. The motives have been a mixture of profit and the strengthening of allies. From the point of view of the manufacturer, sales to foreign armed services have two evident advantages. One is the economy of scale that comes from mass production. The other is the opportunity for the testing of the weapons in real battle conditions. A third advantage is enjoyed by the government of the country supplying arms, namely, the political influence it can exert over the purchasing state.

The most buoyant period for this trade in recent years has been the decade from the mid-1970s to mid-1980s. Since then massive international debts in many Third World countries have forced them to economise. And it has been arms imports by Third World states that has accounted for the bulk of the trade.

By far and away the greatest share of the arms business has been cornered by the two massively armed states of the cold war, the United States and the USSR. Partly this trade was a dimension of the cold war. The United States supplied Israel and Pakistan; the Soviet Union supplied Cuba and Angola, for example. During the 1980–4 quinquennium American and Russian exports of major weapons accounted for over 70 per cent of all such trade. The West European arms manufacturing countries – France, United Kingdom, Germany and Italy – accounted for a further 20 per cent. During the same period over half of the Third World's major weapons imports were bought by half a dozen states: Egypt, Syria, Iraq, India, Libya and Saudi Arabia. Only a few Third World states are themselves exporters of weapons: South Africa, Brazil and Israel (if she may be so classified) are the most significant.

The proliferation of conventional weapons through the domestic arming of the arms-producing nations and the export of their products has caused many worries and protests. The proliferation of nuclear weapons, however, poses an even more horrendous threat.

Nuclear weapons

The potential effects of conventional weapons, especially chemical and biological devices, are horrifying to contemplate. However, it is the total 'lethality' of the world stock of nuclear weapons that has been most petrifying.

The original American decision to embark on the development of an atomic bomb was taken during the Second World War against the background of fear that Nazi Germany was engaged in such work. During the two decades immediately after the Second World War the tensions of the cold war led the USSR, the United Kingdom, France and China to join the United States as members of the 'nuclear club'.

Since those early years proliferation has continued in two ways. First, there has been 'vertical proliferation', which means an increase in the total number of such weapons in existence. In 1946 the United States had the world's complete stock – nine. Forty years later it was estimated that there were more than 50,000, mainly in the possession of the two superpowers.

Secondly, the spread of nuclear weapons to an increasing number of states is called 'horizontal proliferation'. In addition to the five declared nuclear states, four others are unofficially known to have produced these weapons. They are India, Israel, Pakistan and South Africa. Furthermore, numerous states are believed to be in various stages of nuclear weapons development. These include Argentina and Brazil in South America, Egypt. Iraq and Iran in the Middle East and North Korea, South Korea and Taiwan in East Asia. In 1992, however, this pattern was complicated for two reasons. One was the UN-supervised destruction of Iraqi bomb-making facilities. The other was the attempt to transfer all of the former Soviet nuclear weapons to Russia.

The term 'nuclear weapon' is in fact shorthand for an immense variety of devices in terms of military purpose, explosive 'yield' and method of delivery. It is usual to classify their military purposes into three categories. The first is battlefield or theatre weapons. These are small devices like mines, artillery shells and short-range rockets. The second are shorter- and medium-range and are usually referred to as INF (Intermediate-range Nuclear Forces). They are designed for use over distances between 500 and 5,500 kilometres. The third type are long-range, intercontinental systems usually called strategic weapons. These are subdivided into a 'triad' of bomber aircraft, submarine-launched ballistic missiles (SLBMs) and ground-launched intercontinental ballistic missiles (ICBMs).

Not only are the warheads of strategic missiles of very high yield, many of the missiles are also MIRVed. This means they are fitted with several warheads or, in the jargon, Multiple Independently targetable Re-entry Vehicles. As an example, let us take the American Trident SLBM to be used to arm British nuclear submarines. One missile can be fitted with eight warheads with a combined explosive force equivalent to nearly 10 million kilotonnes of TNT. As a yardstick of comparison the atomic bomb which destroyed Hiroshima in 1945 had a TNT equivalent of 11,500 kilotonnes – 853 times less powerful.

Nuclear weapons in such vast numbers and in so many different sizes have been developed in response to several urges. One is the doctrine of deterrence: if we have the capacity for 'massive retaliation' no enemy would dare use their weapons against us. The second is 'graduated response': if we have small nuclear weapons we can use these in any initial exchange as a warning to try to prevent resort to the nuclear Armageddon of strategic devices. The third is technological and military pride: the ICBM, it has been suggested, is the most potent of all phallic symbols.

There are arguments that nuclear weapons are beneficial inventions. The case is that without them the cold war tensions (particularly in Berlin and in Cuba in 1962) would have burst into a hot, fighting war – a Third World War in fact. Only the awesome deterrence of their nuclear arsenals kept the United States and the USSR from each other's throats. Moreover, the destructive force of modern conventional weapons is devastating yet little recognised. Consequently, it is fortunate that nuclear-armed states are restrained from fighting conventional wars that could be terrible in their effects for fear of escalation to nuclear combat. In other words, nuclear weapons, by virtue of the very terror they inspire, serve as stabilising influences in a volatile world.

Yet lurking behind these arguments, both rationally and irrationally held, are mortal fears that nuclear weapons might actually be used. Worries and warnings have been voiced at a number of levels. Most gruesome is the apocalyptic scenario of the detonation of the whole world's nuclear arsenal. It is capable of destroying all human beings many times, perhaps even the whole of life, rendering the planet utterly sterile. But even a limited exchange of nuclear weapons would have catastrophic effects. The wide dispersal of radioactive fall-out would contaminate virtually the whole hemisphere in which the explosions occur. Moreover, the persistence of a thick veil of dust sucked up into the atmosphere by the explosions would so blot out the sun as to create a 'nuclear winter' with devastating effects on food production.

These hypothetical events have been guarded against by strict systems of control over the several nuclear 'buttons' (that is, the firing codes). But can we be sure that these safety measures can hold good in the future? There are five main concerns, as follows:

1. One is the basic, inherent possibility of human or technical failure. And as the number of states possessing nuclear weapons multiplies so does the chance of a failure in the built-in safety systems.
2. Secondly, any temptation by a head of state to delegate authority to theatre commanders to use their nuclear weapons also highlights the danger. The decision by a general to use a few nuclear artillery shells, for example, to stem an enemy advance could lead to uncontrolled escalation.
3. Thirdly, the political leaders of the nuclear states have so far been balanced personalities. But supposing a psychologically disturbed dictator were to take control of a state armed with these devices? The Gulf War against Saddam Hussein of Iraq in 1991 (see p. 71) was partially provoked by the fear that he might acquire a nuclear capability which he might well have no compunction about using.
4. Fourthly, related to this fear, is the dreadful possibility of terrorist groups obtaining compact nuclear devices and using their possession and even detonation as a means of blackmailing governments into political concessions.
5. Finally, although deterrence has worked, it might not continue to do so. For instance, hypothetically technology might be able to render a country totally impervious to nuclear bombardment (this was Reagan's dream of the Strategic Defense Initiative (SDI)). A state with such a perfect defence might be tempted to use nuclear weapons itself to achieve its ends.

These worries are very much alive in the world today. It is hardly surprising, therefore, that the basic idea of disarmament, which has been reiterated at intervals over the centuries, should have taken on an added sense of urgency during the past decade or so. The nuclear stockpiles of the world are far too perilous to be left only partially controlled and undiminished.

Arms control

Was the ancient Roman military analyst Vegetius right? If we wish for peace must we prepare for war? Or do military preparations, arms races, in fact heighten tension and therefore help to provoke war?

Certainly from the early nineteenth century there have been episodic attempts by various governments to promote disarmament or arms limitation agreements as a means of defusing international tension. Almost all until recent years have been unsuccessful. Tsar Alexander I made a proposal in 1818, Napoleon III in 1863, Tsar Nicholas II in 1899.

The outbreak of the First World War was attributed at the time, and by some historians since, to the arms race between Germany and her rivals. In drawing up his blueprint for a peaceful world – the Fourteen Points – President Woodrow Wilson therefore incorporated the requirement for 'Adequate guarantees given and taken that national armaments will be reduced to the lowest point consistent with domestic safety' (Point 4). One significant treaty was signed in the inter-war period, at Washington in 1922. The United States, the United Kingdom, France, Italy and Japan agreed to restrict their navies' strengths. However, attempts at general disarmament conferences in the 1920s were killed, destroyed by the dilemma presented in the first paragraph of this section. Britain argued for disarmament to provide security; France argued for rearmament to provide security.

The framers of the Charter of the United Nations were not, nevertheless, to be deterred. They incorporated Article 26, which states: 'In order to promote the establishment and maintenance of international peace and security . . . the Security Council shall be responsible for formulating . . . plans . . . for the establishment of a system for the regulation of armaments.' It must be said that the UN has had little success in implementing this article.

Since 1945 efforts at producing international agreements for arms reduction and control have inevitably been concentrated on the problems raised by nuclear weapons. (We commented on chemical and biological weapons on p. 31.)

After the explosion of the first atomic bombs in the summer of 1945 it was absolutely evident that a weapon of a quite different order of power from conventional explosives had been developed. Almost immediately proposals were shaped in the United States for the creation of international controls. These were presented to the UN as the Baruch Plan in 1946. The plan provided for international control of research, development and use of atomic energy together with sanctions against any state attempting to bypass the regulations. The Soviet Union objected to the inspection system this would involve and felt that development of their own weapons would be a better insurance against America's use of hers. The Soviets made a counter-proposal that all nuclear weapons should be dismantled. The United States was unwilling to agree to this: they would lose their advantage of a head start in the event of other states (notably the USSR) developing theirs at some later date. The scene was set for the nuclear arms race between the two superpowers.

Until the early 1970s the United States and the USSR were unwilling to agree to any effective restrictions on their development of more and more nuclear weapons with which to threaten each other. True, in 1963 the evidence of increasing radiation pollution from the testing of nuclear devices brought them to an agreement on a Limited Test Ban Treaty. This prohibited nuclear tests in outer space, under water or in sites which would lead to fall-out beyond the testing-state's own territory.

Most progress in the period 1954–71 was made in the signature of treaties banning the deployment of nuclear weapons in various geographical locations outside the immediate strategic interests of the superpowers. The first, the Antarctic Treaty, was signed in 1959 and renewed in 1989. The Outer Space Treaty came in 1967. In the same year a treaty prohibiting nuclear weapons in Latin America was signed at Tlatelolco. In 1971 there was produced the Sea-bed Arms Control Treaty.

The year 1968 was significant in the history of nuclear arms control. At that juncture the Nuclear Non-Proliferation Treaty (NPT) was signed and the Strategic Arms Limitation Talks (SALT) were started. However, both of these events promised more than they delivered.

The NPT distinguished between the then five nuclear powers and the rest. The former promised not to transfer nuclear weapons to the latter nor to assist them in constructing their own. The non-nuclear powers in turn agreed not to seek to procure such weapons. Because the non-nuclear powers were worried about the rapid piling up of nuclear stocks by the United States and the USSR particularly, they insisted on the insertion of Clause 6 into the treaty: by this article the superpowers agreed to start talks on strategic arms limitation.

The SALT talks lasted for a decade and produced three treaties. SALT I, signed in 1972, was composed of two agreements. One restricted the number of various categories of offensive missiles that the Soviet Union and the United States could hold. The other was the ABM treaty, which severely limited the number of defensive Anti-Ballistic Missiles they could deploy. SALT II, signed in 1979, extended the types of weapons embraced in the agreed limitations.

Were these treaties of any real significance? Some very obvious arguments can be marshalled to deny their worth. The NPT did not prevent the export of nuclear technology to other states as the argument that such transfers were for civil use could be and indeed was used. We have already seen that a number of formerly 'non-nuclear powers' are acquiring a nuclear capability (p. 34). And in any case, by no means all states signed the treaty. SALT I was a very incomplete agreement: it omitted bombers and provided no effective restraint on MIRVs. The number of strategic warheads significantly *increased* after this *limitation* treaty. The US Senate did not ratify SALT II (though in practice it was substantially observed).

Gromyko, Soviet Foreign Minister for nearly three decades (1957–85), has written enthusiastically about the SALT process. He has emphasised the 'openly expressed mutual understanding that informed the work'; the intrinsic value of SALT I ('enormously important in limiting the arms race'); and the way negotiations were kept in train (Gromyko, 1989, pp. 280–1). On the other hand, some commentators have been highly critical. One group of authorities has expressed its scepticism about the SALT era in the following way: 'Neither SALT I nor SALT II committed either superpower to surrender any weapon that it really wished to keep. . . . The ABM Treaty . . . was an agreement not to do what neither side intended to do' (Prins, 1983, pp. 127–28).

In a very real sense the apparent imperfections of the SALT I and ABM treaties were central to the negotiating strategy. The purpose was to stabilise the structure of nuclear deterrence. It was of paramount importance to preserve the balance between the two sides. In particular it was crucial to maintain their known capacity to launch a 'second strike' in the event of a nuclear exchange – a key element in deterrence theory at this time. The ABM treaty provides strong evidence of this thinking. Each side was permitted one such defensive site – to protect its second-strike capability.

Obviously the next objective had to be the positive reduction rather than the limitation in the increase in numbers of nuclear weapons. This work was accelerated by the ending of the cold war (see Chapter 1). The new atmosphere had three elements conducive to the conclusion of agreements for the significant scaling-down of both nuclear and conventional forces. The first was the amelioration of the political relationship between the United States and the USSR, including the toning down of the ideological commitment of the Soviets. The second element was the consequent recognition that many of the mobilised troops and much of the conventional and nuclear armoury were now surplus to the defensive needs of the two sides. And thirdly, the United States and more especially the Soviet Union had pressing financial/economic reasons for reducing military expenditure: the need to enjoy the so-called peace dividend.

Three treaties emerged from these new circumstances: Intermediate-range Nuclear Forces (INF) in 1987; Conventional Forces in Europe (CFE) in 1990; and Strategic Arms Reduction Treaty (START) in 1991.

The INF treaty was a breakthrough in nuclear disarmament for two reasons. In the first place, it provided for a reduction in numbers by the physical destruction and non-replacement of one category of weapon. This category was that of land-based missiles with ranges from 500 to 5,500 kilometres. Secondly, the United States and the USSR agreed to thorough verification of the dismantling processes: 'Each Party shall have the right to conduct inspections . . . within the territory of the other Party and within the territories of basing countries' (Article XI.2); and 'Each Party shall have the right to conduct inspections . . . for 13 years after entry into force of this Treaty' (Article XI.5).

One of the problems which has always faced the negotiators is the complexity of the nuclear armouries of the two sides. How should individual weapons be categorised? How should a weapon particular to one side be equated with one on the other side? If there is heavy imbalance of one category on one side, how can that be 'traded off' against a heavy imbalance in another category on the other side?

These questions exercised the minds of the negotiators in the START talks which began in 1982 and did not result in a signed treaty until nine years later. Even then the juggling with the numbers of launchers and warheads, 'accountable' and 'non-accountable' systems led to the text being difficult to summarise with precision. Basically it provided for a reduction of the Soviet strategic nuclear arsenal by more than 35 per cent and the American by about 25 per cent. Limits were also imposed on various categories. The relationship between the SALT and START figures in terms of warheads may be seen in Figure 3.1. A supplementary agreement was reached in 1992 which arranged further reductions in the United States and Russian strategic armouries, especially the numbers of land-based missiles. By the beginning of the next century each state would have just over 3,000 strategic warheads.

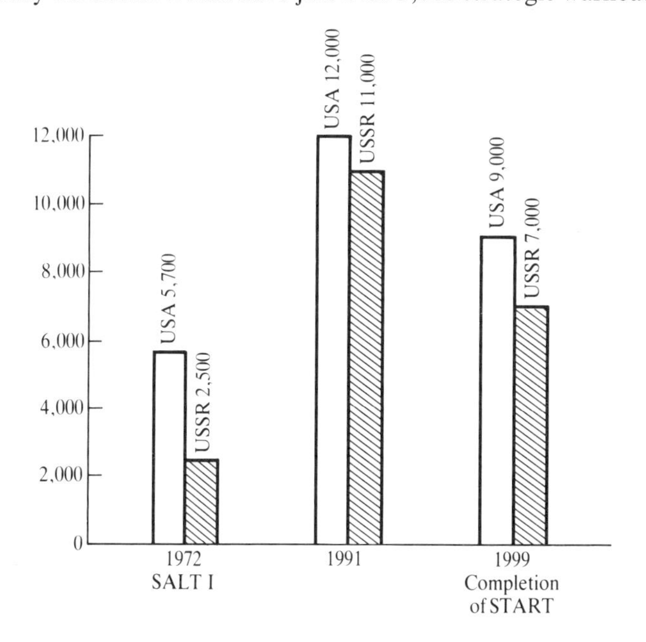

Figure **3.1** Numbers of strategic warheads

In the meantime, talks got under way to reduce the Conventional Forces in Europe (CFE). By 1991, however, these agreements had in some respects been superseded by the wishes of the Americans and Russians (not to mention other states such as Britain) to engage in further measures of disarmament unilaterally. In the autumn of that year President Bush made a dramatic announcement concerning the scaling down of American nuclear forces, particularly short-range systems; President Gorbachev responded by announcing sizeable reductions in troop levels and Soviet nuclear weapons.

By this time, too, a new disarmament agenda was taking shape. We may discern five main concerns. One is the proliferation of nuclear weapons to an ever-increasing number of states. Can international trade in fissile material and manufacturing and weapons components be further tightened? The second item concerns the stocks of chemical and biological weapons. These are sometimes called 'the poor man's nuclear bombs': they are relatively cheap to produce yet gruesomely lethal. Is it possible to persuade countries like Chile, Iraq, Libya and Vietnam, who are thought to have stocks of poison gas, to surrender them? And what about the stocks held by the United States, Russia and France?

The third problem is the massive international trade in arms, which we have already outlined (pp. 32–3). Huge quantities of munitions are sold each year. Much of this weaponry is purchased by Third World countries. This trade contributes signally to continuing poverty of these lands by the diversion of funds from peaceful use and by intensifying the destructiveness of the wars waged in the southern hemisphere. For the arms manufacturers and the chief exporting states, however, the trade is enticingly lucrative. Can the conscience-pricking arguments of morality overcome the temptations of greed? One idea is for a UN register of arms transfers so that supplying and purchasing nations may be monitored.

Fourthly, we should note the spread of missile technology. Defence against rocket-propelled missiles is extremely difficult. Yet increasing number of states are producing, selling and buying such weapons.

This brings us to the fifth item on the current agenda – the conversion of arms factories to civilian use. It was all very well for Isaiah to predict the beating of swords into ploughshares. Modern armaments and consumer goods production techniques and management are not quite so basic. Will the decommissioning of weapons factories lead to heightened unemployment? Can factories easily be retooled for civilian production? Can arms manufacturers adjust to the marketing of civilian goods? With the ending of the cold war great expectations were harboured in many countries, formerly keyed up by that tension, of the forthcoming enjoyment of the 'peace dividend'. Nevertheless, the hoped-for diversion of funds from defence to welfare, infrastructure and consumption purposes was disappointingly slow in materialising. Are there ways of accelerating the process? In 1992 Western states started to provide financial and technical assistance to the CIS republics both for the dismantling of nuclear weapons and to prevent unemployed nuclear scientists and engineers from seeking posts in other countries. But in that same year the Stockholm International Peace Research Institute (SIPRI) predicted job losses in Western Europe of approximately a quarter of a million between 1991 and 1995 as a result of the scaling-down of armaments manufacture.

Since the age of the club mankind has scarcely ever been without weapons with which to mete out injury and death to his fellows. It is useless to dream of a world stripped of armaments. What the international system can try to achieve is greater restraint on their proliferation and use.

4

Crises and Diplomacy

An international crisis is a condition of extremely bad relations between two or more states, so bad in fact that the outbreak of war between them cannot be ruled out. It is the more serious for the world if the antagonists are major powers, and the more serious still if they are members of different alliance systems. Crises may develop slowly (as between China and the Soviet Union in 1969) but are generally provoked by a sudden move by one party that is regarded as damaging or at least seriously threatening to a vital interest of another. In such circumstances routine disintegrates, top-level policy-makers go into virtually permanent secret conclave with their chiefs of staff, emergency sessions of the UN Security Council are demanded, ambassadors are recalled 'for consultation', military forces are placed on a high state of alert, press management is tightened to the point of strangulation, and propaganda exchanges become vitriolic. In the cold war (see Chapter 1) famous crises occurred over Berlin, Cuba and Afghanistan, and more recently a major crisis was prompted by the sudden invasion of Kuwait by Iraqi forces in August 1990.

It is in such circumstances that diplomacy is put to its most severe test. However, it is a mistake to regard crisis diplomacy as in some way essentially different from more ordinary kinds of diplomacy, which is the implication of applying the term 'crisis management' to the former. It is also a mistake to concentrate attention on crisis diplomacy at the expense of the more normal kind. Crisis diplomacy is distinguished only by its greater urgency and speed, and the active involvement of higher level policy-makers; and it would never work at all if there were not already wide understanding of the language, functions, and methods of everyday diplomacy. This chapter, therefore, will present a general treatment of modern diplomacy while providing illustrations from crisis diplomacy where appropriate.

The functions of diplomacy

Diplomacy has a good many functions but there is wide agreement that its chief one is negotiation, a technique of controlled argument which normally occurs between delegations of officials representing states, international organizations or other agencies. Negotiation takes place with a view to achieving one or both of the following objectives: the identification of common interests and agreement on joint action in their pursuit and compromise on an issue where interests are in conflict. A dramatic example of compromise is provided by the Cuban missile crisis of October 1962. This developed rapidly after US intelligence caught the Soviet Union in the act of installing nuclear weapons in what Washington considered to be its own backyard. An acknowledged common interest in avoiding nuclear war offered an encouraging background to a search for compromise. In the event, this was achieved by agreement on Soviet withdrawal in exchange for the lifting of the US blockade of the island and an American promise not to invade Cuba.

Negotiation is not an activity that can proceed fruitfully in any conditions. The time must be ripe, which means that the parties should have abandoned hope of achieving their objectives by other means (for example, by war). Less obviously, the talks must also take place *in secret*. The first reason for this is that they unavoidably reveal weaknesses as well as strengths. It is bad enough having to reveal weaknesses to the other side; having to reveal them to the whole world might prove highly damaging. Secondly, negotiations involving conflicting interests have to be conducted in secret because success in such negotiations inevitably means that each side will have to settle for less than its ideal requirements. This means that certain parties – a domestic interest or a foreign friend – will have to be in some measure betrayed. If they are aware of this at the time they might well be able to sabotage the negotiations. As Kissinger says: 'The sequence in which concessions are made becomes crucial; it can be aborted if each move has to be defended individually rather than as part of a mosaic before the reciprocal move is clear' (1979, p. 803).

Negotiation is not an activity for which everyone is fitted. Most international negotiations – even between allies – are difficult enough without being made more so by abrasive and discourteous behaviour. Neither can negotiation be successful unless there is a minimum of trust between the parties; trust in the truth of what is being said and trust in the promises being made. Hence honesty is among the other attributes of the successful diplomat. and so, too, is precision of language. Vagueness and muddle can lead to misunderstandings likely to result in actions inconsistent with agreed objectives; and these misunderstandings can lead to the charge of bad faith and thus vitiate subsequent negotiations. Indeed, such is the importance attached to precision of language in diplomacy that Harold Nicolson (1969), the most widely quoted twentieth-century writer on the diplomatic art in the English language, goes so far as to say that diplomacy is 'a written rather than a verbal art' (p. 60). However, lack of precision due to carelessness must not be confused with deliberate ambiguity. This can sometimes play a constructive role in negotiations when the parties concerned are in agreement on the more important issue confronting them but cannot reconcile their differences on a lesser, though related, matter on which the world nevertheless expects them to pronounce. In such circumstances it is better to fudge or 'paper over' these differences with deliberately vague language rather than to allow them to undermine the whole negotiations. An important case in point is the vagueness concerning the future of the Palestinians of the 1978 Camp David Accords.

Negotiation typically proceeds through three stages, though 'back-tracking' to an earlier stage often occurs and in crises the stages may be severely truncated. The chief stages of negotiations are pre-negotiation (putting out feelers and agreeing the format of the talks); the formula stage (agreeing the broad shape, or general principles of a settlement); and the details stage. Negotiation may be assisted by a carefully chosen venue, appropriate deadlines, mediation by third parties (see below) and, in some cases, the assurance of great power guarantees of any settlement that the powers can endorse. Such guarantees, albeit vague and very guarded, have been a marked feature of recent settlements in regional conflicts – for example, in Afghanistan and south-western Africa.

Diplomacy, however, is by no means concerned exclusively with negotiation, Among its other important functions are the conveying and clarifying of messages between governments (vital in the first days of 'crisis management'), the gathering of information, the symbolic demonstration of the state's legitimacy and splendour, the protection of a state's citizens abroad (strictly speaking, 'consular' work), and the cultivation of friendly relations. The latter should not be scorned or regarded simply as an excuse for staggering from one cocktail party to the next. Feelings of respect and 'cordiality' between states can smooth the general course of business and may sway a nicely balanced argument the right way in a crisis. But the less tangible functions of diplomacy are often overlooked, and many diplomats today find themselves in the absurd position of having to engage in export promotion in order to stave off political attacks.

Surviving the ideological attack

Diplomacy was practised in ancient Greece but it only began to assume the character of an 'institution' of the states-system with the creation of the resident ambassador in the city states of Renaissance Italy. By the eighteenth century the modern system of diplomacy was clearly recognisable, and at the Congress of Vienna in 1815 was placed on a more secure foundation by the elimination of arguments over the precedence to be accorded to different missions in the same capital city. In 1961 the Vienna Convention on Diplomatic Relations tidied up and modernised the international law that had reflected and shaped the development of this new institution.

The main reason why a diplomatic network became a permanent feature of the states-system was simple enough; only rarely was any one state simply able to seize what it wanted. In the absence of overwhelming power, negotiation was inescapable. Diplomacy, in other words, took root in centuries of multipolarity. Nevertheless, in the twentieth century the very principle of diplomacy has been under attack.

The principle of diplomacy has come under attack from ideologists of all hues. It was attacked by the Bolsheviks after the Russian Revolution in 1917, the Chinese Communists between 1949 and the early 1970s, and the Islamic fundamentalist regime in Iran following the overthrow of the Shah in 1979. Diplomacy was also held in low regard in the United States until the late 1960s, when disasters in Vietnam produced unprecedented feelings of national weakness. However, this was an antipathy fostered as much by geographical isolation and enormous power as by the pronounced moralistic and legal strains in American foreign policy. Ideologists, whose tests of truth are unique and whose arrogance is absolute, cannot reason and compromise with their opponents but only kill, convert or – if their power is too great – ignore them.

The unusually ideological character of the twentieth century has certainly contributed to long periods in which diplomacy was at a discount; war and propaganda have often seemed to be the hallmarks of this epoch. However, the balance of power has preserved the states-system through thick and thin and thus maintained the situation in which diplomacy is unavoidable – namely, that in which not even the strongest power is able simply to seize what it wants. Within months of the October Revolution the Bolsheviks had realised that the social structure of the rest of Europe was not going to be razed to the ground. They consquently started to conduct a diplomacy of their own with the surrounding capitalist states, thus swiftly reversing the famous announcement of the first People's Commissar of Foreign Affairs, Leon Trotsky, that he would just 'issue a few revolutionary proclamations to the people and then close up shop' (Uldricks, 1979, p. 17).

During the 1960s the cold war gave way to serious negotiations, first on the ground rules of the conflict and then on more substantive issues. Imperial distractions and economic disintegration in the late 1980s confirmed Moscow's disposition to seek negotiated solutions with the Americans. Furthermore, at the height of its isolation from the West, in 1966, China retained diplomatic missions in forty-eight states, while during the 1970s, fearful of Soviet attack and less and less impressed by the merits of self-reliance, it came in from the cold altogether. By this time, too, most of the new states had well and truly lost any early suspicions of traditional diplomacy and were as heavily involved in it as their slender budgets would permit. Though it is true that embassies have been attacked by mobs, this has only occasionally (as in Tehran and Tripoli) been with the connivance of governments.

Modern methods

Diplomacy as such, then, has manifestly survived. Nevertheless, it is true that in its *methods* there have been considerable changes. Though different changes are to be explained in part by reference to different reasons, all have been in significant measure influenced by the multiplication of international crises in the twentieth century, their more apocalyptic implications, and the new opportunities provided by advances in transport and communications (including, not least, television). The much greater use of summitry is the most spectacular of these changes but is probably not the most significant.

Summitry

Politicians now play a much greater role in diplomacy relative to the professionals than they did before the Second World War. A distinction should be made at once, however, between 'summits' of political leaders and meetings of politicians at lower levels. Thus while the latter may make serious individual contributions to international negotiations, especially when an impasse has been reached, summitry usually plays a somewhat different role, though in part a *diplomatic* one none the less.

Heads of government, especially if they are also heads of state, are usually in no position to make any individual, direct contribution to international negotiations and it is as well if they do not try. As David Watt says: 'with their massive egos, their ignorance of the essential details and their ingrained belief in the value of backslapping ambiguity, [they] simply mess everything up' (*The Times*, 3 July 1981). Besides, since heads of government personify regimes and always attract great publicity, it is difficult for them to contemplate bringing a summit to a scheduled end without something substantial to present to their followers. Hence they are always in danger of falling into one of two traps. One is the making of unwise concessions in order to achieve a 'success', which, because of the greater loss of face, are more difficult to retrieve when made by a head of state rather than a professional diplomat. The other is the breaking off of negotiations prematurely if it seems that they will not be able to gain everything they had promised. The unfortunate results of the personal encounter between Hitler and Chamberlain on the eve of the Second World War is a sobering illustration of the risks of summit meetings.

Fortunately, the pitfalls of summitry are now widely recognised and therefore usually avoided. This is achieved by ensuring that excessive expectations are not previously aroused; that the greater part of the negotiations is concluded before the summit actually begins; and that any remaining details are wrapped up by the professionals prior to the scheduled signing ceremony. But if the heads of government thus have little to do other than sign any agreements and pose for the cameras, what, if anything, is the positive contribution of summitry to diplomacy?

Summits certainly allow government leaders to take the measure of each other in person. They also force heads of government to see problems in their international context, that is, they discourage parochialism. They make 'linkage' easier, that is, trade-offs between different areas ('we'll make concessions to you on trade if you'll give ground to us on arms control'); this is because they involve the person who has to carry all of the otherwise bureaucratically separate strands of policy in his own head. And summits can be very helpful in setting deadlines for important negotiations and breaking last-minute deadlocks. Certainly, great quantities of midnight oil were burned in order to bring the SALT (arms control) negotiations to virtual completion before the arrival in Moscow of President Nixon in May 1972, while the proximity of leaders on this occasion allowed for a relatively speedy settlement of remaining differences. A similar process preceded the signing of the INF Treaty during the Reagan–Gorbachev summit in Washington in December 1987.

In short, it is clear that especially when summits are held regularly, when they are in effect institutionalised, they are of the first importance in maintaining diplomatic momentum on an issue or range of issues. Following the advent of Mikhail Gorbachev, summitry became an institution in East – West relations – and arms control, the settlement of regional conflicts, and other matters have benefited accordingly. But it should not be forgotten that for varying lengths of time summitry has also been an important institution of the Commonwealth, the 'Front-Line States' in Africa, the Arab League, the European Community (the 'European Council'), the 'Group of Seven' Western economic powers, Central and South America (the 'Rio Group'), francophone Africa (the annual 'Franco – African summit'), and other regional groupings.

Another important diplomatic function of summits (and meet-the-people foreign tours) is to clarify intentions by dramatic *symbolism*. The purpose may be to underline an existing commitment, as when President Kennedy visited West Berlin in 1962 and addressed the words 'Ich bin ein Berliner' to an increasingly hysterical crowd in the Rudolph Wilde Platz. It may be to emphasise the sincerity of a new policy priority, as when the Egyptian President, Anwar Sadat, made his 'historic' visit to Jerusalem in November 1977, or when President Bush met the leaders of the South American drug-producing countries at the 'Cocaine Summit' held in the Colombian seaside resort of Cartagena in February 1990. Or it may be to set the seal on a new friendship, as when Benazir Bhutto of Pakistan met Rajiv Gandhi of India in December 1988. Summits are also probably the best way to demonstrate solidarity between friendly governments in a crisis, as in the one-day summit between Soviet and American leaders held on 9 September 1990 in Helsinki in order to discuss the Gulf crisis.

Multilateral diplomacy

Summitry and multilateral diplomacy are to some extent overlapping categories since many summit meetings (such as those of the Arab League) regularly involve more than two leaders. Nevertheless, it is conventional to treat this method separately, which is entirely right since it raises separate issues.

As the twentieth century has witnessed a huge growth in summitry, so it has also seen a substantial switch to diplomacy in conference at which many states are represented, that is, to multilateral rather than bilateral diplomacy. As well as being encouraged by the general developments mentioned at the beginning of this section, this was also a response to the great increase in the number of states and to the naïve liberal idea that diplomats required to debate in a public assembly would be creative and pacific in their outlook.

There are two main kinds of multilateral conference, *ad hoc* and permanent. The *ad hoc* conference, such as that convened in Madrid in November 1991 in order to discuss the Arab–Israeli dispute (see Chapter 10) is one called up when the occasion demands and dissolved when agreement is reached or failure to agree is acknowledged. Such conferences, however, have other distinguishing features, which align them squarely with traditional diplomacy. Only interested parties are invited, the agenda is agreed beforehand, the chairman is usually a dignitary of the host government, and – most importantly – unanimity is required for agreement. By contrast, permanent, or standing conferences (sometimes known as 'international organisations'), such as the United Nations, the International Monetary Fund (IMF) and the Organisation of African Unity (OAU), have diplomatic delegations permanently accredited to them and a permanent secretariat typically headed by a 'Secretary-General'. In further contrast to *ad hoc* conferences, permanent conferences of ten have a deliberative group which is wider than that of the 'interested parties' and characteristically adopt a 'parliamentary' style of proceeding; they debate in public; they have a non-specific agenda; and they wield votes (only rarely, as in the World Bank, weighted to give more influence to the bigger members) in order to determine the outcome.

It will be clear from the foregoing that permanent conferences in practice often have little to do with diplomacy – and certainly not with crisis diplomacy – and even exacerbate tensions between states. The General Assembly of the United Nations – where each member state is encouraged to speak up even on issues that have only the remotest connection with its interests – is particularly notorious for conducting propaganda in the name of diplomacy. Among its more significant consequences in this regard it contributed to the general deterioration in relations between the United States and the Third World in the 1970s. It was awareness that the United Nations was a diplomatic minefield which produced the early reluctance of Finland and Mexico to serve on the Security Council and clearly contributes to the continuing refusal of the Swiss people to join the UN at all. However, proper attention to the anti-diplomatic side of permanent conferences such as the United Nations should not be allowed to obscure the fact that they usually have a pro-diplomatic aspect as well. The UN – despite the reputation which it acquired in the United States in the 1970s for being 'a dangerous place' – is no exception to this rule.

Apart from mediation by the Secretariat (see below), the United Nations fulfils two main diplomatic roles. First of all, and because it is widely regarded as the world's most important shrine to peace, the UN makes acceptable ('legitimises') diplomatic contact between states who do not normally like to be seen in each other's company. The Security Council itself is the most obvious example of this role in operation; but the same function is being fulfilled when the UN puts its imprimatur on an *ad hoc* conference such as that held on the Middle East in Geneva in December 1973 and essentially run by the Americans. States can also retreat from dangerous positions if it can be made to *look* as if they are deferring to the UN rather than to their enemies.

Secondly, the UN provides a convenient forum for general diplomatic activity. The UN facilitiates diplomacy because almost all states have permanent representation at its New York headquarters, and because many world leaders attend the annual opening of the General Assembly each September. This is especially important both to states that are too poor to afford world-wide diplomatic networks and to those who cannot afford to be *seen* talking to each other even under UN auspices. In the late 1970s New York was used by the Americans to make contact with the Palestine Liberation Organisation, with which they had sworn to have no dealings until it recognised the state of Israel; a decade later they used it to make contact with the Marxist government of Angola (which they did not recognise) in the context of the negotiations being brokered by the Reagan administration to bring peace to south-western Africa.

Unconventional diplomacy

The United Nations (together, it should be added, with certain other permanent conferences) is by no means the only vehicle that hostile states may employ in order to preserve, or re-establish, discreet diplomatic contact. Crises followed by an abrupt severance of diplomatic relations, as well as the severance of relations merely to make a political gesture in the absence of any genuine crisis, have been so common since the 1960s that old alternatives to the exchange of ambassadors have been used more extensively than ever. These include mediation by third parties, the special envoy, the diplomatic corps in third states, and funeral diplomacy. Furthermore, at least one new method has been invented, the interests section.

States have long entrusted their interests in a hostile state to the embassy of a state with which both are on friendly terms. Because of their policies of neutrality, Switzerland and Sweden have been especially popular choices for the role of 'protecting power'.

However, it is now common to find a state's interests in a hostile state being protected by a small group of its *own* diplomats operating under the flag of the embassy of a third state. *Interests sections*, as they are known, were first employed by the United Kingdom when seven African states broke off relations with London as a protest at the weakness of its response to the unilateral declaration of independence in 1965 by the white supremacist party controlling its self-governing colony of Rhodesia. With the agreement of these states, 'British Interests Sections' were established in the embassies of third states in their capitals.

Though the effectiveness of interests sections is impaired by their smallness (though not all are miniscule), the junior status of their members, and the extreme hostility – in some cases – of their immediate environment, at least they ensure that a presence *inside* the countries concerned is maintained. This makes it easier to conduct the general business of diplomacy. Some interests sections occupy their own buildings and are virtually embassies in all but name.

During the Falklands War a British Interests Section was established in the Swiss Embassy in Buenos Aires. Following the severance of relations with the United States by Egypt and other Arab states in the aftermath of the Arab–Israeli war of 1967 an American Interests Section was opened in the Spanish Embassy in Cairo. And following the rupture in United States–Iran relations consequent upon the overthrow of the Shah, an Iranian Interests Section was opened in the Algerian Embassy in Washington. However, as well as being employed as a means to salvage something from a dramatically deteriorating relationship, interests sections may be created as the first step towards normality in an improving one. Thus in 1986, against the background of a thaw in relations between Israel and Eastern Europe, the governments in Jerusalem and Warsaw, which had enjoyed no diplomatic relations for almost twenty years, agreed to exchange interests sections. Their first tasks were to process visa applications and foster cultural links but it was clear that, if things went well, the new diplomatic connection woud be upgraded.

Direct contact between hostile states may also be made within the *diplomatic corps in a (third) state* with which each has diplomatic relations. This was an important means employed by the United States and the People's Republic of China during the long years of their bitter rivalry following the revolution in 1949; Geneva, Warsaw, and finally Paris were the cities where their diplomatic proximity was most usefully exploited. It is true that the 134 formal Sino–American meetings held in Warsaw prior to January 1970 (mainly to do with the US relationship with Taiwan) seemed sterile. Nevertheless, the 135th meeting witnessed a breakthrough after both powers had decided to explore, with great caution, the possibilities of a *rapprochement*. The Warsaw channel was soon supplanted by Paris, where contact between the Chinese Embassy and the US Military Attaché, General Vernon Walters, was deliberately established, on American initiative, in 1971. (Paris was less vulnerable to KGB eavesdropping and already the site of the secret Vietnam negotiations.) A great improvement in Sino–American relations took place in the years following and there was soon a permanent American mission in the Chinese capital. Beijing itself, it is interesting to note, is now the setting for diplomatic contacts between the United States and one of the last remaining Communist regimes, North Korea.

The strategy of exploiting coincidental proximity in third states has the obvious disadvantage that the diplomats of the unfriendly states are likely to have been chosen for their knowledge of the third state rather than for their knowledge of each other's country. Walters was unable to speak Chinese and the Chinese Ambassador in Paris could not speak English (oddly enough, he could not speak French either). On the other hand, great secrecy can attend these meetings.

Direct contact between hostile states may also be made by the high-powered teams of mourners which they dispatch to attend the funerals of foreign digitaries. *Funeral diplomacy*, which goes back at least to the Feast of the Dead celebrated by the Algonkians of the Upper Great Lakes of Canada in the seventeenth century and probably much further, is a special case of summitry. It began to become important in the 1960s and became an especially pronounced feature of international politics in the 1980s as a result of the highly advanced age profile of the Soviet leadership. Brezhnev, Andropov and Chernenko all died in fairly quick succession between late 1982 and early 1985, and their funeral rites were attended by huge numbers of foreign dignitaries and professional diplomats. As well as taking the opportunity of talking with each other, almost all of them wanted discussions with the new

Soviet leadership (allies seeking reassurance that there would be continuity of policy; rivals looking for signs of change). Particularly worthy of note in the category of talks between the bereaved and the delegations of mourners were the encouraging conversations held between Andropov and the Pakistani leader, General Zia ul-Haq, at Brezhnev's funeral in November 1982. These were important because Islamabad was embroiled indirectly with Moscow over the bitter conflict then raging in Afghanistan. Interesting as an illustration of the category of talks between the mourning delegations themselves were the fruitful discussions held between the East German leader, Erich Honecker, and Chancellor Kohl of West Germany at the funerals of both Adropov and Chernenko. These were the first occasions on which the leaders of divided Germany met.

'Working funerals' as they are now known, are important because even the enemies of the bereaved government can attend without serious fear of attack from supporters at home or friends abroad; paying respects to the dead (unless exotically depraved or the object of religious anathemas) is above reproach in probably all cultures, including that of the New York mob. These funerals are times of political truce. It is true that the short notice given for them means that attendance will upset the diplomatic schedules of busy leaders, and that, in the rush, rebuffs and mistakes may be courted. (Zia, who had been so well received by Andropov at Brezhnev's funeral, was humiliated by Chernenko at the wake of Andropov himself.) Nevertheless, self-confident and agile leaders (hosts as well as visitors) now find them occasions that provide great diplomatic opportunities, and precisely *because* normally only a few days elapse between the death of the foreign dignitary and his funeral.

To begin with, this means that there is little time for political opposition to be mounted against attendance; it also means that circumstances are unlikely to have deteriorated between the decision to attend and the funeral itself (compare the student occupation of Tiananmen Square which formed the embarrassing backdrop to the long-announced Gorbachev–Deng summit in Beijing in 1989). Secondly, and above all, it means that diplomatic schedules *can* be broken without causing serious offence in order to seize the opportunitiy for discussions with foreign leaders on an issue of immediate urgency. Mrs Thatcher became a regular diplomatic mourner in the 1980s, though President Reagan was wisely kept at home. It should also be noted that these funerals present first-class opportunities for the signalling of intentions. Hosts do this via the style in which mourning delegations are received; mourners via their ability to attend or not to attend, and if to attend at what level to attend. The Egyptians, who had been substantially ostracised in the Arab world after making peace with Israel in 1979, were able to extend an obvious olive branch to the Saudis by sending President Mubarak himself to the funeral of King Khalid in 1982.

Finally, direct contact between hostile states may be made by the simple expedient of dispatching a high-ranking government official (or even minister) on a temporary visit. The *special envoy* may go in public or in secret, depending upon the odium which the visit might be expected to attract or the alarm which it might be reckoned to excite. Secret ones, of course, tend to be better known after the event. We may cite several interesting cases. Henry Kissinger paid a secret visit to China during the fragile early stages of the *rapprochement* with the United States. An extraordinary visit was made to Tehran by President Reagan's own National Security Adviser, Robert MacFarlane, who was trying to put together the notorious arms-for-hostages deal. South Africans made forays into black Africa in 1974. Israel's new Foreign Minister, Moshe Dayan, made an excursion to India in 1977, travelling on scheduled Alitalia flights and disguised by dark glasses and a large straw hat. (In the same year he also travelled to Morocco, disguised this time – incredibly enough – as a beatnik.) By contrast, in the 1970s no secret was made of the travels to Eastern Europe of the Vatican special envoy, Cardinal Casarole, nor in the early 1980s of those of Richard Stone, United States Special Envoy to Central America.

Special missions of high-powered officials are valuable where deeply suspicious enemies need to be convinced of each other's good faith in seeking an accommodation. Nevertheless, they are fraught with perils. Such missions may seriously damage a state or an international organisation's prestige if they are made with public knowledge, especially if they fail to produce results. This is even more likely if they are made to the home territories of other parties rather than to arranged meetings on neutral ground, since those launching the missions are placed in the position of supplicants. This was painfully illustrated by the visit to Baghdad of the UN Secretary-General himself on the eve of the Gulf War. Besides, public missions invite sabotage of the policy initiatives which are behind them. For these reasons, unless their visits are intended to be symbolic (as when a British diplomat visited Pnom Penh, capital of Communist Cambodia, in 1990, in order to defuse the charge that the West was in effect aiding the come-back of the murderous Khmer Rouge), special envoys normally make their trips in secret. However, if they are made in secret, the high rank of the envoy means that there are formidable obstacles to be overcome in order to ensure that they remain secret. And if caution dictates a secret meeting on neutral ground, the host government will normally have to be told a good deal of what is going on. The French government seemed to know a lot more about Kissinger's secret talks with the Chinese and the North Vietnamese in Paris than most administration officials in Washington. Finally, the contact provided by special missions is, by definition, spasmodic. They can, therefore, never be the only form of contact between states seeking to repair long-embittered relations.

There are thus a variety of methods whereby hostile states may make direct diplomatic contact. But in addition to these there are, of course, various *indirect* ones. When *mediation* is employed, hostile states vest in a third party more or less limited powers to help them achieve a settlement, ranging from acting simply as a bearer of messages to being in the chair of the talks and an active supporter of a specific solution. The mediator is normally a state, or the secretariat of a body such as the UN or the OAU (these two have acted jointly in the Western Sahara dispute). However, non-governmental organisations such as the International Committee of the Red Cross (ICRC), together with private individuals, may be employed in limited capacities as well. Among the latter, journalists and businessmen, whose work provides them with legitimate reasons for foreign travel and contact with governments, are particular favourties. During the Cuban missile crisis the Soviet Union used both to convey messages to Washington.

The hostile states themselves may or may not be prepared to negotiate face-to-face following the intervention of the third party. If 'recognition' of one or more of the states is an issue, this will certainly not take place. In such circumstances 'proximity talks' are employed: that is, negotiations in which a mediator carries messages between hostile delegations, usually located in separate rooms in the same building. A recent example is provided by the UN-mediated talks on the conflict in Afghanistan between Pakistan and the

Soviet-backed regime in Kabul, which started in 1981 and finally reached agreement in April 1988.

What are the qualities (other than those required in any diplomacy) of the ideal mediator? Impartiality in the dispute is normally important, though this should not be taken to imply that the mediator needs to be indifferent to the nature of the solution. Power, whether military or economic, is also a very important asset if the mediation involves active chairmanship. This argues for mediation by a superpower or a larger medium power (though Algeria – which is neither – has achieved a reputation for modest success in mediation efforts). A considerable part of Jimmy Carter's achievement at Camp David is explained by his ability to offer both the Egyptians and the Israelis large amounts of money – 'side payments'. A decade later, in 1988, the pressure which the United States was able to bring to bear on both the Angolans and the South Africans was also an important ingredient in the success of the mediation efforts in South-Western Africa of US Assistant Secretary of State for African Affairs, Chester Crocker. The mediator also requires staying power because if the conflicts were not intractable they would not have required mediation in the first place. This argues for mediation by international organisations or stable autocracies, rather than democratic regimes subject to periodic changes in direction after elections. This is where the United States falls down, as witness the essentially episodic nature of its efforts in the Arab–Israeli conflict.

States which assume the role of mediator rarely do so out of high-mindedness but because they expect to benefit from it. They may hope that by helping to defuse a conflict they will remove the risk of being dragged into a dangerous military intervention in it themselves. They may anticipate an increase in their international prestige. Or they may be looking for a quid pro quo of one sort or another from either or both parties. All of these considerations influenced the American diplomatic intervention in the Angola–Namibia negotiations, while Yahya Khan's good offices in the early stages of America's *rapprochement* with China were repaid by President Nixon's 'tilt to Pakistan' (relative to its long-standing differences with India) in 1971. It is because mediation by a state usually requires payment of some kind that mediation by the UN or a regional organisation or the Vatican, each of which – under different charters – has an obligation to engage in mediation, may be advisable. Besides, agencies such as these can bring *continuous engagement* to mediation – and sometimes more power, too, than is commonly supposed. The importance of continuity is borne out strikingly by the achievements finally won by UN mediation in the Iran–Iraq conflict and in Afghanistan in the second half of the 1980s.

The survival of the resident embassy

Despite the fact that modern diplomacy has witnessed substantial changes, these do not include the disappearance of the permanent ambassador, so confidently predicted in the 1960s. Bilateral diplomacy is alive and well and its servants are to be found in every national capital in the world, as well as at the seats of major international organisations. Some of them not long retired, such as Anatoly Dobrynin (Soviet Ambassador in Washington from 1962 until 1986) and Sir Anthony Parsons (British Ambassador in Tehran from 1973 until 1979), were figures of considerable influence in the relations between their own governments and those to which they were accredited.

Most of the central functions of diplomacy cannot usually be performed adequately by anyone other than the permanent ambassador and his increasingly expert staff. This does not apply, it is true, to negotation, in which – especially in fairly well 'integrated' regions such as Western Europe – embassies have been substantially replaced by politicians and home-based experts. Nevertheless, if the latter were to be called on to negotiate on every matter which cropped up in bilateral relations their mental and physical resources would soon be exhausted. Hence embassy staff are still frequently employed to negotiate on matters of lesser importance even in regions where direct government contacts are highly developed. Where this is not so, embassies still commonly play an important role in high level negotiations as well. Dobrynin's role in Soviet–American negotiations, at least during the Nixon years, was clearly pivotal.

For political reporting to the sending government, the resident embassy is indispensable; this is especially true in crises, during which the embassies of the parties concerned often remain open throughout or at least until it appears that fighting is imminent.

Provided its senior staff have been carefully selected, the embassy will have a better understanding of local realities than the foreign ministry at home, easier access to high government officials (including heads of government) than either secret intelligence agents or the media, and obviously a greater inclination than the latter to ask the questions in which its government is interested. The embassy's local knowledge plus its privileged access in turn place it in a better position than anyone else to *lobby* on behalf of its government and locally resident citizens (as we saw in the case of the Western embassies in Baghdad during the recent Gulf crisis). Furthermore, while others – for example, sportsmen – may be 'great ambassadors for their country' in the creation of goodwill abroad, only the embassy can be relied on to make this a continuous priority. Finally, though many governments may find this a dispensable function, the resident embassy is a permanent reminder of the fact that beyond the state there is a states-system, a political order to which all states owe some allegiance.

Nevertheless, as this chapter has tried to demonstrate, the resident embassy is now only one important element in an increasingly dense network of contacts between professional diplomats. This testifies to the inescapability of diplomacy in a world where power is dispersed rather than concentrated. It also makes crises easier to manage because of the greater choice of lines of communication, and because a signal sent along one can be reinforced by sending the same signal along another. Altogether, the world diplomatic network reduces the ignorance which nurtures fear, cushions the collision of elephantine political egos, and – more often than not – eventually produces agreements where none was initially thought possible.

5

Regional Powers and Tensions

Regional power politics

We live in a world in which all the component states are, according to international law and convention, equal. Yet they range in size of population from China with over 1 billion inhabitants to the Pacific island of Nauru with fewer than 10,000. Their armed strength varies from the intimidating superpower might of the United States to the military impotence of the forty or so micro-states. In wealth too, whether measured in gross national product (GNP) or GNP per capita, a huge gap separates the richest from the poorest states.

The international system has to take account of these wide variations. Different ages display different configurations of power relationships. The classic European system from the mid-seventeenth to the mid-twentieth century revolved around the existence of a handful of major powers. The half-century from the end of the Second World War was the era of superpower bipolarity (see pp. 3–4). Since about 1990 the United States alone has survived as a truly world superpower.

Nevertheless, whatever the context of great power dominance, there have always been second-rate powers – below the strength of the dominant states, yet with economic and military resources that have been by no means negligible. The concept of middle or minor powers was first officially recognised in the post-1815 German Confederation. But although a state may be a middle power in comparison with the great powers on the world stage, it may in its own regional context play the role of a major power in relation to the even smaller states in its immediate geopolitical environment. Martin Wight commented on this situation. He wrote:

> in certain regions which are culturally united but politically divided, a subordinate international society comes into being. . . . In such sub-systems as these, there will be some states with general interests relative to the limited region and a capacity to act alone, which gives them the appearance of local great powers.
>
> (Wight, 1979, p. 63)

The ambition to attain or retain local great power status may have either a stabilising or destabilising effect on a region depending on the circumstances. If one state is indisputably stronger than the rest, then it may be able to use its influence to sustain the status quo, a condition that is in its own interests in any case. On the other hand, if two or more states are in contention for regional domination, they may be drawn into fighting to decide the issue. Nor must it be forgotten that first-rank powers may intervene in regional affairs to affect the local power relationship.

These generalisations can be illustrated most vividly from the recent history of the Gulf (see also pp. 68–70). During the 1970s the United States built up Iran as a regional power. American motives were the need to stem Soviet influence in the area and to ensure a secure supply of oil. After the overthrow of the Shah in the 1979 revolution, the United States began to cultivate Iraq, a long-standing Soviet client and leading rival of Iran, instead. Iraq and Iran then fought a bitter eight-year war. The United States, however, fearful of the lust for power of the Iraqi leader, Saddam Hussein, attempted to destroy his military might in the second Gulf War of 1991, and set about bolstering Saudi Arabia in turn as the regional power.

If one great power intervenes in a region, it is usually for the purpose of acquiring or consolidating influence for itself. If two or more great powers intervene, the motive can be the more altruistic one of promoting peace for its own sake. The end of the cold war in the late 1990s enabled the United States and the USSR to collaborate in reducing or ending conflict in numerous places. These included Afghanistan, Cambodia and South-West Africa (Angola and Namibia). They also combined in efforts to bring greater peace and justice to the Middle East. (For great power collaboration, see Chapter 12.)

The study of regional international relations such as these raises questions about regional co-operative associations, the nature of power and the nature of sovereignty.

During a period spanning little more than two decades large areas of the world were provided with regional organisations devoted to trying to solve their own quarrels and enhancing co-operation. The Arab League was founded in 1945; the Organisation of American States (OAS), in 1948; the Organisation of African Unity (OAU), in 1963; and the Association of South-East Asian States (ASEAN), in 1967.

The Arab League was established to foster links among the Arab states from the Straits of Gibraltar to the Persian Gulf. In its early years it was concerned mainly with the continuing influence of France in some of its member-states and the creation and policies of Israel. Since about 1970 the attitudes and policies of the members have diverged to such a degree that the League's potential for co-ordinated action has been reduced to being just a mouthpiece for moderation.

The OAS evolved from organisations created at the turn of the century. With the exception of Canada, which has never been a member, and Cuba, which was expelled in 1962, the organisation embraces all the states of the Americas and Caribbean. Its ostensible purpose is collective defence. In practice, however, it has been mainly used as a vehicle for the United States' concept of regional peace: that is, preservation of the status quo so favourable to US interests. The OAS has successfully cooled some intra-regional conflicts, notably arranging a cease-fire between Peru and Ecuador in 1981. It has also made some small efforts at encouraging economic and human rights improvements.

The OAU owes its origin to the desire of newly independent states to co-operate and to promote the process of decolonisation in Africa still further. It has largely succeeded in establishing the principle of maintaining the state boundaries inherited from the colonial era. Since the 1970s, however, the organisation has declined in effectiveness and prestige.

ASEAN is composed of Brunei, Indonesia, Malaysia, Singapore, the Philippines and Thailand. Its main purpose is to promote economic co-operation and development. The association has been most successful in its relations with Japan. Progress towards the integration of members' economies along the lines of the European Community and much favoured by Singapore has been exceedingly slow.

Political power, our second major question, is the ability to bring influence to bear so as to ensure that the outcome of a given course of events is what one desires. That power may be exercised in an international arena either through peaceful, diplomatic persuasion (scc Chapter 4) or by the threat or actual use of military force. It is usually understood that the status of 'power' (of whatever rank) can be attributed to a state only if it has the forces to exercise the military option if it so wishes. But can it really be denied that a state of great economic strength but of modest military capability is a power in the sense of wielding influence?

The cases of Germany and Japan since 1945 have made it necessary to pose this question. The constitutions of these two defeated former Axis powers have precluded the deployment of their armed forces outside their own territories. Japan, indeed, spends only a tiny proportion of its massive GNP on armed forces. Moreover, neither Germany nor Japan is equipped with nuclear weapons. Partly because of this relative military weakness and partly because of their need to tread delicately on the international stage because of their black Second World War records, these two states have not exercised political influence in recent decades in proportion to their formidable economic performance. Germany has often been called 'an economic giant but a political dwarf'.

In the conventional sense Germany and Japan have not been great powers as they were, for example, from the early 1930s to 1945. Yet the strength of the Deutschmark and the yen in international financial markets has significant global ramifications. It is sometimes wryly noted that, insofar as the motives for the ultimately unsuccessful aggressive policies of Hitler and Tojo were economic, their successors have brilliantly achieved those objectives by peaceful means. Is this not power?

Our second problem concerns sovereignty. The myth of international law is that all states are equal in sovereignty. But as in Orwell's literary allegory, *Animal Farm*, some, in reality, are very much more equal than others. One of the attributes of sovereignty is that the sovereign state's borders are impermeable. No other state has a right to interfere (except in a condition of war) in the internal affairs of a fellow sovereign state. Yet power can be and is exercised locally by relatively stronger states against weaker ones to achieve their ends.

Acting as a hemispheric regional power the United States has a long history of intervening, both openly and covertly, in its own 'back-yard': the Caribbean and Latin America. In defence of its own ideological, economic and security interests the United States has shown scant respect for the sovereignty of a number of states in the region. The most recent example was the invasion of Panama in 1989. Sovereignty was the issue in the war in the South Atlantic in 1982. Britain claimed sovereign right over the Falkland Islands while the local regional power, Argentina, argued that the same archipelago, which it called 'the Malvinas', were part of her sovereign territory (see also p. 72).

An interesting example of local intervention in the domestic affairs of a sovereign state occurred in East Africa in 1979. In that year President Nyerere of Tanzania, sickened by the bloodshed perpetrated by his maniacal neighbour Idi Amin of Uganda, ordered Tanzanian troops to invade that suffering country to overthrow its ruler.

In the Middle East there is no doubting the status of Israel as a formidable regional power, yet its very right to exist as a sovereign state was for long denied by its Arab neighbours (see Chapter 10). And Israel itself has virtually institutionalised – for security reasons – its own intervention in the affairs of Lebanon.

The most instructive example of sovereignty as a regional issue was occasioned by the policies of Saddam Hussein of Iraq in 1990–1. His invasion and capture of Kuwait in 1990 was universally condemned as an act of unacceptable aggression against a sovereign member of the community of nations. Then, after the subsequent war (see p. 71), Saddam renewed the brutal treatment of the Kurds of northern Iraq in which he had periodically engaged throughout his dictatorship. Several nations, prompted by Britain, sent troops and relief workers via Turkey into Iraq to establish 'a safe haven' for the Kurds. Officially the state of war between Iraq and the anti-Iraqi coalition no longer obtained. Yet these foreign personnel violated the borders of the sovereign state of Iraq. Many questions were raised at the time as to whether sovereignty could any longer have any real meaning.

It must be emphasised, of course, that in considering these examples of the role or violation of sovereignty in regional conflicts, the issue has been the legal not the moral validity of the actions. Let us now consider some examples of the regional powers and conflicts not dealt with elsewhere in this book.

The Gulf

The region of the Middle East known in shorthand as 'the Gulf' (see Figure 5.1) lies at the intersection of several dangerous conflicts. Moreover, inter-state and intra-state discontents and hatreds contribute further to the instability of the area.

Figure 5.1 The Gulf region

In the nineteenth century the Ottoman and British Empires exercised a virtual *de facto* condominium over the region. The

Turkish sultan was suzerain over Mesopotamia and the Arabian peninsula. The British, in pursuit of their Indian interests, occupied Aden, gradually exercised increasing influence in southern Persia and policed the Persian Gulf itself. Several sheikhdoms on the Arabian coast of the Gulf became British protectorates,

The collapse and dismemberment of the Ottoman Empire at the end of the First World War led to a political fragmentation of the region and incipient instability. The British withdrew from their Persian zone of influence and retained a League of Nations mandate over Iraq for only a few years. Both Persia (now called Iran) and Iraq were, by virtue of the size of their populations and potential oil wealth, regional powers-in-waiting. But the region remained quiescent internationally for a few decades more largely because oil, the subsequent source of intense interest, remained of relatively minor importance even as recently as about 1950.

Western influence, verging on partial control, of the Gulf region has continued. Britain retained a substantial presence in the petty princedoms from Kuwait to Oman until 1971. Increasingly, British power was supplemented, then supplanted by that of America. Part of the motivation, for over a century, until about 1990, was fear of a Russian drive to the Indian Ocean – initially tsarist, subsequently Communist.

Colouring this fear of Russian imperialism was the growing concern to preserve Western oil interests – both the profits of the predominantly British and American companies operating in the area and the assured supply of the precious fluid. We may take as indices of the increasing importance of Gulf oil the following figures. In 1938 the subsequent major producers of the region, namely Iran, Saudi Arabia, Kuwait and Iraq, accounted for 14.9 million tons or 5.3 per cent of the world total. A generation later,in 1969, these figures had risen to 521.3 million tons and 24.4 per cent.

As Britain withdrew from direct government of sundry territories in the region, more indirect ways of exercising influence were devised in London and Washington. Partly these were covert activities by the US Central Intelligence Agency (CIA); partly, the support of friendly rulers by military advice and *matériel*. The most notable example of this policy was the American build-up of Iran in the 1970s. The *New York Times* explained in 1971:

> Acting with British-American blessings, Shah Mohammad Reza Pahlavi has accepted responsibility for the security of the Persian Gulf after Britain removes its protection and armed forces. . . . By 1975, when the present programme of military deliveries and training is completed, Iran is expected to be a major Middle Eastern power and an element of stability in the volatile Gulf region, American officials say.
>
> (quoted, Halliday, 1974, p. 484)

The plan did not outlive the decade as the Shah's regime foundered in the Islamic revolution in 1979. By 1990 the behaviour of Saddam Hussein had disqualified Iraq for the role of US-supported regional power. Therefore, in the months following the second Gulf war (see p. 71) the American administration pumped over 800 million dollars' worth of sophisticated military equipment into Saudi Arabia in order that she might perform this function.

However, all this Western attention was not entirely welcome. Powerful nationalist movements were already expressing anti-Western feelings in Iran and Iraq by the 1950s. Sometimes these were directed primarily against Western political influence, sometimes against Western economic control, sometimes against Western cultural infiltration. For instance, the creation of the Organisation of Petroleum Exporting Countries (OPEC), including six Gulf States, in 1960 was an attempt to defend these countries' economic interests against the Western multinational oil companies. A more dramatic example may be found in the Iranian revolution of 1979. In the capital Tehran, this assumed violent anti-American overtones, including the seizure of the US Embassy staff as hostages.

Peace in the Gulf region is intermittently threatened not only, or even chiefly, because of hostility to Western influence. There are also many antagonistic cross-currents within the region.

First, we may recall the enmity between Iran and Iraq. This has a number of causes. One is the ethnic difference between Arabs and Iranians. It may be noticed that the wide, long inlet of sea which partially divides the region has traditionally been named the Persian Gulf. Persia – that is, present-day Iran – does indeed provide its eastern shore. But because of the susceptibilities of the various Arab states which line the western littoral, the adjective 'Persian' has fallen into disuse. And because Iran and Iraq have a long common border, Iraq is the obvious representative of the Arab 'nation' in this unfriendliness. This common frontier includes, at its southernmost stretch, the Shatt-el-Arab river. Navigation rights on this waterway, crucial for Iraq's access to the Gulf, has been a bone of contention ever since the nineteenth century. Another cause of conflict between Iraq and Iran is religious. True, both states are predominantly Muslim. Indeed, the majority of the populations of both are of the Shi'a branch of that religion. However, in recent years the Iraqi government has favoured the minority Sunnis and has in consequence been fearful of Shi'ite co-religionists in Iran. These tensions led to the gruesome and gruelling first Gulf war (1980–88).

More needs to be said on the matter of religion – the second of our antagonistic cross-currents. As in other Islamic countries, so in the Gulf region Islam is a cardinal factor in the shaping of personal and group identity. Moreover, it is an all-encompassing creed embracing faith, culture and politics. By adhering to such a holistic code a Muslim in a Gulf state, for instance, cannot but recognise his or her distinctiveness from those people who hold other faiths or none. They find the materialism and immorality of the Americanised West offensive especially as it infiltrates into their own lands. The United States is 'the Great Satan'. However, we are here primarily concerned with Islam not as a source of cohesion against the outside world, but as a cause of tension within the region. There are two main, related reasons for this. One is the division between Sunnis and Shi'ites; the other, between radical fundamentalists and moderates.

The division between Sunnism and Shi'ism originated over a quarrel concerning the succession to the caliphate soon after the death of the Prophet Muhammad. Within Islam as a whole ('Dar al Islam') the Shi'ites have always been a minority. They have also identified with the underdogs, the impoverished and oppressed. They are conscious of predictions in the Qur'ān (Koran) about the less fortunate; for example: 'Yet We desired to be gracious to those that were abased in the land, and to make them leaders, and to make them the inheritors' (quoted, Hiro, 1988, p. 145). Shi'ism is also a more emotional style of religious faith than Sunnism.

The 1970s witnessed an intensification of worry amongst some Christians and some Muslims alike that their religions were losing their purity of belief. The solution to what they perceive as this dangerous trend is a return to the sacred texts as the receptacles of revealed truth. In Islam it is the Shi'ites who have adopted this fundamentalist position, rejecting particularly any accommodation with Western modes of life. Moreover, it was Shi'ism that provided the motive force behind the Iranian revolution. While the Ayatollah Khomeini governed Iran (1979–89) Shi'ite fundamentalism had a powerbase from which to preach and act on behalf of the Shi'ite commitment to fundamentalist doctrinal purity and radical championing of the cause of the oppressed. Nor have the fundamentalists been averse to using violence to achieve their objectives. In the Gulf region these developments have made the privileged rulers of Sunni lands such as Saudi Arabia, Kuwait and the United Arab Emirates decidedly nervous. More generally, the majority of Muslims reject the paths of fundamentalism and violence.

A third source of internal tension in the region is the discontent of the Kurds. Denied the nation-state they had hoped they would be allowed after the First World War, they have remained discontentedly partitioned amongst several states, most numerously in Turkey, Iran and Iraq. Their ill-treatment at the hands of Saddam Hussein of Iraq in the aftermath of the second Gulf war led to the international intervention already recorded (see p. 66).

Fourthly, by about 1990 the lack of any truly democratic style of government in most of the states of the region has been considered a dangerous feature. The extraordinarily rapid collapse of the Communist autocracies of Central and Eastern Europe at the turn of the decade (see p. 9) has raised popular expectations in many other parts of the world. A military dictator like Saddam, an autocratic monarch like King Fahd of Saudi Arabia or a petty emir like those of the Gulf coast are all vulnerable to these pressures.

In the Gulf crisis of 1990–1 many of the issues discussed in this section became manifest. Saddam launched an Iraqi invasion of Kuwait because of a quarrel over oil extraction and revenues. Iraq needed extra income because of the huge expense of the first Gulf war – the eight-year conflict between Iraq and Iran. Partly because of this blatant seizure of a sovereign state, partly because of the vital importance of the local oil to the world economy a US-led international force was launched to drive Iraqi troops from Kuwait. At the end of the war the United States encouraged Shi'ite and Kurdish opponents of Saddam's regime to rebel. The rebellions failed. But because of media protests assistance was dispatched to the Kurds.

But it should also be noticed that the war to oust Iraq from Kuwait was sanctioned by a UN Security Council Resolution of

25 August 1990. A fortnight later President Bush made a speech. He asserted that: 'Out of these troubled times . . . a new world order . . . can emerge; a new era – freer from the threat of terror, stronger in the pursuit of justice, and more secure in the pursuit of peace', and built upon 'a United Nations that performs as envisaged by its founders' (quoted, Roberts, 1991, p. 520).

Was that a feasible scenario? Is it possible to envisage UN law and US strength being deployed against regional powers in regional conflicts elsewhere in the world?

Some other regions

Apart from the extraordinarily difficult problems of South Africa and the Palestinians (on the latter see Chapter 10) few other regions of the world contain such potentially dangerous tensions as the Gulf. It will nevertheless be useful to look briefly at three regions where powers of some strength exist in more or less strained relations with their neighbours.

In South America Argentina is the dominant regional power. All three of her armed forces are, by local standards, strong and she is considered to be potentially capable of developing nuclear weapons. In the 1970s and 1980s the country's military junta pursued quarrels with both Chile and Britain over the disputed possession of groups of islands, the latter escalating to actual war (see p. 66). The return to civilian government in 1983 helped to calm these disputes. By 1990 Argentina was negotiating with her major neighbours, Chile and Brazil, for the creation of a common market.

Across the Pacific ocean three mighty regional powers uneasily co-exist in north-east Asia: the USSR, China and Japan. Although the Soviet Union was suffering from debilitating economic and political difficulties from the late 1980s, it must not be forgotten that it was the most formidable Asiatic military power, a status now inherited by Russia. Along the border with China, and on the coast and in the waters of the Pacific are deployed substantial conventional and nuclear forces. China too has political and economic problems. The suppression with no quarter shown of vocal discontent in Tibet and in Peking (Beijing) has revealed a distinct nervousness about ethnic minority and democratic objections to centralised Communist Party rule. Even so, China has both the largest population and army in the world, and her forces are equipped with nuclear weapons. Japan's strength, as already mentioned (p. 65), lies in her extraordinary economic success. In his great study of *The Rise and Fall of the Great Powers*, Paul Kennedy makes the following observations:

> Just how powerful, economically, will Japan be in the early twenty-first century? . . . the consensus answer seems to be: *much* more powerful. In computers, robotics, telecommunications, automobiles, trucks, and ships, and possibly also in biotechnology and even aerospace, Japan will be either the leading or the second nation. In finance, it may by then be in a class of its own.
>
> (Kennedy, 1988, p. 602)

Now between these very different regional powers there are stresses and strains. The former USSR and China share the longest land frontier in the world – some 4,000 miles. There have been disputes over this in some places and fighting even broke out in 1969. Sino–Soviet disputes since the 1960s have been exacerbated by ideological differences. The retention of a hard, albeit less doctrinaire, regime in China while Communism is obsolete in the republics of the old Soviet Union perpetuates this difference. On the other hand, the settlement in 1991 of Cambodia's internal conflict (where both supported different sides) provided evidence that Sino–Soviet relations had much improved.

Between the USSR and Japan there is a dispute over the Soviet seizure after the Second World War of the southern half of Sakhalin and, more particularly, the Kurile Islands. The Japanese consider the Kuriles as a natural part of their homeland.

The legacy of war also makes Sino–Japanese relations uneasy. The two countries were at war from 1937 to 1945. During this time the Japanese captured much territory and perpetrated many atrocities – behaviour which the Chinese still find it difficult to forgive.

The third region for us briefly to consider is Southern Asia. Ever since the withdrawal of Britain from the Indian subcontinent after the Second World War the region has been prone to international and internal, communal antagonisms, which have periodically burst into violence.

The two regional powers, India and Pakistan, have often been at loggerheads. They have indeed fought three wars since their creation as independent states. Their disagreement over possession of Kashmir – the cause of their first war in 1948–9 – remains unresolved. Since the late 1980s, however, relations have been less cantankerous.

Both states suffer from internal ethnic divisions. Pakistan is composed of five main linguistic groups. The Sindis and Mohajirs are on particularly bad terms, while the province of Baluchistan has chafed at the control exercised from the central government in Islamabad. The bewildering ethnic, linguistic and religious divisions in India are better known. The state is an extraordinary patchwork. Resentment at Hindu dominance has led to endemic communal violence, local fighting and assassinations. The Muslim minority (about 11 per cent of the population) are fearful of a burgeoning Hindu fundamentalist movement. The Sikhs (about 2 per cent of the population) want the Punjab to be an independent state of Khalistan. The Kashmiris and Assamese also seek independence. The Hindus are afraid of a backlash against their supremacy. In this turmoil two prime ministers have already been assassinated, Indira Gandhi (in 1984) and her son Rajiv (while out of office, in 1991).

The frightening danger is that India might at some time in the future prove ungovernable. In the event of a bloody disintegration, the temptation of Pakistan to intervene might be irresistible. It is constitutionally an Islamic state. And although Muslims are a minority in the huge Indian population, they number more than the Muslims of Pakistan. Pakistan has a tutelary interest in their safety. Furthermore, India has already tested a nuclear weapon; and Pakistan is known to be developing her own. India's horrendously difficult communal problems are consequently of more than internal interest.

In such circumstances the affairs of regional powers and the tensions between them assume the proportions of global concerns.

6

Economic Power

The use of economic power in support of foreign policy is now usually referred to as 'economic statecraft'; this is not to be confused with foreign economic policy. In furtherance of a state's *political* objectives abroad, economic resources may be used as rewards (promised or delivered) or punishments (threatened or carried out); in short, they may be given, denied, or taken away (see Box 6.1). When rewards are given openly and on a politically significant scale, we tend to speak of 'foreign aid'. When punishments are meted out in the same way, whether by states in pursuit of their own interests or by international organisations in defence of international norms, we now tend to speak of 'economic sanctions'. This chapter will consider the requirements of successful economic statecraft ('the bases of economic power') and the utility of its most controversial components: foreign aid and economic sanctions.

The bases of economic power

No state can employ economic statecraft with any prospect of success unless it has a fair degree of economic power. This in turn depends upon four things: economic strength; the will to use it; skill in its application; and a reputation for its successful employment.

'Economic strength' is the most important base of economic power and exists to the extent that a state, say state A, has either a monopoly over some economic good regarded as vital by another

Box 6.1 The forms of economic statecraft

Economic rewards	Economic sanctions
Financial	
Capital grants	Freezing bank assets
Soft loans	Suspending aid
Investment guarantees	Banning capital exports
Debt rescheduling	Expropriation
Encouraging private capital exports	Refusing to reschedule debt
Commercial and technical	
Granting MFN status	Export embargoes
Reducing tariffs	Import boycotts
Export or import subsidies	Increasing tariffs
Export or import licences	Withdrawing MFN status
Technical assistance training	Blacklisting of firms that trade with target state
Joint projects	Dumping
Trade agreements	Imposing quotas
	Refusing licences
	Pre-emptive purchase
	Suspending or cancelling joint projects, trade agreements
	Cancelling technical assistance training
	Banning 'high-tech' exports

state, say state B, or has a monopsony (monopoly purchasing position) over some economic good which state B needs to sell in order to survive – *provided* state A is not similarly dependent on state B. Since most goods and services are in wide demand throughout the world economy, only very large states or groups of states like the EC are likely to have any real degree of monopsony, or market, power. However, even relatively small states may possess monopoly power if they are well endowed with natural resources in high demand, the known occurrence of which is limited. States which have only a low ratio of foreign economic transactions to gross national product, for example, the United States, are likely to be less vulnerable to monopsony power (exports being relatively insignificant to the economy as a whole) than 'trading states', for example, Britain and South Africa. On the other hand, both kinds of state may be equally vulnerable to monopoly power exerted by a foreign rival.

To have 'economic strength'' *vis-à-vis* a foreign target is not, however, sufficient. Economic statecraft also requires the absence of strong cultural resistance to political interference or 'meddling' in foreign commerce and finance, together with adequate government control (direct or indirect) over them. If the will exists and the skill is available, it is likely that the state in question will already have a diplomatically serviceable reputation for the political manipulation of economic strength. Soviet-style 'command economies' have traditionally been better endowed with these 'non-economic attributes' of economic power than market ones. As a general rule, this suggests that market economies are more likely to obtain political influence via the dispensing of economic rewards than the threatening of sanctions (except where direct aid – 'tax-payers' money' – is concerned), providing they extract the political price before the reward is granted.

Where the pre-conditions for sanctions are concerned, it should also be noted that even if a state has both a substantial degree of economic strength in relation to its target and the non-economic attributes of economic power, sanctions are unlikely to serve it well unless the target state regards the costs of compliance as less than the costs of stubborn resistance. Thus, while serious economic losses are not likely to be thought worth incurring in order to resist some small change in foreign policy, they may well be endured if the price demanded is a humiliating reversal or an obvious and significant modification of domestic policy.

How useful is foreign aid?

Foreign aid may be employed in the service of foreign policy either by holding out the prospect of its donation, its continuation or its suspension. When used in the latter way it is best thought of under the heading of 'economic sanctions' (see below). 'Foreign aid' is a rather elastic term but normally means the transfer of goods, services or investment capital from one state to another either without charge or (more frequently) at a rate somewhat below the market price. This may be done directly ('bilateral' aid) or via the medium of some international organisation such as the World Bank ('multilateral' aid). Because they have sole control over it and because this makes it easier to extract a political price (or 'tie' it to purchase of their own exports), states normally prefer to give aid bilaterally (see Table 6.1). However, the major powers also have great influence over the inter-governmental aid agencies, so this rule needs qualification. Indeed, donor influence over recipients may be exerted more discreetly via the aid agencies.

Table 6.1 Official development assistance by type and as percentage of GNP, selected countries, 1989

Country	*Bilateral* %	*Multilateral* %	*Aid as % of GNP*
Canada	68.1	31.9	0.44
Denmark	55.7	44.3	0.94
Finland	61.6	38.4	0.63
France	82.3	17.7	0.78
Germany	64.2	35.8	0.41
Italy	60.6	39.4	0.42
Japan	75.6	24.4	0.32
Kuwait	87.3	12.7	0.54
Netherlands	72.2	27.8	0.94
Norway	60.1	39.6	1.04
Saudi Arabia	94.8	5.2	1.46
Sweden	70.9	29.1	0.97
United Kingdom	56.6	43.4	0.31
United States	88.9	11.1	0.15
European Community	91.9	8.1	–

Source: Adapted from OECD, *Development Cooperation, 1990 Report* (OECD, Paris, Dec. 1990), Tables 47 and 52.

According to the conventional definition, 'aid' is not the only way in which a state can provide economic rewards to another state that it wishes to strengthen or cultivate. It is the most controversial, however, and embraces most of the techniques listed in the left-hand column of Box 6.1. It was regarded as a useful instrument in the struggle for influence in the Third Word between the Soviet bloc and the NATO powers during the cold war, and also (especially in Africa) between the Soviet bloc and China after the Sino–Soviet split developed in the late 1950s. Its potency – political as well as economic – was generally believed to have been demonstrated by the contribution made by American assistance ('Marshall aid') to the recovery of Western Europe after the Second World War. During the cold war the radical left usually described Western foreign aid to the Third World as a 'tool of imperialism' and inflated its significance. Others saw it increasingly as a product of liberal guilt which was making little or no impact on the economic problems of the Third World and paid surprisingly few political dividends either. In the early 1990s foreign aid is again at the top of the international agenda, but now as a possible means by which the Western powers might sustain reform in the former Soviet Union.

How useful is foreign aid as an instrument of economic statecraft? Since the conditions for the successful employment of economic statecraft in general are exacting, it is not surprising that the record of foreign aid is mixed. Marshall aid certainly reinforced American policy goals (such as stabilising non-Communist governments and promoting European integration) after the Second World War; this was at a time when European governments could turn to no other quarter for help. On the other hand, the influence purchased by the superpowers via their aid programmes to the Third World during the cold war was less obvious and certainly more fragile. The chief reason for this, of course, was that neither superpower had a monopoly on the kinds of aid (including arms and training in their use) which were sought by the developing countries. The result was that any attempt to attach political strings to aid risked the recipient's desertion either to the Non-Aligned Movement or – worse – to the other camp. This problem was compounded by the instability of many regimes in the Third World. Egypt provides a classic example, first relying on Western aid (especially in the construction of the Aswan High Dam), then switching to the Soviet bloc in the mid-1950s, and finally returning in the mid-1970s to reliance on the West. Throughout this period Egypt retained considerable freedom of movement, both at home and abroad – and got the High Dam built!

Foreign aid is not only difficult to utilise for political purposes because of the problems of achieving a monopoly over it. The will to employ it can be eroded by domestic hostility. This is likely to be considerable if the recipients of aid are believed to be ungrateful, or not using it for the purposes for which it was intended, and if aid programmes are thus *seen* – whether rightly or not – as 'ineffective'. ('Development aid' can actually lead to increased military spending if it frees resources that would have had to go into, say, agriculture in the absence of the aid. This is a well-known consequence of disbursements through the United States' Economic Support Fund.) Congressional opposition to the aid budget, which began to mount in the 1960s, has been a headache for successive American administrations; by 1989, under the impact of the budget and trade deficits, it had succeeded in reducing aid to only 0.15 per cent of US GNP (see Table 6.1). As Baldwin (1985) stresses, the less generous the aid is (other things being equal) the less effective it is likely to be; and the fact is that, contrary to popular belief, the size of American aid to the Third World has been at best moderate and at worst trivial when judged by various significant criteria. It was also minuscule compared to Marshall aid to Europe (pp. 298 and 320–2). US aid, which acquired an increasingly military flavour during the Reagan years, is now concentrated on a relatively small number of countries of special political importance (see Table 6.2).

Table 6.2 The top six recipients of US official development assistance (%), selected years

1970–1		*1980–1*		*1988–9*	
India	13.9	Egypt	12.6	Israel	12.5
S. Vietnam	10.5	Israel	11.5	Egypt	9.5
Indonesia	7.8	India	3.3	Pakistan	3.9
Pakistan	5.0	Turkey	2.8	El Salvador	3.3
S. Korea	4.5	Bangladesh	2.2	India	1.9
Brazil	3.6	Indonesia	2.1	Philippines	1.8

Source: Adapted from OECD, *Development Cooperation, 1990 Report* (OECD, Paris, 1990), Table 43.

To be politically effective, aid programmes also have to be skilfully and sensitively administered. Neither superpower found this particularly easy during the long years of their cold war rivalry in the Third World. In Egypt, for example, Soviet advisers did not acquire a reputation for happy relations with the local population.

Nevertheless, it would be a mistake to conclude that because of the considerable problems facing the use of foreign aid as an instrument of economic statecraft its utility is generally low, and that the success of Marshall aid to Europe was a special case. To revert to the example of Egypt, it is clear that while the loss of Western influence here in the mid-1950s demonstrated the limitations of foreign aid, the subsequent increase in Soviet influence (which lasted for many years) testified to its potential. For if Moscow had been unable to step in with offers of arms and finance for the High Dam it is highly unlikely that the Egyptian leader, Nasser, would have severed his links with the West and continued to be in a position to disrupt Western defence planning in the Middle East. When aid recipients change sides it is as mistaken to believe that this is evidence of the ineffectiveness of aid as to conclude that military defeat is evidence of the disutility of force – it is for one party (on that occasion) but not the other.

Moreover, in assessing the effectiveness of aid it is vital to ask: for what purpose was it granted? If attention is confined to the employment of aid to change a recipient's behaviour, especially since politically tolerable levels of aid are generally not high, it should not be surprising if the results are poor. But aid is granted for a whole variety of purposes, and it is clear that in pursuit of some of these it is very effective. Aid (like propaganda) may reinforce existing patterns, which is why the former colonial powers concentrate their own dispersals on former colonies – Britain on those in the 'new' Commonwealth, France on francophone Africa, and Holland on Indonesia. Alternatively aid may help to consolidate changes in direction which have been initiated for other reasons. Even if it has unintended consequences in the target country, aid may also be of great symbolic significance for the donor. Thus food aid donated to a famine-ravaged country such as Ethiopia may in effect do little more than keep a brutal military regime in power, but it will also underscore the benevolent intentions of the donor. Equally, military aid, which merely allows resources that would have gone to the army to go instead into some other sector, may still have the advantage of signalling an especially close relationship.

The moral and economic collapse of Communism in the 1980s, together with the increasingly desperate economic plight of most Third World countries, placed the West in a much stronger position to extract a political price for aid. In Southern Africa, for example, an increasing aid-dependency on the West has contributed to the shift towards multi-party democracy, free enterprise and a more accommodating attitude towards South Africa on the part of such erstwhile clients of the Soviet Union as Mozambique and Angola. (In 1988–9 'official development assistance' was equivalent to an astonishing 76.1 per cent of Mozambique's GNP.) It is in this sort of situation that threats to cut off existing aid programmes are especially credible. Nevertheless, different sources of aid within the West – the United States, the EC, Japan and the Nordic countries, as well as the aid agencies – still provide some latitude for recipient-country manoeuvre.

In sum, the utility of foreign aid depends on a whole host of factors. The only sensible question is thus not 'How useful is foreign aid?' but 'How useful are particular levels of particular kinds of aid for particular purposes in the context of particular distributions of economic power?'

Economic sanctions

The popularity of sanctions

Although economic sanctions are by no means a wholly twentieth-century phenomenon, there seems little doubt that since the First World War they have been used in support of an increasingly broad range of foreign policy objectives. Initially they were employed only as an auxiliary to military action or – as with the League of Nations – in attempts to halt military aggression. But since the Second World War they have also been employed to weaken the military potential of adversaries and 'destabilise' the governments of hostile smaller states. More recently sanctions have also been employed in order to encourage states to observe human rights (notably in Poland and South Africa), stop the spread of nuclear weapons, settle expropriation claims, and attack the growing problem of terrorism. Not surprisingly, the general incidence of their employment has grown and, despite mounting scepticism about their utility, 'the imposition of a whole range of economic sanctions and energetic diplomacy to persuade other countries to follow suit' is now, as Mayall (1984) points out, 'the standard reaction to a crisis' (p. 631) – at least in the West. The first UN response to Iraq's invasion of Kuwait in August 1990 once more proved this point. Why did this reflex grow?

Probably the most important reason, ironically enough, was the triumph of liberal political theory – of which both the League and the UN were products – that occurred in the West during the course of the nineteenth century. This held (among other things) that war was irrational because it destroyed and interrupted commerce. Economic sanctions were thus preferable, not least because no state could long survive without the inestimable benefits of free trade. Since liberal theory blossomed at a time when economic 'interdependence' was believed to be growing rapidly and weapons were becoming more and more destructive, the appeal of economic sanctions is not difficult to understand. The alleged success of economic warfare in the two world wars was held to have provided substantial confirmation of its view, while the subsequent deveopment of nuclear weapons seemed to have proved beyond doubt the liberal claim that alternatives to war were more urgent than ever.

If it was liberal theory which spawned the idea of economic sanctions as an alternative to war, it was, in a further irony, an anathema to early liberalism that made possible its growth to maturity: the appearance of the interventionist state. In the East command economies were established, while in the Western market economies, particularly in Western Europe, the state sector grew considerably and indirect government control of the private sector became substantial. As a result, the political manipulation of foreign trade and international financial flows became much easier than hitherto. Furthermore, in the later 1970s and early 1980s objections to such manipulation were weakened by the economic nationalism provoked by recession.

Finally, economic sanctions are popular because, as with force, they have uses other than that of putting pressure on foreign states. Indeed, they may be employed even if they are believed to be ineffective in this regard. They may for example be used to *symbolise* opposition to an unpopular regime and to deter others thinking of going down the same road; they are usually introduced in the hope that both of these purposes, and possibly others as well, will be achieved. A detailed study of the United States' boycott of Castro's Cuba shows that American goals embraced all of the following: re-election for the Republicans in the presidential contest of 1960; showing other Latin American countries what they could expect if they chose the same path as Castro; symbolising the American belief in a *right* to exercise influence in Latin American affairs; cutting down on Castro's ability to *export* revolution as a result of poverty and preoccupation with domestic economic problems; and making it more difficult for the Cuban regime to portray itself as a successful model of Communism (Schreiber, 1973).

How effective are economic sanctions?

Despite the multiplicity of purposes, particularly symbolic ones, which sanctions may serve, there remains great interest in their ability to influence the behaviour of target states, which is invariably the purpose for which they are ostensibly employed. How effective are they in this role?

On the face of it, the record of sanctions here has been poor, especially when employed in issues in which the stakes were high. League of Nations sanctions failed to prevent Mussolini's annexation of Abyssinia in 1935–6 and were abandoned with terminal implications for the League's authority. The NATO embargo on the supply of 'strategic goods' to the Communist countries, which was introduced in 1949, did not prevent the emergence of the Soviet Union as a nuclear superpower and was gradually scaled down. American economic measures against Cuba were no more effective in getting rid of Castro than were CIA covert operations. UN sanctions against Rhodesia, which lasted from 1966 until 1979 and, until August 1990, represented the only attempt by the world body to implement comprehensive, mandatory sanctions, were certainly not the major reason for the ending of white rule in that country; credit here must go principally to the revolutionary warfare of the 'Patriotic Front', which started at the end of 1972. The Arab League boycott of Israel failed to undermine Zionism; and, while the oil embargo imposed on Western states 'supporting Israel' following the 1973 war had some impact on the policies of Western Europe, it signally failed to move the United States, Israel's chief backer. The boycott of South Africa by the Organisation of African Unity, which dates from 1963, had no discernible impact on apartheid; it was not so much official sanctions as the collapse of the confidence of private Western banks in South Africa in 1985, together with rising domestic violence, that in the end forced Pretoria to start negotiating with the African National Congress. American sanctions against Panama in the late 1980s were no more effective in displacing General Noriega than they had been in the attempt to remove Castro. And UN sanctions against Iraq were rejected in favour of force by the 'Coalition' in January 1991, when it seemed unlikely that they would persuade Saddam Hussein to leave Kuwait.

As already noted in the discussion of foreign aid (the suspension of which may itself be an important sanction), the chief problem confronting sanctioning states is the difficulty of obtaining anything like a monopoly position relative to their targets, whether in supply or market terms. For example, the UN oil embargo on Rhodesia (as well as other aspects of the UN campaign) was undermined by the oil conduit provided by friendly South Africa; the American boycott of Cuba was vitiated by Castro's ability to find an alternative market for his country's sugar in Russia; Arab sanctions against Egypt following Sadat's peace with Israel in 1979 were nullified by a massive rise in American aid and increased trade with Israel; and President Carter's attempt to punish the Soviet Union for its invasion of Aghanistan by the imposition of a grain embargo in 1980 was utterly defeated by the extent to which other producers – notably Argentina and Australia – succumbed to the temptation of the high price offered to replace American grain in the Soviet market.

Sanctioning states face other problems as well. Being highly visible (like the use of force), sanctions tend to provoke a strong patriotic response in the target state, which stiffens the resistance of its regime. (However, sanctions also tend to raise the morale of any internal opponents of the regime; depending on the balance of forces, this may be more significant, as was the case in Rhodesia.) Some sanctions, especially commercial ones (see Box 6.1), also take time to mobilise and thus allow the victim opportunity to make defensive dispositions (see Box 6.2). Sanctions tend, furthermore, to

Box 6.2 How states defend themselves against trade sanctions

When states are threatened with boycotts of their exports and restrictions on their ability to buy key commodities abroad (such as arms, oil, food, electronic and transport equipment), they characteristically resort to some or all of the following measures:

- stockpiling
- diversification of trade (markets and sources of supply)
- domestic substitution
- exchange control
- rationing
- concealment (e.g. of quantities of oil stored, international trade statistics)
- transport diversification
- 'sanctions busting' (clandestine trading)
- counter-sanctions (i.e. commercial and/or financial retaliation)

produce administrative and juridical problems of great complexity and thus require extraordinary 'bureaucratic tenacity' to see them through – particularly, of course, in the market economies (Renwick, 1981, pp. 78–9). And where the sanction being threatened is the reduction or termination of aid, there is often such a strong bond of common interest between donor and recipient that the threat is simply not credible. (This has been all too apparent in the relationship between creditor and debtor countries since the onset of the debt crisis in the early 1980s; failure to grant re-scheduling could have led to the collapse of the existing international financial regime.) Finally, unlike most kinds of conventional military force, economic sanctions tend to be undiscriminating in the damage which they inflict; in the complex and intricately intermeshed world economy, economic missiles, once more the commercial variety in particular, are almost by definition unguided. Not only do they have a nasty tendency to explode in the faces of those who launch them (a rise in unemployment figures following a trade embargo, for example), but they are likely to do as much harm to states adjacent to the target states as to the targets themselves. 'In the Rhodesian case', says Renwick, who was a senior official responsible for Rhodesian affairs in the British Foreign Office and subsequently a highly successful Ambassador to South Africa, 'it is at least arguable that they did *more* damage to the neighbouring countries than to the one to which they were applied' (p. 91, emphasis added).

However, while it is true that it has been rare for economic sanctions to have been *decisive* in any major inter-state conflict, it is illogical to conclude from this – though this was often done until quite recently – that they are rarely *effective*. Indeed, it is now coming to be recognised that, though unlikely to be much use on their own in conflicts involving high stakes, sanctions may well be important when introduced in such conflicts *in conjunction with* force, propaganda or diplomacy, especially if the target is small and weak. Hufbauer and Schott's (1985) quantitative study claims that one in two efforts to destabilise the governments of foreign rivals (usually 'small and shaky') succeeds and that economic sanctions make a modest contribution to this goal (p. 80).

There is now also ample evidence that economic sanctions are a still more effective weapon when employed in pursuit of modest policy goals, even when used alone. (Hufbauer and Schott record that 'in not quite half of the modest policy change cases, the sender country made some progress in achieving its goals through the use of economic sanctions' (p. 42).) This is helped by the fact that in such cases it is easier to employ sanctions with less fanfare and thus to make it possible for the target to comply without major loss of prestige. A good example is the US economic pressure on China which probably helped secure the release of the leading dissident, Professor Fang Lizhi, in June 1990. In conflicts over issues of relatively low priority, it is also more difficult for the victim to gain international support.

The successful use of sanctions in pursuit of relatively modest policy goals is, of course, a common feature of the relations between great powers (including 'regional great powers') and their clients. This is because for *political* reasons clients find it difficult to make defensive economic adjustments with the help of other states. A case in point is provided by Soviet-Cuban relations in the late 1960s. At odds with Castro over the issue of encouraging armed revolution throughout Latin America, in late 1967 the Soviet Union slowed down deliveries of oil to Cuba and also insisted on more difficult terms in the trade agreements signed in the following March. These measures evidently hurt (gasoline rationing had to be introduced on 2 January 1968) and subsequently Castro not only moderated his position on armed revolution but adopted the unpopular position of support for the Soviet invasion of Czechoslovakia. In 1969 Soviet economic pressure was relaxed (Schreiber, 1973, pp. 403–4). In Southern Africa in 1976 the regional great power, South Africa, used unaccountable 'bottlenecks' on its railways to put the Rhodesians in more accommodating mood towards the settlement that it was then anxious to promote.

It is not only in the relationship between great powers and their clients that sanctions are successfully employed. To speed the downfall of the Chilean Marxist, Salvador Allende, the United States applied economic pressure across a broad front in the aptly termed 'invisible blockade'. For its part, especially in the 1960s and 1970s, South Africa employed economic pressure not only to stiffen its faltering friends in the West but also to underpin its dominance of the entire Southern African region. With the former it found its lucrative market and its ability to manipulate gold sales impressive weapons, while with the latter its transport network played an invaluable role (as with Rhodesia). Eloquent testimony to the potency of South African economic pressure on the black Front

Line States was supplied in 1980 when they were obliged to establish the Southern African Development Co-ordination Conference, in order to free themselves from the political consequences of economic dependence on the white south.

In sum, because of the exacting requirements of economic strength and the contingent difficulties of translating it into sanctions, this aspect of economic statecraft does not have any decisive punch in disputes between states involving high stakes. Nevertheless, economic sanctions are a useful auxiliary to other instruments of policy in such conflicts, especially when the victim is a small state with a weak regime. When used in a limited and discreet manner, even alone, they may also be effective in pursuit of modest policy goals, particularly in the relationships between great powers and their clients.

Part II

Justice

7

Human Rights

International documents

'Natural rights is simple nonsense, natural and imprescriptible rights, rhetorical nonsense, – nonsense upon stilts.' Thus wrote the English political and legal philosopher Jeremy Bentham two centuries ago. Yet the signatories of the Universal Declaration of Human Rights did not consider human rights to be nonsense. That document speaks of the 'recognition of the . . . inalienable rights of all members of the human family'. When the representatives of the members of the United Nations signed the Declaration in 1948, they pledged 'every individual and every organ of society . . . to promote respect for those rights and freedoms and . . . to secure their universal and effective recognition and observance'. If the notion of human rights is not arrant nonsense, two main questions arise for us. These are: what are the rights which all human beings should be able to enjoy; and what can the community of nations do to try to ensure that they are observed?

The idea of rights became commonplace from the late seventeenth century. The English philosopher, John Locke, defined them as life, liberty and property. The American Declaration of Independence defined them as 'life, liberty and the pursuit of happiness'. The French Declaration of the Rights of Man and the Citizen (which provoked Bentham's irascible comment) defined them as 'liberty, property, security and resistance to oppression'. It was the duty of the state to respect these rights.

However, at no time before 1948 did the whole international community formally and collectively commit itself to protecting and pursuing human rights. It was the Universal Declaration that introduced the crucial change of establishing human rights as a recognised international concern. It is this international focus on the topic in which we are primarily interested here. We need to make another distinction also. There is obviously a very real moral difference between governments who deliberately persecute their opponents and those who, for reasons beyond their control, cannot, for example, provide their citizens with minimum nutritional and health standards. It is the first category of government that is culpable in the eyes of those (predominantly the liberal democracies of the northern hemisphere) who espouse the cause of human rights. What we are mainly, though not exclusively, concerned with in this chapter therefore is the international protection of individuals whose human rights are violated by their own government agents.

The world is now by no means short of documents proclaiming and defining the rights that human beings should expect to enjoy. The Universal Declaration itself contains thirty articles. The basic proposition is that all human beings have an equal right to 'life, liberty and security of person'. There follow more detailed expositions of particular rights. These include freedom from slavery, torture and arbitrary arrest, freedom of speech and to practise a religion. These could be found in eighteenth-century documents. However, a characteristically twentieth-century flavour is present too. For example, the individual is declared to have the right to a national identity and to the opportunity to participate in the government of his/her own country. Social and economic rights also feature prominently. Thus, everyone has a right to marry, to receive an education, to enjoy rest and leisure and be assured of 'a standard of living adequate for the health and well-being of himself and of his family'. Also, the right to work and to do so for a proper remuneration are proclaimed.

The Universal Declaration was the work of the UN Human Rights Commission, which has continued its activities and produced many more documents. Some of these are declarations, that is, statements of principles, which member states are invited to approve. However, they do not require of states anything more than good intentions. Other documents do. Conventions and covenants have the force of international law. All signatory states bind themselves to implement their contents and they are therefore more significant than Declarations.

Conventions and covenants are of two kinds. Some deal with specific topics. They include: the Convention on Genocide (1948); the Convention on the Status of Refugees (1951); the Convention on Slavery, the Slave Trade and Institutions and Practices similar to Slavery (1957); the Convention on the Elimination of All Forms of Racial Discrimination (1966); the Convention on the Elimination of All Forms of Discrimination against Women (1979); and the Convention on the Rights of the Child (1990). The other kind are general covenants: on civil and political rights; and on economic, social and cultural rights. Basically they expand on the Universal Declaration, though one novel feature is the recognition of the *collective* right of a people to national self-determination, as distinct from the traditional emphasis on the rights of individuals. Unfortunately, however, as we shall see (pp. 99–102), securing the honouring and enforcement of these instruments of international law is by no means as easy as securing signatures.

In the meantime, a number of European states founded the Council of Europe and soon (in November 1950) committed themselves to their own regional European Convention on Human Rights. As the definition of rights in this convention was closely modelled on the UN Declaration, it might well be asked why another document was thought to be necessary. The clue lies in the preamble, which refers to the signatories' resolve 'to take the first steps for the collective enforcement of certain of the Rights stated in the Universal Declaration'. Indeed, nearly two-thirds of the text is given over to arrangements for the operation of a European Commission of Human Rights and a European Court of Human Rights. The Council of Europe correctly foresaw that the UN was to prove ineffectual in bringing to book those regimes guilty of offending against the declarations, conventions and covenants. In contrast, the Europeans were determined to make a better effort at actual enforcement. To these practical matters we shall return (pp. 101–2).

Membership of the Council of Europe has steadily expanded from the original mainly Western European states. There is, nevertheless, a European body concerned with human rights which has an even wider membership. This is the Conference on Security and Co-operation in Europe (CSCE) (see also pp. 20 and 22). The 'Final Act' of this body, signed at Helsinki in 1975, was divided into four sections or 'baskets'. Baskets One and Three dealt with human rights issues.

Basket One contained 'Questions relating to security in Europe'. These included a declaration of ten principles to guide relations between states. The seventh of these was entitled 'Respect for human rights and fundamental freedoms, including the freedom of thought, conscience, religion or belief'. In expounding this principle the signatories acknowledged the international importance of human rights:

> The participating states recognise the universal significance of human rights and fundamental freedoms, respect for which is an essential factor for the peace, justice and well-being necessary to ensure the development of friendly relations and co-operation amongst themselves as amongst all states.
>
> (Keesing's Contemporary Archives, 27302A)

Also, Principle VIII affirmed the 'equal rights and self-determination of peoples'. In Basket Three were placed those matters relating to 'Co-operation in humanitarian and other fields'. Here a few particular human rights issues were highlighted. These included the freedom of members of separated families to meet or reunite, freedom of travel and improvements in the dissemination of information.

In addition to these universal and European documents we should note that many states have constitutions containing bills of rights. Moreover, two other continents besides Europe have their own documents: namely, the Inter-American Convention on Human Rights and the African Charter of Human and People's Rights.

Clearly, human rights are in our own day widely expounded. How may they be succinctly delineated? First, we must recognise that rights can be conceived as relating either to an individual or to a group or a nation. Secondly, rights may be political-legal in nature or socio-economic. Next, we may conveniently take the Universal Declaration's triad of categories, namely, the rights to life, liberty and security. Of these, liberty requires further explanation. Liberty may be of a negative kind – to be free *from* abuse or discrimination. It may also be of a positive kind – to be free *to* live and act in certain ways. This somewhat abstract picture of human rights may be clarified by Table 7.1.

Table 7.1 Analysis of human rights

Category	*Life*	*Security*	*Liberty*		
		Political and Legal			*Economic, social and cultural*
Rights of the individual	No unlawful killing or executions	No torture or degrading treatment	Freedom from: Slavery Exile Arbitrary arrest Retroactive laws/ punishment Discrimination because of race, religion or sex	Freedom to: Express political opinions Hold meetings Participate in government Be tried fairly Worship Marry Travel	Freedom to: Work, and for just remuneration Enjoy a reasonable standard of living Benefit from social security Enjoy a life of dignity, with rest and leisure Benefit from a free education Enjoy culture Own property
Rights of groups or countries	No mass killing or genocide		Freedom from: Discrimination because of race or religion	Freedom of: Collective existence National self-determination	

Attitudes towards human rights

Just as in a religious society everyone is against sin, so in a humane society everyone must surely be against violations of human rights. Thus Christians have the Decalogue as a guide for avoiding transgression. Similarly, should not governments have moral guidance to help them to treat their citizens humanely – and in order to be condemned if they violate these accepted standards? The matter is not quite so simple. It is indeed possible to marshal a formidable array of arguments against the drafting of human rights declarations and conventions.

First and fundamentally, it is often pointed out that these documents are in any practical sense worthless. Their terms cannot be enforced. Their value is nullified when governments who have, by their signatures, promised to abide by humane codes of conduct, do in fact practise the most nauseating barbarities. To persuade tyrannical governments to agree to lists of hypothetical rights is pointless; worse, it is an encouragement of hypocrisy. Those who adopt this sceptical attitude towards the very principle of broadcasting human rights standards have only to refer to the endless evidence of human rights violations revealed almost daily by the news media.

If, however, conventions and covenants were to be enforced, would not the preceding argument be undermined? Not necessarily. The argument then merely shifts, secondly, to the question of justification for intervention. There is a powerful case that would deny the legitimacy of one state interfering in the affairs of another – the so-called reserve domain – even for the purposes of upholding human rights. Whatever the motive, such intervention could be construed as an unacceptable violation of the offending state's sovereignty (see p. 202). The principle of non-intervention is enshrined in Article 2 (7) of the UN Charter. This declares that: 'Nothing contained in the present Charter shall authorize the United Nations to intervene in matters which are essentially within the domestic jurisdiction of any state.'

Furthermore, attempts to impose human rights standards could actually be counter-productive. Their very publication could incite disaffection in societies where conditions, especially economic conditions, render them unattainable on a short time-scale. And the suppression of discontent of either a political or economic nature could cause increased misery. External pressure on oppressive and unjust governments to improve conditions might provoke an even more violent backlash: in order to save face the offending government must not be seen to be making concessions.

A third counter-argument relates to foreign policy objectives. Supposing state A wishes to condemn state B for human rights abuses and to exert pressure to force it to mend its ways. Would this be a wise policy if state A was reliant on state B for trade or mutual defence arrangements? It would surely be contrary to the national interests of state A to provoke resentment in state B in this manner. This tension between foreign policy realism and human rights idealism can lead to hypocritical stances on the latter issue. For example, during the cold war Western governments were more critical of human rights abuses in the Soviet Union than in South Africa, and turned a blind eye to the horrors perpetrated in Cambodia because of its conflict with its neighbour, Vietnam, America's *bête noir*.

In any case, and fourthly, are we really so sure that a catalogue of rights can be universally acceptable? Is it truly possible to assert that the rights as listed, for example, in the Universal Declaration, are valid for all times, places and cultures?

There are, in fact, two worries under this heading. One is the attitude of Bentham. This is that rights should be pragmatically derived from actual state laws. Working to increase the justice of the law and its operation must take account not of high-sounding generalised phrases, but of what is practicable. The other element, most often voiced today, is that the Universal Declaration and other UN documents betray their origin in Western liberal thinking. For example, when the Universal Declaration was approved, there were some abstentions. One was Saudi Arabia, on the grounds that it was insufficiently sensitive of the principles of Islam. How can a list of human rights be universal if it fails to incorporate the beliefs of 800 million of the present world's population? Some Communist states also abstained in 1948. One of their reasons was the weak emphasis on socio-economic rights. Third World countries have added their voices to this complaint. A right to eat is more important than a right to vote.

Yet each one of these arguments may be countered. In the first place, to submit to the view that human rights documents are useless is sadly defeatist. It is an attitude that leads to the rejection of morality as a feature of international relations. The countervailing case is that, however difficult it might be, moral standards should be set, proclaimed and enforced. By constant reiteration the value of human rights can become increasingly accepted and evidence of their violation, an embarrassment to the delinquent state. For this reason, slavery has been abolished, Nazism was condemned and the moral validity of Soviet-style Communism has foundered. Certainly since the 1970s the issue of human rights has been prominent in international relations. The US President Jimmy Carter was notable for giving the matter high priority. When he announced his decision to run for the presidency, he expressed the wish: 'That this country set a standard within the community of nations of courage, compassion, integrity, and dedication to basic human rights and freedoms' (Carter, 1982, p. 143).

But, secondly, is interference in another state's affairs justified? The principle of non-intervention is, in fact, less rigid than is sometimes suggested. On the matter of human rights there is the famous historical example of Gladstone's 1876 pamphlet, *The Bulgarian Horrors and the Question of the East*. Because of the atrocities in the Balkans he had no hesitation in urging that: 'our government . . . shall apply all its vigour to concur with the other states of Europe in obtaining the extinction of the Turkish executive power in Bulgaria' (quoted, Morley, 1903, vol. II, p. 554). Since 1975 the 'Helsinki process' has made human rights problems a legitimate inter-state matter. Nor is there much evidence in practice that cruel regimes intensify their persecution as a result of publicity. Especially in the contemporary world, which has become so receptive of the ideals of human rights, imprisonment, torture and killings flourish rather in the darkness of secrecy.

The third question concerns the justification for using diplomatic methods to achieve human rights improvements. The argument that the initiating state might suffer needs to be tested by actual cases. It will depend on the way negotiations are conducted and how anxious the offending state is to maintain good relations with the state exerting pressure. Sometimes it may be a matter of balancing self-interest with self-respect.

On the general problem of balancing the effects of a human rights foreign policy with other objectives, let us quote President Carter again:

> I was often criticized, here and abroad, for aggravating [*sic*] other government leaders and straining international relations. At the same time, I was never criticized by the people who were imprisoned or tortured or otherwise deprived of basic rights. When they were able to . . . they [pointed] out repeatedly that the worst thing for them was to be ignored or forgotten.
>
> (Carter, 1982, pp. 146–7).

Finally, can human rights be universal? There is much less hesitation about this idea now than hitherto. Capitalist states have generally come to accept the need to complement legal and political rights with social and economic rights. Former Communist states have generally come to accept that individual rights are as important as group rights, and political, as economic rights. Furthermore, many Muslims are as unhappy about the denial of 'Western' human rights in Islamic states of the Middle East as Christians have been about similar problems in Catholic South America or Protestant South Africa.

However, the ultimate justification for declarations and conventions is the success with which their terms are in practice implemented.

Implementation

Despair comes easily to the observer of the human rights scene. Periodic starvation; slaughter of political opponents; systematic torture of political dissidents; absence of democratic procedures – because of these and other conditions millions of human beings lack the most basic rights in scores of states. Clearly conditions are worse in some states than in others; and conditions vary according to the government in power (or in the case of economic well-being, according to climatic variations). Comparisons between states are difficult, partly because of the problems of acquiring accurate information, partly because of the large number of variables in the human rights catalogue.

An interesting attempt was made at quantifying human rights ratings in *World Human Rights Guide* (Humana, 1983). Notional perfection represented 100 per cent. While it showed sixteen states scoring over 90 per cent, five scored abysmally less than 30 per cent. Denmark and Finland were top of the league; Ethiopia, at the bottom.

The UN, various governments, several unofficial bodies and numerous journalists make it their business to uncover human rights abuses with a view to forcing reforms. Constant publicity about these problems is most famously provided by Amnesty International (AI). This organisation was set up in 1961 to press governments to release 'prisoners of conscience'. Both AI pressure and some bilateral government negotiations have succeeded in securing the release of unjustly jailed political prisoners.

When it comes to pressurising a regime to change its overall style of oppressive government, a whole range of actions of increasing severity is open to a concerned government. The late Evan Luard, who was a British Foreign Office minister responsible for human rights questions in the 1970s, has listed thirteen of these, from 'confidential representations to the government concerned' to 'trading sanctions' (Luard, 1981, pp. 26–7).

The most celebrated attempt to employ economic sanctions to induce human rights reforms has been against South Africa. Governments, businesses and private individuals in many countries were all caught up in the controversy from the early 1960s: should South Africa be boycotted because of its apartheid system? In Britain, for example, the government introduced a partial arms embargo in 1963 and strengthened it in 1964; in the 1980s especially a number of organisations 'disinvested', that is, withdrew their wealth invested in South African companies; and housewives refrained from buying South African produce such as fruit. From 1989 the new South African President, de Klerk, started to introduce reforms for the relaxation of apartheid and the release of political prisoners. The economic difficulties caused by sanctions – allied to acute domestic unrest and a collapse of confidence in South Africa which this provoked in international financial circles – was probably a factor in bringing about this change of policy.

The introduction of human rights questions into the West's relations with the Soviet Union in the Helsinki Final Act produced a number of reactions. It immediately encouraged agitation in the Soviet bloc for the end of human rights abuses. Most notably a body which called itself Charter 77 was founded in Czechoslovakia. This activity prompted a backlash. In the Soviet Union a number of famous dissidents were 'punished', including the Nobel physicist Sakharov. However, these acts of repression put the Communist regimes in bad odour with liberal world opinion. When Gorbachev came to power in 1985 he was determined to repair his country's reputation and relaxed its authoritarianism in many ways.

In Europe the most impressive international machinery for the protection of human rights was already in motion. In order to promote the standards pronounced in the European Convention on Human Rights a Commission and a Court were established in Strasbourg. If it is thought that the actions of any member-government has infringed the Convention, the case may be investigated by the Commission. Another government may present the complaint; in addition, most member-states allow their own citizens to lodge complaints against them. If the case appears to be valid, it is transmitted to the Court. This consists of judges from each of the member-states.

The most common complaint about the system is that it takes an inordinate time from the initial presentation to the Commission to the judgment of the Court: some five to six years on average. On the other hand, the usefulness of the arrangements is shown by the increased frequency with which they are used. In 1988, on the occasion of the thirtieth anniversary of the creation of the Court, its President explained that:

> between 1959 and 1975 16 cases were referred to the Court and 20 judgments were delivered, whereas between 1976 and 1988 the corresponding figures were 144 and 160. What is significant is that this progression has been not only quantitative but also qualitative, in that our cases today concern a widening spectrum of subject-matters and are often far more complex.
>
> (Ryssdal, 1989, p. 12)

Although it is remarkable that a group of states allow a certain amount of their dirty linen to be washed in public in this manner, it is important to keep the system in perspective. With very few exceptions the members of the Council of Europe rank extremely high in their reputations for honouring human rights. (The main exception is Turkey, which, not surprisingly, does not allow individuals to present complaints.) The level of embarrassment caused by adverse judgments is therefore quite low. The cases do not concern horrendous violations of rights such as systematic use of torture and mass executions. Rather they are on the level of corporal punishment in schools and phone-tapping, to cite two examples of judgments against Britain. Indeed, the whole purpose is not to arraign governments as guilty but, as often as not, to persuade them to reform outdated laws and practices. The importance of the Council of Europe Commission and Court is therefore to remind governments and citizenry of the need for constant vigilance in protecting human rights and to effect minor improvements.

Would that such civilised procedures were suitable for many other regions of the world. They are utterly incompatible with the brutal regimes of Indonesia, Iraq or Zaïre, for example. In some states there has been a marked decline in respect for human rights in recent years. In addition to Iraq and Zaïre, we may mention the Sudan, Kenya and the inhumane behaviour of Serbian troops in the Yugoslav civil war. Yet, since the late 1980s many states have in fact undergone changes which have enhanced their citizens' human rights. Governments in the former Soviet Union, Eastern Europe, Argentina, Paraguay, Chile, Ethiopia and South Africa are decidedly less oppressive than hitherto. One of the reasons for the pace and extent of reforms has been the speed with which hopes can be transmitted via the news media. International relations are no longer the preserve of governments; peoples also interrelate. And once improvements are enforced by popular pressure in one country, despair fades before confident expectation in others. For, as Victor Hugo recognised: 'An invasion of armies can be resisted, but not an idea whose time has come.' Perhaps the belief that all human beings are endowed with natural rights which no government can legitimately deny is an idea whose time has now come.

8

The Force of Nationalism

European nationalism

Nationalism has been the most powerful political force in the world for two centuries. The appeal of the nationalist ideology in so many different historical and geographical settings may be explained by its protean nature: it readily adapts its shape to fit the circumstances. This extraordinary versatility derives from the manifold components that constitute the basic idea.

Human beings have a fundamental need to live together, to identify themselves with a group of similar people. Families, villages, tribes are such communities. The nation is a more sophisticated form built upon shared cultural experiences such as a common language, mythology and history. The nation-state is the political organisation of a people thus consciously self-defined and of the territory they inhabit. Nation-states started to emerge in Europe in the Middle Ages, England and France being two of the earliest.

But national*ism* as a dynamic political ideology had to await the emergence of the doctrine of popular sovereignty in the late eighteenth century. The idea that the will of the people and not the monarch is law was given potent, indeed violent, expression by the French Revolution. And by defining 'the people' as 'the nation', the will of the nation became the supreme fact of political life. Nationalism must therefore be distinguished from patriotism. Patriotism is love of and loyalty to one's country irrespective of its cultural content or the theoretical political foundation of the state's authority.

The application of nationalism to an established, compact nation-state like France was relatively easy. But in 'Germany', which was fragmented into well over three hundred separate states until about 1800, it was necessary to supplement the basic message by broadcasting with loud conviction the splendid cultural traditions which the people of all these political entities shared. The message soon became mystical, strident and arrogant. Listen to the words of Herder writing of the Germans in about 1790: 'Their stature amongst other peoples, their warriors' leagues and inborn character have become the foundations of Europe's culture, freedom and safety' (reprinted, Kohn, 1955, p. 106).

By the time of the First World War the principle of national self-determination had become a cardinal feature of political and international thinking. The US President Woodrow Wilson set the agenda for the post-war settlement in a speech in which he declared that: 'National aspirations must be respected; peoples may now be dominated and governed by their own consent. Self-determination is not a mere phrase, it is an imperative principle of action' (quoted, Macartney, 1934, p. 190).

Nationalism expresses itself in the following four main ways:

1. One is by the unification of the nation into a single state. This occurred, classically, in nineteenth-century Germany and Italy.
2. A second mode of expression is by securing independence from a multinational empire. This occurred in the break-up of the Austrian Habsburg, Russian Romanov and Turkish Ottoman Empires after the First World War; and of the British, French, Dutch, Belgian and Portuguese Empires over a longer time-span after the Second World War. Most recently we have witnessed the same force in operation in the USSR. But it is rare for so-called nation-states to be truly ethnically homogeneous.
3. Consequently, and thirdly, nationalist movements grow in minorities that are resentful of their perceived subordinate position. They demand their own national autonomy or even sovereign independence. This phenomenon is very common in contemporary Europe, as we shall notice below. We may also mention the uncomfortable twin European legacies in Canada

leading to demands for autonomy or even secession by the Québecois.

4. The fourth face of nationalism is aggression, so evident in the history of Germany from 1870 to 1945. Aggression is sometimes justified in the consciences of the nationalists as a means of bringing neighbouring minorities into the fatherland, as occurred in Germany 1938–9; sometimes it has no other basis than a welling-up of militaristic pride in the greatness of one's own nation and xenophobic hatred or scorn of another.

Since the age of the French Revolution cartographers have been kept intermittently busy redrawing boundaries to accord more closely with ethnic distribution. Yet there are still plentiful examples of unsatisfied nationalist demands. It is interesting to classify these according to the origins of the dissatisfaction with present conditions.

Our first cluster of problems derive from arrangements made before the present century. Many Corsicans chafe at being part of France: their island was purchased from Genoa for 2 million livres in 1768, a transaction which provoked one of the first truly nationalist resistance movements. Recent use of terrorist methods forced the government in Paris to concede a substantial measure of devolution in 1982. Constitutional changes have been made in Belgium too: a federal system has been introduced because of the incompatibility of the Walloon and Fleming populations of this state artificially created in 1831. Meanwhile, in Spain the Basque separatist movement ETA (an abbreviation of the words 'Basque homeland and freedom') continue their terrorist campaign. A more peaceable Catalan movement is also now growing in vigour.

After the First World War, at Woodrow Wilson's instigation, a sustained effort was made to apply the principle of nationality in Eastern and Central Europe. The map then devised, however, has left a legacy of nationalist discontent. The transference of the mixed province of Transylvania from Hungary to Romania still rankles with the Hungarian people who have since suffered from being a minority in an alien land. The creation of two totally new states, Czechoslovakia and Yugoslavia, can now be seen as storing up trouble for the future. Many Slovaks feel that they are treated as inferiors by the government in Prague. (As this book goes to press the division of the Czechoslovak state into its two components appears imminent.) The situation in Yugoslavia has been much more serious. A glance at Figure 8.1 will reveal just what a national patchwork was created in 1919. In 1991 the two northern provinces of Slovenia and Croatia declared their independence. The Croatian President coined the slogan, 'national individuality of even the smallest nations'. The problem escalated to civil war and set up waves of fear that similar events might occur in other European states. By 1992 Slovenia, Croatia and Bosnia-Herzegovina were all internationally recognised as independent states. By the middle of that year the situation, most particularly in Bosnia-Herzegovina, had deteriorated so much that the process of Yugoslavia's disintegration had caused more deaths and refugees than any other European conflict since the Second World War. And we may add a footnote to these 1919-vintage problems. The partition of Ireland, about which the IRA still so bloodily protests, took place because the outbreak of the First World War prevented the enactment of the Home Rule Bill for the whole of the island.

At the beginning of the Second World War the Soviet Union seized substantial areas of non-Russian territory on her western border which had been lost to Russia in 1918. These included what became the Soviet republics of Estonia, Latvia, Lithuania and Moldova (Moldavia), which declared their independence from Moscow's control in 1991.

At the end of the Second World War devising arrangements for the future of Germany was a major problem. Her eastern provinces were transferred to Poland. To prevent the difficulty of a large non-Polish national minority in Poland the German population was expelled to the rest of Germany. This country itself came to be divided into two states, Western and Communist. This arrangement, the result of the cold war, made no sense in nationalist terms. Therefore, with the collapse of the East European Communist system (see pp. 9–10), the two Germanys were reunited in spite of the severe economic difficulties entailed.

The downfall of Communism in Eastern Europe in 1989–90 is usually explained in terms of its economic inefficiency and political authoritarianism. However, the powerful demand for change derived not only from a desire for more prosperity and freedom. A

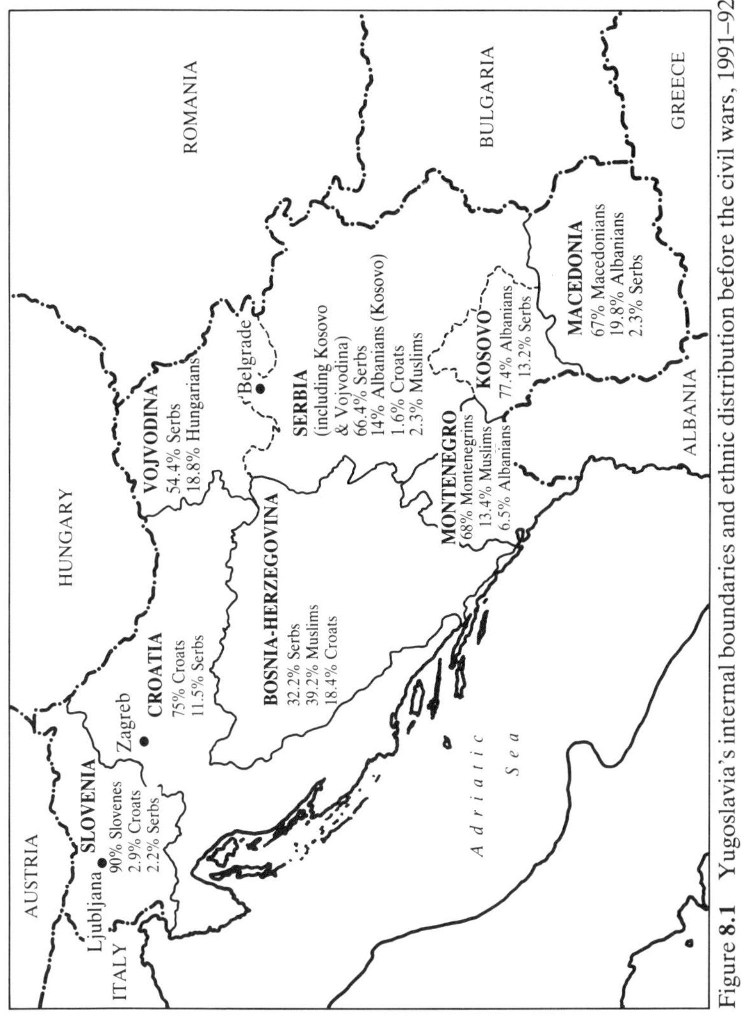

Figure **8.1** Yugoslavia's internal boundaries and ethnic distribution before the civil wars, 1991–92

deep nationalist resentment of the Soviet hold over her 'satellites' had been smouldering for decades. It had indeed burst into flame, most notably in the uprisings in Budapest in 1956 and Prague in 1968.

Just as the nations of Eastern Europe have kicked against a supranational control from Moscow established largely against their will, so there have been voices raised in Western Europe against negotiated and agreed transfers of authority to the central institutions of the European Community. The loudest nationalist protests have been made by President de Gaulle of France in the 1960s and Mrs Thatcher of Britain in the 1980s. In a speech at Bruges in 1988 the latter declared: 'To try to suppress nationhood and concentrate power at the centre of a European conglomerate would be highly damaging. . . . It would be folly to try to fit [the nation-states] into some sort of identikit European personality' (reprinted, Freedman, 1990, p. 269). That speech has been both praised and condemned as a clear expression of unbending West European state nationalism.

Afro-Asian nationalism

By the end of the nineteenth century scarcely a state in the world had escaped being a colony of a European power at some time in its history. And even the main exceptions, Japan and China, were coming increasingly under European influences. But ever since the late eighteenth century imperial political control has provoked successful surges of demands for independence. Initially the United States and Latin America; then south and south-east Asia and Africa. By the mid-1970s the only examples of European control of substantial numbers of non-European peoples were the Caucasian and central Asian provinces of the Soviet empire; and nationalist demands for autonomy burst forth here in 1991.

Merchants, missionaries and the military effected the European penetration and conquest of so much of the other continents. As well as Christianity, European secular culture was also infiltrated into these lands. Sometimes the impact was merely superficial and symbolic, as with the adoption by middle-class Asian and African men of European-style dress.

Of much deeper significance was the spread of the languages and laws of the metropolitan states. In many imperial territories this was necessary in order to recruit members of the indigenous populations to the European-style administrative structures – as clerks, civil servants and police. One result of this policy was to adulterate the indigenous cultures. Inevitably this process affected the more highly educated people more deeply than the bulk of the population. The great Indian leader, Pandit Nehru, complained that, having been educated at Harrow and Cambridge, he was neither truly Indian nor truly British.

The spread of Western goods and technology has proceeded apace since the achievement of independence from colonial status. These influences have tended to consolidate the hybrid nature of Afro-Asian societies. True, various attempts have been made to restore the purity of indigenous cultures, though with limited success. In Africa Julius Nyerere tried to restore traditional family and village structures in Tanzania under the slogan '*Ujamaa*', which he translated as 'familyhood'. Similarly Léopold Senghor adopted the slogan of '*négritude*' (blackness, though ironically using a *French* word!) in Senegal. More widespread and of greater popular force has been the recent upsurge of religious fundamentalism as a militant reiteration of Muslim principles endangered, as it is feared, by less virtuous Western culture. This crusade for cultural purification found its initial and most dramatic expression in the Iranian revolution from 1979. Its example has inspired (or enflamed) Muslims in several other lands since.

One of the European ideas exported with imperialism was nationalism. There was a paradox here. At the very core of nationalism lies the belief that ethnic culture should be celebrated in the political context of the state; furthermore, that the nation, in the sense of a state, should occupy the same territory as the nation, in the sense of a culturally homogeneous people. Yet this nationalist call to give culture political meaning was alien to those very Afro-Asian cultures it sought to enhance. Therefore nationalism took root in these continents by means of the hybridisation of the peoples' cultures we have already noted: a European idea was grafted on to indigenous traditions. Admittedly nationalism provided the necessary impulse for the acquisition of independence. But the post-independence regimes have had the problem of living with the consequences of the paradox, as we shall now indicate.

As the European imperial powers withdrew from their overseas possessions, the borders they had marked out for their former colonies were, by and large, maintained. The major exception was India, where Muslim fears of post-independence subordination to the majority Hindus led to partition and the creation of Pakistan. Elsewhere, artificial as the boundaries were in local ethnic terms, the dangers inherent in trying to change them appeared more daunting than those that might attend their retention. The Organisation of African Unity (OAU) went so far in 1963 as formally to recognise all existing boundaries in that continent.

On the other hand, some challenges have been thrown down to the status quo. These have been of two kinds. There have been a few examples of states claiming border territory in the possession of a neighbour. Some of these disputes have degenerated into wars: for instance, between India and Pakistan, India and China, Somalia and Ethiopia, Libya and Chad.

More frequently, ethnic conflict has occurred inside states. Inter-ethnic tensions, often caused by the domineering manner of one group, have generated numerous bloody conflicts. Let us take just three examples. In Sri Lanka the minority Hindu Tamils and majority Buddhist Sinhalese have co-habited most uneasily since the end of British rule. Violence has continually erupted since 1958. In the Horn of Africa a grinding civil war between the largely Amhara central government of Ethiopia and the minority peoples of the north-eastern portion of the country led eventually in 1991 to the secession of the Red Sea littoral and its hinterland as the independent state of Eritrea.

In many ways the most horrific of these ethnically motivated civil wars occurred in Nigeria in 1967–70. Nigeria was created by the British – a vast patchwork of some two hundred and fifty ethnic communities and categories, though the three major ones (Hausa-Fulani, Yoruba and Ibo) account for about 60 per cent of the population. The leaders struggled with the virtually impossible task of trying to create a sense of Nigerian national identity. In the autumn of 1966 a Hausa-Fulani delegation to a constitutional conference warned:

> We have pretended for too long that there are no differences between the peoples of this country. The hard fact which we must honestly accept as of paramount importance in the Nigerian experiment

> especially for the future is that we are different peoples brought together by recent accidents of history. To pretend otherwise would be folly.
>
> (quoted, Forsyth, 1977, p. 75)

The following summer the Ibo-populated Eastern Region declared its independence under the name of Biafra. In the ensuing civil war upwards of a million Ibos were killed in battles or massacres or died of starvation or disease, provoking charges of genocide against the federal government and forces.

Even so, for all the arbitrariness of the boundaries of so many states in Asia and Africa, an effective sense of national identity has been haltingly evolving. Two policies have assisted this process. One has been the use of education to socialise the younger generation out of their tribal or regional attachments to a primary loyalty to the nation-state. The other has been the policy of dissociation from, even antagonism towards, the former imperial power. Diplomatic non-alignment in great power quarrels and campaigning against the continuing economic dominance of 'neo-colonialism' have helped to consolidate a sense of national self-interest and therefore cohesion in many Afro-Asian states.

The search for national identity has also led to its being understood as existing in more than one layer. In the nineteenth century an idea of 'super-nationalisms' developed with the growth of 'pan' movements. For instance, the Pan-Slav movement emphasised the 'family' similarities of Russians, Poles, Serbs and so forth. In more recent years Pan-Africanism and Pan-Arabism have had similar objectives. For example, people from the Atlantic coast of Africa to the Persian Gulf speak forms of Arabic and are committed to the Islamic faith. Yet this wide-ranging cultural identity exists in tension with the national identity at the lower layer of the nation-states such as Algeria and Egypt.

Before leaving the topic of Afro-Asian nationalism, we must take note of the splitting up of the Soviet Union. The Communist regime claimed to have 'solved the nationalities problem' by conceding *cultural* autonomy as a counterbalance to centralised political power. The sudden revival of nationalist desire for *political* autonomy in 1991–2 revealed how false that claim had been. Even so, the replacement of the USSR by the CIS did not solve the nationalist problem either. Three major difficulties remained: the non-Russian peoples in the Russian Federation; the ethnically Russian inhabitants of many of the other republics, both European and Asiatic; and inter-state ethnic quarrels, most seriously between Armenia and Azerbaijan.

If nationalism has been so difficult to define with accuracy and to implement with justice, should one be searching for a different principle for the organisation and coherence of states? Is movement beyond the age of nationalism yet possible?

Nationalism: for and against

In our own century it has been widely assumed that the ideal political system requires that every nation should have its own state and every state should contain but one nation. This assumption is based upon two main beliefs. One is that the arrangement is just; or, to express the point negatively, it is unjust to deny people the right to live in nation-states. The second argument is that a world composed of nation-states is beneficial to the international community as a whole. This is because the satisfaction of nationalist demands will make the world more peaceable by eliminating this cause of conflict.

As a result of this second argument the issue of national self-determination has become a matter of universal international interest. We have already seen how the peace settlement after the First World War was based upon this principle (see p. 104). It is now enshrined in key United Nations documents. The Charter declares that one of the purposes of the organisation is: 'To develop friendly relations amongst nations based on respect for the principle of equal rights and self-determination of peoples' (Article 1.2). The Covenant on Civil and Political Rights is more forceful: it opens with the clear declaration that: 'All peoples have the right to self-determination' (Article 1).

But is the ideology of nationalism and its application in the form of national self-determination just and beneficial? The classic defence of the principle was made by the English philosopher John Stuart Mill on the basic ground 'that the question of government ought to be decided by the governed'. He continued:

> One hardly knows what any division of the human race should be free to do if not to determine with which of the various collective bodies of human beings they choose to associate themselves. . . . Free institutions are next to impossible in a country made up of different nationalities. Among a people without fellow-feeling, especially if they read and speak different languages, the united public opinion, necessary to the working of representative government, cannot exist.
> (Mill, 1861: 1910 edn, p. 361)

Two generations later it was widely held that it was the frustration and denial of the right of national self-determination in Central Europe and the Balkans that had plunged the continent, then much of the rest of the planet, into the horrors of the First World War.

Yet equally powerful arguments may be marshalled to the contrary. One of the elements of the case against nationalism is the exact reverse of the belief that by conceding its justice peace will ensue. The opposite point of view is that nationalism can be, and often is, aggressive, as already noticed (see p. 105). One of the reasons that nationalism promotes violence is that there can never be an end to its demands. Pure nation-states cannot in practice exist because ethnic groups are so scattered and mingled. Even such a long-established 'nation-state' as the United Kingdom contains English, Welsh, Scots, Irish, not to mention the descendants of successive waves of refugees and immigrants with different cultural backgrounds. It is quite impractical for every ethnic minority in every state to become independent. However, to raise national self-determination to the level of an incontrovertible principle is to arouse ambitions and expectations whose disappointment can be explosive.

Whether nationalism is a beneficent or malignant force is a matter of continuing debate. But what of its strength in practice? Are there any signs of its waning or being superseded? If we had been viewing the scene a generation ago we would probably have suggested that nationalism was a spent force in the northern and western portions of the globe and would soon become so in the southern and eastern portions as soon as the process of decolonisation had been completed. Since then, however, in the words of Professor Smith:

> In North America, Europe and the Soviet Union undergoing *perestroika* the interventionist state has rekindled amongst its ethnic minorities those aspirations for autonomy or even separation that had

> previously been muted or repressed. No wonder many observers were surprised by the vigour of this nationalist renewal.
>
> (Smith, 1991, p. 138)

The USSR is a particularly interesting example of the continuing potency of nationalism because the Communists asserted that they had solved the problem. They claimed to have progressed beyond nationalism by separating political power from cultural identity and centralising the former while devolving the latter. But nationalism had not been permanently sublimated, only temporarily submerged. Not only have powerful nationalist movements developed in the obviously non-Russian republics of the Baltic and Transcaucasia, but even in the Slav-populated Ukraine.

On the other hand, the world, including Europe, is being shaped by very different influences from those which brought forth the ideology of nationalism. Two features of the contemporary world particularly affect the nationalist ideal and may be said to undermine it.

One of these is the extraordinary mobility of people today. Whether refugees fleeing from personal danger or 'economic migrants' seeking a better life, many millions of people have settled in states other than their homelands in recent years. Afghans to Pakistan, Hispanics to the United States, Palestinians scattered in many lands. Moreover, leaving aside future waves of refugees that might be produced by unforeseen crises, millions more harbour ambitions to migrate to wealthier lands: Mexicans to the United States, East Europeans to Western Europe, for instance. This resettlement further dilutes the ethnic homogeneity of many so-called nation-states. Even within a firmly established nation-state like France opposing trends are clearly evident. While immigrants from the Caribbean and the Maghreb are diversifying its culture, this very process is provoking a nationalist, not to say racist, backlash led by the populist politician Jean-Marie Le Pen.

The other characteristic of the contemporary world tending to weaken nationalism is the growing interdependence of states and societies in so many different ways. International finance, multinational industrial and trading companies, global communications systems, the spread of English as a lingua franca are all pulling in the opposite direction to national differentiation. Both state sovereignty and ethnic cultures are having to give in varying degrees in the face of these forces.

The forces of nationalism and cosmopolitanism are currently indeed in a state of interesting tension. Europe provides the most fascinating arena. While the federalist thrust of the European Community is knitting up the member-states into some form of political union, re-energised nationalism has been unravelling the state in the Soviet Union and Yugoslavia.

Is it possible therefore to conceive of a post-nation-state political system? The zealous nationalist has perceived the nation-state as a self-contained and self-sufficient political and cultural entity. Any alternative to this arrangement would necessarily involve a dispersal of some functions, powers and loyalties to other entities. The late Professor Hedley Bull conceived 'a new medievalism' along these lines – 'a modern and secular equivalent of the kind of universal political organisation that existed in Western Christendom in the Middle Ages'. He explained that:

> If modern states were to come to share their ability to command their loyalties, on the one hand with regional and world authorities, and on the other hand with sub-state or sub-national authorities, to such an extent that the concept of sovereignty ceased to be applicable, then a neo-medieval form of universal political order might be said to have emerged.
>
> (Bull, 1977, pp. 24–5)

Since he wrote these words the European Community, with its increasing emphasis on a Citizens' Europe and the principle of subsidiarity, has been moving in this direction (see Chapter 16).

Even so, however much the nation-state surrenders political and economic sovereignty to other geographical units or functional organisations, nationalism will persist with great vigour all the while people think and feel in primarily national terms. The sense of national identity is sturdily consolidated by the mutually reinforcing strengths of language, folklore and history. A true sense of multiple loyalty can only be said to have evolved when the psychic attachments to province, region, and even the world, can command influences of comparable power over human sentiments. These have not yet fully developed. The age of nationalism is not yet dead.

9

Sustainable Development

Development and underdevelopment

Hundreds of millions of people, mainly in the northern hemisphere of our planet, live lives of some comfort. Hundreds of millions of other people, mainly in the southern hemisphere, live lives of bare subsistence. This is unjust. Yet to raise the living standards of the poor to any marked degree could involve so much greater industrialisation as to cause global ecological catastrophe. In the words of a founder of the German Green Party: 'if the industrialisation of the world were to be completed, life on earth would be destroyed' (Rudolf Bahro, quoted Barnaby, 1988, p. 190). How can a more equitable distribution of the world's wealth be achieved without incurring disaster? That conundrum is the subject of this chapter. The key to its solution, it is often argued, is 'sustainable development'. However, that requires for its success, besides technical advance, international political will, wisdom and skill of the highest order.

But first, what is the nature of development and underdevelopment? They are deceptively simple labels. A developed society is one with a high gross national product (GNP); and the source of much of that wealth is industrial production. Present-day Germany and Japan, for example, would obviously be poorer without their automobile and electronics industries. However, industrialisation, and consequently development, involves social as well as economic changes. It requires a geographical shift from a predominantly rural, agricultural society to an urban, manufacturing and entrepreneurial society. It both requires and produces an acceleration of social mobility.

Many commentators, however, would have it that the essence of development lies not simply in wealth creation, but in an improvement in the quality of life. The material benefits of development, whether they be refrigerators or telephones, are easily quantifiable; qualitative advantages such as education and health are not so susceptible to statistical comparison. They are none the less often asserted as crucial features of development. The United Nations Development Programme has, in fact, produced a comparative measure called the human development index (HDI) by combining figures for literacy, life expectancy and gross income. Other qualitative features of development, such as freedom and stable government, defy measurement. Yet, as the Tanzanian statesman Julius Nyerere wrote: 'Freedom and development are as completely linked together as are chickens and eggs . . . . Without freedom you get no development, and without development you very soon lose your freedom' (Nyerere, 1974, p. 25).

We shall, however, be using the words 'development' and 'underdevelopment' here mainly in the economic sense. By the 1950s a number of politicians, journalists and scholars began to comment on the wide divergence of living standards between the wealthy and poverty-stricken countries of the world. The Frenchman, Alfred Sauvy, coined the term 'the Third World', which is still fashionable as a label for the poor states of the planet. In 1980 an independent international commission under the chairmanship of the German statesman Willy Brandt produced a report entitled *North–South*. This helped to popularise the term 'South' as an alternative to 'the Third World' as a means of identifying the underdeveloped countries.

These terms are, nevertheless, shorthand. It must be understood, for example, that 'the South' does not include wealthy Australasia. Nor are all Third World countries equally impoverished. A recent device is to refer to a 'core' of wealthy states and a 'periphery' of the poorer as being more useful. However, we shall employ the words 'developed' and 'developing' because of their wide currency.

One of the advantages of the word 'developing' is that it recognises wealth-creation as a process; and, implicitly, accepts that different individual countries will progress along this path at different rates. The oil-rich states of the Middle East are clearly in a different category from the desert lands of Saharan Africa unendowed with mineral wealth. Moreover, in general terms of economic growth, analysis of recent performance reveals that there are a dozen or so fast developers. These include the so-called Asian tigers – South Korea, Taiwan, Singapore and Hong Kong (a separate polity until reabsorbed into China in 1997). These four Newly Industrialising Countries (NICs) are being joined by Malaysia, Thailand, the Philippines and Indonesia, whose rates of economic growth have accelerated remarkably since the mid-1980s. Also China and India improved their growth rates in the 1980s.

The forty or so states with very weak economic performance are mainly in Africa and Latin America. The indices of poverty are all to be found as startling evidence of underdevelopment in these lands. These measurements include not just the cold statistical yardstick of GNP. There are also the powerful indicators of human deprivation and misery such as percentage of illiterates, average daily calorie intake and average life expectancy at birth. Even averages, of course, mask the desperate conditions of those below the average. Furthermore, no statistic reveals the terrible episodic impact of events such as mass starvation in the Horn of Africa and the Sudan; cyclonic destruction in the Bay of Bengal; and eruptions of civil war in many African states. Because of these experiences and a variety of constant factors, some of which we shall touch on below, the wealth gap between the richest and poorest countries has continued to widen in recent decades. To give just one example, the GNP per head of the population of Ethiopia rose from the equivalent of $55 to $130 per annum from 1965 to 1981, while the equivalent US figures were $3,540 and $12,675.

The word 'underdeveloped' implies potential for development which has not as yet been exploited. Here again there are wide variations. For some states like Zaïre, which are rich in mineral resources, this is true; for others like Mali, which consists of large areas of wilderness, the term is something of a cruel euphemism.

However diverse underdeveloped or developing countries are in both realised and potential wealth, three interesting questions arise. First, how has the gulf between developed and underdeveloped countries come about? Secondly, what have been the recent relationships between the two halves of the world? And thirdly, in what sense is this disparity an international issue rather than a national problem for each of the destitute states? Detailed answers to these questions are beyond the scope of this book because the debate over explanations has been muddied, and therefore complicated, by political controversies concerning blame and by economic controversies concerning the relative importance of the various factors that have been at work.

A few generalisations are possible. A broad sketch of the causes of the divergence of levels of wealth between developed and developing states must take account of the following considerations. For a variety of reasons the Industrial Revolution began in Western Europe and North America and gave those countries a head start on the road to modern development. One of the reasons why these states were able to renovate and expand their industrial production was the availability of cheap raw materials and of ready markets in Asia, Africa and Latin America. When these colonial or quasi-colonial territories became independent they were unable to follow the rapid path of industrial development pioneered in countries like Britain, the United States and Germany for a number of reasons. These included: adverse climatic conditions; the incompetence of their political and economic leaderships; the problem of effecting the necessary social reconstruction; and the difficulty of transforming the established, imperially imposed, trading relationships.

The persistence of the gap between the developed and the underdeveloped worlds has been a dominant theme in the relations between these two groups of states during the second half of the twentieth century. And because the problem has proved to be chronic it has led to feelings of frustration and consequently acrimonious disputes over responsibility.

The wealthier countries have provided aid in various forms and for a variety of purposes. Sometimes in the form of loans, sometimes in the form of technical assistance; sometimes for capital modernisation, sometimes as charitable relief. Donor countries have complained that aid monies have been culpably misused – for instance, for the purchase of arms and for bribes and excessive profits, instead of for the benefit of the poor in the recipient countries. In their turn, the countries in receipt of aid have complained that it has too often been 'tied' by the requirement to trade with the donor state and that loans have carried crippling interest rates.

As a result of these experiences the governments of the Third World started in the 1970s to demand a New International Economic Order (NIEO) and, in some cases, a remission of their debts. An NIEO would involve fairer trading practices including higher prices for primary products (namely, raw materials and food). Remission of debts would involve a recognition that there has in fact been a 'negative flow' of funds to the Third World: that is, the underdeveloped countries have paid more to the richer countries in the form of interest and repayment of loans than they have received. The figures for the 1980s are startling: plus $36.5 million in 1981 compared with minus $42.9 million in 1989. In the face of these complaints and demands the donor countries have despaired at the waste and ingratitude in the lands that have received their generous aid; the recipients have despaired at the seeming impossibility of making any progress.

Behind all the heart-rending misery of underdevelopment and all the heart-searching about ways of effecting improvements, three basic considerations reveal the problem to be quite clearly international in its complexity.

In the first place, in terms of commerce and finance, let alone in other spheres of activity, the world is becoming inexorably more and more interdependent. The Brandt Report stated this fact quite categorically:

> More and more local problems can only be solved through international solutions–including the environment, energy, and the coordination of economic activity, money and trade. Above all, the achievement of economic growth in one country depends increasingly on the performance of others.
>
> (Brandt Commission, 1980, p. 33)

The subtitle of the report was 'a programme for survival'. Its core message is that the prosperous North has no cause for complacency. Continuing economic debility in the southern hemisphere will at best retard economic activity universally; at worst, it will cause such bitterness amongst the disadvantaged nations as to explode in violent aggression.

The second reason for categorising underdevelopment as an international issue is the responsibility which the states of the North have for this condition. It is often pointed out that in the imperial era single-crop farming was imposed on some colonies so that the successor states are now painfully vulnerable to fluctuations in the market prices of those goods, such as sugar or coffee. In more recent years, moreover, rich industrialised countries have sold expensive weaponry to Third World states and arranged loans with crippling interest rates. Because of these considerations liberal opinion in the developed world suffers a collective guilty conscience. It therefore strives to adjust the international system to a better balance of advantages for the South.

The basic moral argument is that the principle of distributive justice is as valid for the international community of states as for the internal condition of any individual state. Briefly this is the belief that wildly unequal access to the planet's goods and wildly unequal standards of living are unfair. It follows that the international community has a moral responsibility to level out some of this unevenness. It is an argument which relates back to the subject matter of Chapter 7. If a reasonable standard of living is a universal human right, surely the international community of states has an obligation to ensure that such a standard is universally enjoyed.

The problem is how to achieve this highly desirable moral end without using the highly immoral means of exhausting and polluting the planet upon which we all depend for our very lives.

Resources and environment

Earth is under great strain. An ever-increasing number of human beings are taking much more from the planet than it can naturally replace, poisoning its atmosphere and waters and distorting its climate with their polluting industries. Our planet is endangered by the twin threats of too many people and too many factories – by the population explosion and expanding industrialisation. Moreover, these two threats mutually interact. Industrialisation (in its broadest sense) leads to population increase by lowering the death rate. Technical advances conquer diseases and increased wealth provides improved public health and nutrition. At the same time, growth in population means that there are more customers demanding the products of manufacturing industry.

On the matter of population we must, inevitably, start with some figures. The giddying speed of recent and projected population growth may be simply demonstrated by Figure 9.1.

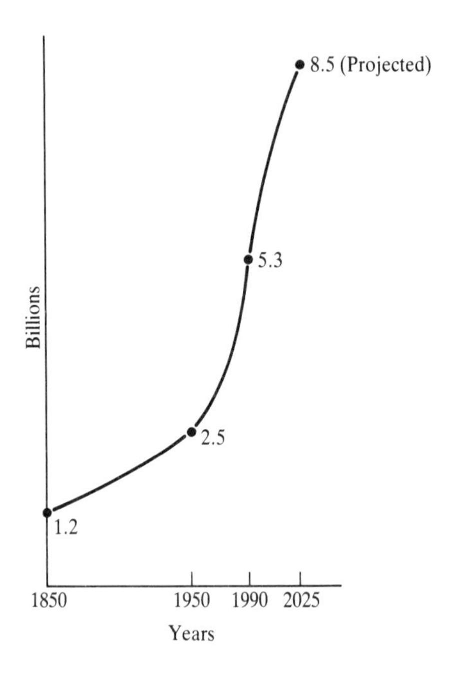

Figure **9.1** World population

Additional human beings mean more mouths to feed, more bodies to warm, clothe, shelter and keep healthy and more minds to educate. That is all very obvious. But we also need to remind ourselves that the extra food, fuel, clothes, houses, hospitals and schools are required extraordinarily quickly. As the graph in Figure 9.1 shows, in the span of a generation from 1990 it is estimated that the world's population will increase by more than 3 billion. Furthermore, the problem of coping with this vast increase will be exacerbated by the fact that it is the poorest countries where the biggest percentage increase is likely to occur, most notably Africa. Thus whereas the world's population is projected to increase from 1990 to 2025 by 60 per cent, the forecast for Africa is 150 per cent – from 640 to 1,600 million. (Though these figures, especially for Africa, may have to be revised downwards if AIDS reaches truly epidemic proportions.) Can the social institutions, transport and economies of the countries destined to expand at such an enormous rate cope with the inevitable pressures?

The second threat to the planet's ecosystem is industry. It is true that in some respects we are entering a 'post-industrial' age; the era of information technology is replacing the era of manufacturing technology. It is also true that the massive expansion of manufacturing industry that characterised the policies of many Third World countries in the 1950s and 1960s is slowing down. Nevertheless, it is quite obvious that much more industrial activity of the traditional kind is under way now than a generation or so ago. (By 'traditional' industry we mean manufacturing, construction, mining and energy-generation.) For example, reporting in the mid-1980s, the Bruntland Commission (see p. 125) noted that: 'As recently as 1950, the world manufactured only one-seventh of the goods it does today, and produced only one-third of the minerals' (Bruntland Commission, 1987, p. 206).

People and industry exert stresses on the global environment for three major reasons. People need food; industry needs raw materials; and both need fuel. To meet these demands the human race is degrading Earth and its atmospheric envelope by the twin processes of exhausting resources, both mineral and biological, and pollution. (Though in a sense pollution is an aspect of resource depletion because pollutants destroy.) The simplified web of examples shown in Figure 9.2 may help to make the argument clearer.

We are not concerned here to give the physical, chemical and biological explanations for these effects. What we do need to notice are the following four features of the situation:

1. The first, as the web demonstrates, is the interconnectedness of so many of the elements in the environmental crisis.
2. The second is that both rich and poor countries contribute in their own ways. Let us take the example of fuel. Many rich countries may imperil the planet by contributing to the 'greenhouse effect' of rising world temperatures by the operation of coal- and oil-fired generators, while the impoverished people contribute to the same effect by cutting down carbon dioxide-consuming trees for their fires.
3. The third feature is that many of the effects of environmentally degrading activities are not confined to the particular localities where these activities take place. Consequently no country, however small its contribution to the problem, can avoid either responsibility or concern.

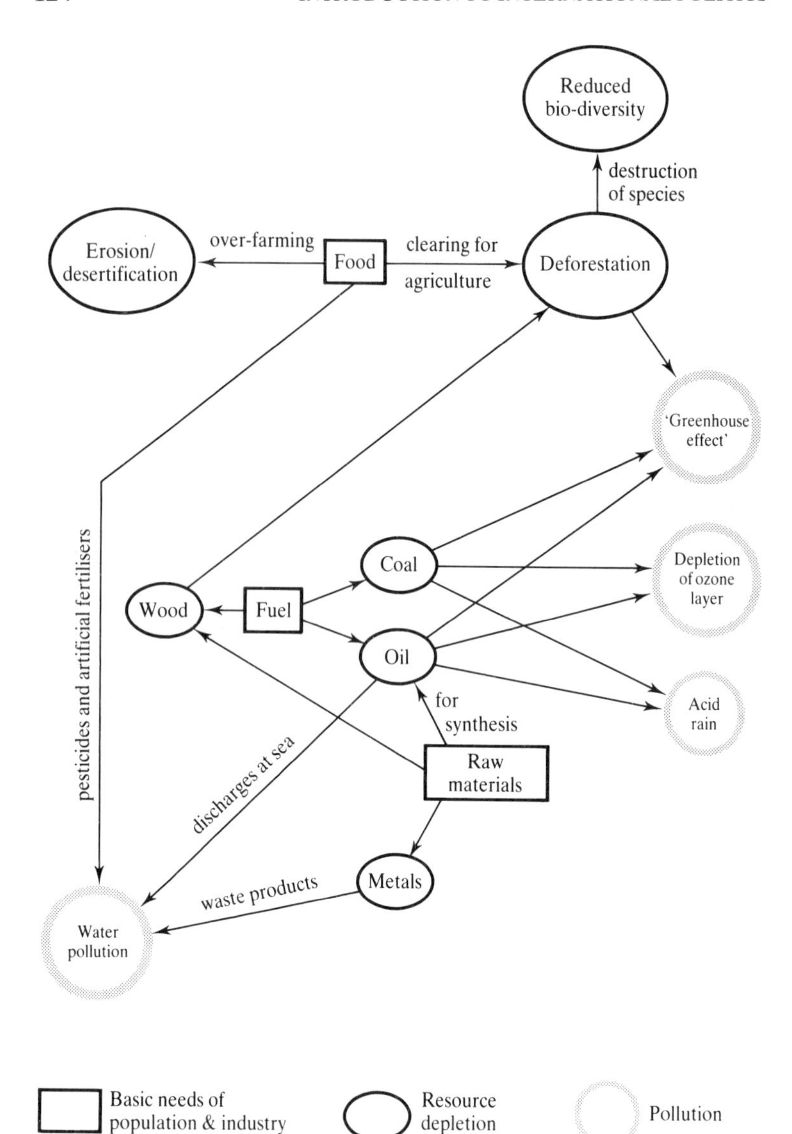

Figure **9.2** Resources and environment

4. The fourth feature is that the problems are becoming increasingly serious. Therefore international action at least to

contain the damage to our planet is becoming yearly more urgent.

Development, environment and international action

Third World poverty and environmental degradation remained for some time separate burdens on the world's conscience. The institutions designed to cope with these problems remained separate too. By the 1980s, however, the understanding grew that the two issues were connected. This insight was expressed by the term 'sustainable development'. The most important exposition of this idea is contained in a report prepared by the World Commission on Environment and Development. This was an independent group drawn from twenty-two different nations and established in 1983 at the instigation of the United Nations General Assembly. Its purpose was to draft 'a global agenda for change'. The chairman of this body was Mrs Gro Harlem Bruntland, the prime minister of Norway. Their report, under the pointed title of *Our Common Future*, was published in 1987.

The Commission's conclusion was guardedly optimistic – provided action was taken to implement policies of sustainable development. The Commission defined this concept as 'not a fixed state of harmony, but rather a process of change in which the exploitation of resources, the direction of investments, the orientation of technological development, and institutional change are made consistent with future as well as present needs' (Bruntland, 1987, p. 9). It is a moral as well as a pragmatic notion: it asserts that the present generation has no right to hand on to future generations a planet savagely degraded by our own greedy exploitation.

The Commission's optimism may be exemplified by the following brief quotation: 'The concept of sustainable development does imply limits. . . . But technology and social organization can be both managed and improved to make way for a new era of economic growth. The Commission believes that widespread poverty is no longer inevitable' (p. 8). However, that optimism has not been universally shared. Some economists believe, contrary to the Bruntland Commission, that growth and sustainability cannot be made compatible. This means that if the ecosystem is to be effectively protected from further depredations, living standards in the wealthy, industrialised countries must be *reduced*.

The Bruntland Report is a detailed analysis of the interrelated economic and environmental problems facing mankind, together with recommendations for legal and institutional changes necessary for their solution. For it is self-evident that, in the words of the Commission: 'The real world of interlocked economic and ecological systems will not change; the policies and institutions concerned must' (p. 9).

Two of the great obstacles to institutional change are the continuing power of the self-regarding nation-state and the profit-motivated industrial company. Sustainable development requires that both restrain their short-term selfish interests in favour of a longer-term altruism. But this is where the optimists and pessimists part company. The optimists argue that states and companies will ultimately benefit from less selfish policies in any case; the pessimists fear that governments and boards of directors are incapable of handling the discontent of reduced or more slowly rising standards of living and profits.

If, however, a shift to a more collaborative attitude is to be effected, it would seem easiest to achieve this in areas free of national sovereign control. These are Antarctica, the oceans, the ocean floor and outer space. These regions have been called the Common Heritage of Mankind (CHM) or, by analogy with medieval land usage, 'the global commons'.

From the perspective of the early 1990s there can be little doubt that the problems outlined in this chapter have caught the imaginations, bruised the consciences and exercised the minds of large sectors of world opinion. Nor can there be any doubt that new bodies, both official and non-governmental, have proliferated in attempts to meet the evident need for institutional reform. But what has in practice been achieved?

At a basic level scientific research into some of the most dangerous developments has been given an added boost. Let us take the serious issue of the greenhouse effect. For some time the cause and speed of this problem was disputed. Then, in 1990, over three hundred scientists – the influential Intergovernmental Panel on Climate Change (IPCC) – wrote a report which showed conclusively that carbon dioxide and other pollutant gas emissions could produce such warming as to raise sea-levels steadily over the next few decades. The report concluded that: 'In the absence of any adaptive measures this could render some island countries uninhabitable, displace tens of millions of people, seriously threaten low-lying urban areas, flood productive land, contaminate fresh water supplies and destroy many coastal wetlands' (quoted, *Observer*, 19 August 1990).

The publicity accorded to evidence and forecasts like this had led to a considerable increase in public awareness and campaigning. 'Think globally, act locally' became the apt slogan. Some 'environmentally friendly' goods have appeared in the stores. Perhaps one of the most remarkable expressions of popular concern has been the incredible increase in the number of Non-Governmental Organisations (NGOs). It is estimated that some 12,000 of these exist to cater for people with international interests; and a large proportion of these have development and/or environmental matters at the heart of their programmes. These NGOs are important both for what they achieve by themselves (for example, Oxfam in famine relief) and for exerting pressure upon governments (for example, Greenpeace in environmental protection).

A number of individual governments are changing their attitudes, though it is sometimes difficult to assess how far this is the result of NGO pressure. One interesting example of collaboration may be given as an illustration: the billion trees programme in Australia in which the government is co-operating with the Australian Trust for Conservation Volunteers.

On a larger scale are the international agreements, very often negotiated within the framework of the United Nations. It is convenient at this point to explain a few technical terms. The first is 'international regime'. The political scientist who devised this term defined it as: 'a set of mutual expectations, rules and regulations, plans, organisational energies and financial commitments, which have been accepted by a group of states' (John Ruggie, quoted in Little and Smith, 1991, p. 108). What are being sought are global and/or regional regimes to cope with environmental/development issues. The second term to note is 'convention'. This is an international agreement rather less binding than a treaty in the strict sense. And thirdly, 'protocol'. This is a follow-up to a convention. For example, the Vienna Convention for the Protection of the

Ozone Layer was signed in 1985. Two years later came the Montreal Protocol on Substances That Deplete the Ozone Layer By 1988, 140 environmental agreements had been concluded.

Let us look at three examples of varying success. The United Nations Conference on the Law of the Sea (UNCLOS) led to the drafting of a convention in 1982 that has failed to obtain the agreement of key states, such as the United States and the United Kingdom, to prevent uncontrolled exploitation of the mineral wealth of the ocean bed.

On the other hand, the United Nations Environmental Programme (UNEP) has had some modest successes. UNEP was created in 1972 with 'a catalytic and co-ordinating role' within the UN system in connection with environmental matters and responsible to the General Assembly (see Chapter 14). It has been extremely active in promoting many a convention. It has persuaded a number of states to combine to combat marine pollution in the Mediterranean and the Caribbean. Under its auspices a large number of states have committed themselves to the Convention on International Trade in Endangered Species (CITES), even though enforcement is proving difficult.

The prevention of pollution can be a costly business if cleaner technology is required. For instance, power stations fuelled by oil or coal (especially low-grade) are notorious generators of sulphur dioxide, which then produces acid rain. In 1984 Canada and a number of European states formed the '30 per cent club', pledging themselves to reduce their emissions by that proportion by 1993. A number of governments of heavily polluting countries such as the United States (primarily), the United Kingdom and Poland refused to commit themselves to this target. The problem of expense was clearly a factor in their non-compliance.

In many ways a greater worry has been the evidence that the ozone layer in the stratosphere is steadily being eroded. This thin cloak protects the planet from dangerous ultraviolet rays. The main culprits in causing this damage are the chlorofluorocarbons (CFCs) used in a variety of manufactures, most notably refrigerators. In 1987 eighty-one nations agreed to the Montreal Protocol to phase out these chemicals by the end of the century. Three years later the agreement was further tightened. One of the most serious problems facing the negotiators of the ozone protocols was that the Chinese and Indians want to provide their huge populations with refrigerators in the foreseeable future, yet could not afford the alternative to the CFC technology. Only financial aid from the richer countries could avert this potentially disastrous development – a vivid example of the interrelationship between development and environment.

By the early 1990s new ways were being considered for helping the poorer countries without causing collateral damage to the environment. For example, in 1991 a general Global Environmental Facility came into operation to provide financial compensation for environment-friendly but expensive policies. It was also becoming recognised that debt remission would be a signal contribution to the same objective.

One of the most interesting examples of this new attitude is the pressure which the United States started to exert on the World Bank in 1991. The United States, a major source of World Bank funds, has threatened to withhold monies for projects that are environmentally damaging. The Bank has instituted Environmental Impact Assessments (EIAs) of proposals as a means of meeting this kind of criticism. It has demonstrated its policy reversal by formally banning all funding of logging projects in tropical rain forests.

At the time of writing we can look forward to a major conference to be held in Rio de Janeiro in 1992 – the United Nations Conference on Environment and Development. If it is to be successful it will need to provide solutions to the following five key questions.

1. Are new international organisations to be created or the existing ones made more effective?
2. Should fines be exacted to deter environmental degradation and if so how is such a system to be organised?
3. How are the industrialised states to be persuaded to reduce their fossil-fuel energy consumption that causes so many problems?
4. How are the developing countries to be persuaded to slow down their industrialisation in the face of the great advantages enjoyed by the industrialised states?
5. Is it possible to finance and organise the transfer of environmentally friendly technologies to the developing countries?

The Rio conference is being organised by the Canadian, Maurice Strong, who has spoken of the need to find a balance between 'ego-systems and the ecosystem'. He is convinced of the need for an 'eco-industrial revolution' led by the developed nations. Expressing the hope that a real commitment to action will emerge from the Rio conference, he has declared that: 'If we fail . . . the prospects of having another chance in our generation will be very slim' (quoted, *Observer*, 24 March 1991). In the event, the vital issue of population-control was too controversial to be included on the agenda, and the agreements that were signed were more anodyne than potentially effective.

10

The Arab–Israeli Conflict

Until very recently this dispute has seemed the most intractable of all 'regional conflicts' and during the cold war it was also probably the most dangerous. This was because the strategic importance of the Middle East, its richness in oil, and the exceptionally powerful Jewish lobby in the United States led the superpowers to take a close interest in the region. With the United States aligned with Israel and the Soviet Union giving its support to the 'radical' Arab states, Arab–Israeli wars, of which there have been six since 1948 (see Box 10.1), at times threatened world war. It is true that a peace treaty was signed between Israel and Egypt (the most powerful Arab state and traditional leader of the Arab world) in 1979, following negotiations mediated by the United States at Camp David, but Egypt was at once ostracised by the Arabs for this breaking of ranks, and Camp David failed to grapple with the heart of the problem. Why has this conflict been so intractable? What solutions have been canvassed? What lessons does this tragic situation contain?

The origins of the conflict

The most important single reason for the start of this conflict is that both Jews and Arabs claim rights in 'Palestine' that are believed to threaten the very survival of the other. 'Palestine' is the territory lying between the eastern shores of the Mediterranean and the River Jordan and which was given to Britain by the League of Nations following the First World War as a mandate to be held in trust (see Figure 10.1).

To understand the Jewish claim to this land it is necessary to

Box 10.1 The Arab–Israeli wars

The War of Independence, 1948 Five Arab armies are repulsed by Israel following declaration of the new state in May.

The Suez War, October–November 1956 Israel launches a ground attack into Egypt in collusion with Britain and France; *fedaveen* bases are cleared and the straits of Tiran opened to Israeli shipping.

The Six-Day War, June 1967 Israel launches a pre-emptive strike against Syria, Jordan and Egypt, seizing the Golan Heights, the West Bank of the River Jordan (including East Jerusalem) and the Sinai Desert up to the Suez Canal.

The War of Attrition, July 1967–August 1970 Principally an artillery battle between Israel and Egypt across the Suez Canal, punctuated by air duels, commando raids and deep penetration bombing by Israel. This culminates in a major clash between Israeli jets and anti-aircraft defences massively reinforced by the Soviet Union in early 1970.

The Yom Kippur War, October 1973 Egypt and Syria launch surprise attacks on Israel on 6 October, the religious holiday of 'Yom Kippur', the Jewish Day of Atonement. Bridgeheads initially seized by the Egyptians on the east side of the Suez Canal, together with early gains made by the Syrians in Golan, are clawed back by Israel after heavy losses and a counter-crossing of the canal which encircles the Egyptian Third Army in Sinai.

The Lebanon War, June 1982–February 1985 Israeli forces drive into South Lebanon in order to expel the PLO and reduce Syrian influence over the country. The PLO evacuates Beirut in September, but then Israeli forces become bogged down in fighting with Shiite Lebanese guerrillas. Complete withdrawal from Lebanon does not begin until February 1985.

understand Zionism. Sometimes described as the ideology of Jewish nationalism, this is the doctrine that emerged against the background of violent persecutions of Jews in Russia and Eastern Europe in the late nineteenth century. It was expressed most famously by

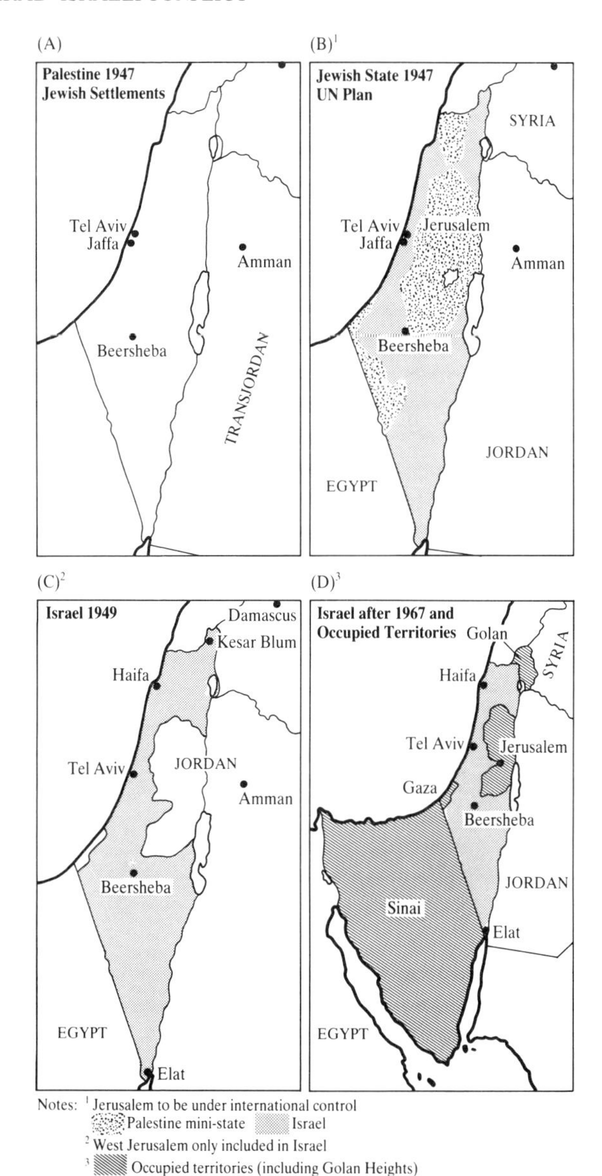

Figure 10.1 The geography of the Arab–Israeli conflict (Source: G. Chaliand and J.-P. Rageau (1986) *Strategic Atlas: World geopolitics*, Penguin Books: Harmondsworth, p. 128)

the Viennese journalist, Theodor Herzl, in his book, *A Jewish State*, which was published in 1896. Provoked by the belief that assimilation into host nations was impossible and that anti-Semitism was ineradicable, Zionism enunciated two main principles. The first principle was that Jews would never be safe until they had the physical protection of a state of their own – a Jewish state. The second was that this state had to be located in Palestine, at that time part of the decaying Ottoman Empire. Palestine had been the homeland of Jews until they had been conquered and scattered by the Romans almost two thousand years before, and – in the Holy City of Jerusalem – contained a relic of central importance to Judaism: the Western or Wailing Wall of the Great Temple. (Many Jews who had no intentions of de-camping to Palestine rejected Zionism since they feared that its nationalist logic would reinforce – as indeed it quite deliberately did – the claims of, say, German nationalists that Jews had no business remaining in Germany.)

The Zionist claim to Palestine was conditionally accepted near the end of the First World War by Britain, which was anxious to enlist world Jewry to the Allied cause and indifferent to the interests of Palestine's Ottoman landlords, who were allied to the Central Powers. Following the notoriously ambiguous Balfour Declaration (it referred to a Jewish 'national home' rather than a Jewish 'state' – see Box 10.2), the end of the war, and British acquisition of the League of Nations mandate in Palestine, Jewish immigration slowly increased. By 1939 the Jewish population of Palestine, which had stood at about only 60,000 at the end of the First World War, had increased to 429,605, or from under 9 per cent of the total population to 28 per cent. This had produced a violent reaction from the Arab majority. At the start of the Second World War London was forced to place severe restrictions on further immigration out of fear of driving the Arabs into the arms of Hitler, a development which would have jeopardised control of the strategically vital Middle East, where British forces were already thinly stretched. After the war, when the full horror of Hitler's death camps was revealed and geopolitical considerations were less weighty, Jewish immigration into Palestine was allowed to resume under intense American pressure, though not on a scale to satisfy the demands of the Jewish Agency, let alone the radical Jewish organisations such as the *Irgun* and the Stern Gang. The result was that Jewish extremists resorted to terror tactics against the British, and Arab residents were increasingly pushed from their lands by a combination of legitimate land purchase, trickery and outright intimidation.

Box 10.2 The Balfour Declaration

This statement of British policy took the form of a letter from the British Foreign secretary, Lord Balfour, to Lord Rothschild:

Foreign Office
November 2nd, 1917

Dear Lord Rothschild,

I have much pleasure in conveying to you, on behalf of His Majesty's Government, the following declaration of sympathy with Jewish Zionist aspirations which has been submitted to, and approved by, the Cabinet.

"His Majesty's Government view with favour the establishment in Palestine of a national home for the Jewish people, and will use their best endeavours to facilitate the achievement of this object, it being clearly understood that nothing shall be done which may prejudice the civil and religious rights of existing non-Jewish communities in Palestine, or the rights and political status enjoyed by Jews in any other country."

I should be grateful if you would bring this declaration to the knowledge of the Zionist Federation.

Yours sincerely,
ARTHUR JAMES BALFOUR

What is the claim to Palestine of the Arabs? This is simply that they had been the great majority in Palestine since the Roman terror had driven out the Jews, and that Jerusalem was also of great religious significance to Muslims. (For Muslims, the Dome of the Rock in Jerusalem marks the spot from which Mohammad ascended to heaven.) Moreover, like the Jews, and for similar reasons, they too had been given vague promises of statehood in Palestine, as well as the other lands that they had peopled under the old Ottoman Empire. Arabs born in Palestine were soon to be known as 'Palestinians', as a new national identity was born in the struggle with Zionism. In the light of their claims to the land they saw no reason why they should be asked to pay, at best with second-class citizenship, at worst with the land of their forebears, for the sins visited on the Jews by Europeans.

By early 1947 the contest between Arabs and Jews for the land of Palestine became too hot for the overstretched British government to handle, and the problem was handed over to the newly created United Nations. The plan with which the UN came up in November had three parts: first, Palestine was to be divided between the two parties (see Figure 10.1); Jerusalem (which contained Christian as well as Jewish and Muslim shrines) was to be internationalised; and the whole of the old mandate was to form an economic union. The decision to give a great slice of Palestine to the Jews infuriated the Arabs, who launched a full-scale war against the new state of Israel once the British had pulled out in May 1948. Badly led and poorly co-ordinated, this assault was repulsed by Jewish forces, which, indeed, seized substantially more territory than had been given to Israel in the UN partition plan (compare maps B and C in Figure 10.1); the remnants of Arab Palestine were absorbed by Egypt and Jordan. Jerusalem, instead of being internationalised, was divided. Arab refugees from Palestine crowded into Gaza and that area between Jerusalem and the River Jordan known as 'the West Bank'. They became the most visible and embittered sections of a Palestinian 'diaspora' scattered through the Arab world, which was, in a tragic irony, crudely analogous to the world-wide Jewish diaspora out of which the idea of a Jewish state was itself born.

In 1967, fearing that the Arabs were about to try to overturn the humiliation of 1948, Israel – by now enormously strengthened by the flood of officially encouraged post-war immigrants – launched its famous 'Six-Day War' (see Box 10.1). The result of this conflict was the creation of a 'Greater Israel', which almost fulfilled the dreams of the wildest Zionists. (Re-creation of ancient Israel would have meant absorption of the whole of Jordan.) Israel now embraced lands traditionally claimed, together with the whole of Jerusalem (after the 1948 war East Jerusalem, which contained the Wailing Wall, had fallen into Jordanian hands). It had also acquired natural defensive lines along its frontiers: the Golan Heights in the north-east (previously belonging to Syria), the River Jordan in the east, and the Suez Canal in the west. Moreover, it had freed the commerce of the southern port of Eilat from the stranglehold imposed on it by Egyptian forces in eastern Sinai and, above all, vastly increased the country's 'strategic depth'. With its major population centres now more remote from Arab military power (especially air bases), early warning of Arab attack was much easier to achieve and the safety of civilians in the event that war should break out again easier to guarantee. Israeli military prestige was also at an all-time high. These were huge prizes.

Greater Israel might have achieved more short-term security for the Israelis, as well as ideological gratification for the Zionists, but its realisation had only intensified the conflict between Arab and Jew. More Arabs were under Israeli occupation than ever before (roughly 1.5 million), the ranks of embittered Palestinian refugees were swollen by an exodus of almost 400,000 from the West Bank, and the enmity between Israel and its Arab neighbours was deepened by the seizure of their lands. To the issue of justice for the Palestinians was now added the issue of the 'occupied territories', some of which (especially the West Bank, East Jerusalem and the Golan Heights) the Israelis clearly had no intention of giving back. The conflict was further intensified at this juncture because it was now seen more than ever – in the Middle East and elsewhere in the Third World – as a major theatre of the world-wide confrontation between the oppressed and the forces of US-led 'imperialism'. Finally, even though the Israelis repeatedly declared their readiness to talk to the Arabs, a clash of cultural styles presented a massive obstacle to dialogue, even had the Arabs been prepared in principle to negotiate. After all, the Arabs are wedded to a collectivist culture in which saving face has exceptional importance, as well as to a picturesque rhetoric and an elaborate civility which appear to Israelis to be by turns menacing and devious. The Israelis, in contrast, are stubbornly individualistic, blunt in manner, and attached to a cult of simplicity, all of which makes them appear to the Arabs to be arrogant, inflexible and above all uncivilised.

It was in these circumstances, then, that the Palestinians' own organisations, disappointed with the efforts on their behalf of the Arab states, began to assume a more prominent role in the conflict with Israel by launching small-scale attacks from bases in south Lebanon and Jordan. Notable among these organisations was the newly radicalised Palestine Liberation Organisation (PLO), which had been created by the Arab League in 1964, though the more extreme Palestinian organisations were responsible for the most spectacular terrorist attacks.

Since the Six-Day War in 1967 stability in the Middle East has continued to be undermined by the Arab–Israeli conflict, not least because superpower involvement meant that local imbalances of power were prevented from deciding the issue by force. When the Israelis had a decisive edge, as in 1967, the Soviets re-supplied the Arabs with even more sophisticated arms; when the Arabs seemed to pose a deadly threat to the Israelis, as at Yom Kippur in October 1973, the Americans rushed more weapons to them. The conflict also sucked in and reduced Lebanon to a state of permanent civil war, constantly threatened the throne of King Hussein in Jordan, and increasingly polarised Israeli society between those who were prepared to make territorial concessions to the Arabs in return for peace and those who felt that this would only encourage the Arabs to demand more and would not, as a result, give an inch. In 1979, following a major personal effort by the American President, Jimmy Carter, the Israelis did in fact agree to return Sinai (with appropriate security arrangements) to Egypt in exchange for a peace treaty. But the Palestinians had no say in these negotiations and the Egyptian President, Anwar Sadat, abandoned his efforts on their behalf when it became clear that the hard-line Israeli leader, Menachem Begin, would not contemplate any significant concessions to them. The Palestinian issue was thus fudged at Camp David, Egypt was ostracised by the other Arab states, and the Arab–Israeli conflict was no nearer to a solution except in one important regard: with Egyptian recognition of the state of Israel, general acceptance of the Jewish state as a permanent political fact of life in the Middle East had moved perceptibly nearer.

The struggle for peace

Despite the huge obstacles that remained, including divisions within Israel, among the Palestinians, and between the Arab states, a negotiated solution to the Arab–Israeli conflict at least became *conceivable* in the early 1970s. This was because both sides were coming to realise that the status quo was insupportable in the long run, and that further attempts to resolve it by force were likely to involve costs which would be excessive relative to any gains which could be reasonably expected.

The Israelis had been considerably sobered by the initial Arab military gains in the Yom Kippur War and many (not all) were in any case apprehensive about the future of a Greater Israel with an expanding Arab population. As for the Arab states, they were on the whole growing weary of the costs which the Palestinian struggle was imposing on them, and increasingly inclined to accept that Israel was a fact with which they would have to come to terms. This was easier to accept – especially for Egypt – as a result of the restoration of pride by the early successes at Yom Kippur. In the face of this attitude and the continuing strength of Israel, the PLO itself was abandoning its previously declared strategy of revolutionary war in favour of diplomacy and propaganda centring on the United Nations. The whole diplomatic process was given a further boost by the United States. The Americans were anxious to defuse the crisis in the interest of stable relations with the Soviet Union and were at the same time happy to increase their influence in the Middle East at the expense of Moscow, which had manifestly failed the Arabs. It accordingly offered itself as a muscular mediator. A very modest minimum of agreement, which provided a 'framework' for a settlement, had also been provided by a resolution of the UN Security Council following the 1967 war. Though necessarily somewhat ambiguous, this stipulated in effect that a settlement of the Arab–Israeli conflict must be based on Israeli concessions of territory in return for recognition of the state of Israel by the Arabs in the context of conditions of genuine peace: land for peace.

The first approach adopted by the United States was the 'step-by-step' method of Henry Kissinger, US Secretary of State in the second Nixon administration. The second was the 'comprehensivist' approach of Jimmy Carter. But before these are considered it is important to distinguish between the various plans that were put forward for a solution to the conflict, which provide the background – as well as much of the substance – of the debate which took place at the historic meeting at Madrid in November 1991. It will be convenient to place these along a continuum starting with the extreme Palestinian position and finishing with the most radical Israeli position. Constant reference should be made to Figure 10.1.

In 1948 the Arabs, rejecting the UN partition plan, fought for a unitary, non-sectarian, democratic Palestine. In such a state Jews would have had no special position and the Arabs would have been in a clear majority. Such majoritarian thinking was summarily dismissed by Zionists as suicidal. The centrist nucleus of Palestinians themselves renounced it, by stages, in the mid-1970s. In his address to the UN General Assembly in November 1974, Yasser Arafat, leader of the PLO since 1969, described it as a 'dream'. Many Israelis, however, still believe that – as a dream – it is the ultimate goal of the Palestinian Arabs.

The more moderate Palestinian position, to which the PLO has been clearly committed since at least 1978, is known as the 'two state solution'. This, with important changes of detail (especially on Jerusalem), amounts in effect to a revival of the UN plan for the partition of Palestine. Israel is accepted as a legitimate state but must surrender the West Bank, the Gaza Strip and East Jerusalem. This would become the territory of a Palestinian mini-state. Gaza (bordering the Mediterranean) and the West Bank would be connected by a corridor, giving the whole of the new state access to the sea. East Jerusalem would become its capital, but would be linked to West Jerusalem by a unified municipal authority. In order to quieten fears in both Israel and the new mini-state, the latter would become a permanent neutral on the Austrian model, UN troops would patrol its frontiers, ports and airports, and the new dispensation would be guaranteed by the superpowers. This, too, has been rejected by Israel, the more so since the hard-line Likud bloc has dominated its politics for most of the time since 1977. The security guarantees for such a shrunken, narrow-waisted Israel were considered a very poor substitute for the presence of the Israeli Defence Force on the River Jordan, not least because Israel had no trust in the Soviet Union (which had severed relations with it following the 1967 war) or the United Nations, where the General Assembly had condemned Zionism as 'a form of racism' in 1975. Besides, Likud had a deep ideological attachment to the West Bank (renamed as Judea and Samaria), where it was determined to make Israel's occupation an irrevocable political fact by allowing – if not positively encouraging – Jewish settlement in this overwhelmingly Arab area.

The third scheme for a settlement of the Arab–Israeli conflict is 'the Jordanian option', which seems first to have seen the light of day in the Hussein Plan of 1972. This is the idea that Israel's security fears and the Palestinians' desire for their own state could both be met *in part* by creation of a *federal* Jordanian state. Israel would surrender the West Bank but to Jordan rather than to the

Palestinians. Since King Hussein was pro-Western and had fought a bloody war to expel the troublesome Palestinians from his territory in 1970–1, it might have been thought that this plan would evoke some sympathy in Israel. As for the Palestinians themselves, they would not get their state but they would get considerable autonomy from Amman in the new 'United Arab Kingdom', as it was to be known in the original Hussein Plan. East Jerusalem would be the capital of the new autonomous province. But this plan – despite periodic American support – has never found sufficient support among the Israelis or the Palestinians. For the former it presents basically the same obstacles as the mini-state plan, while for the latter it founders on distrust of Jordan and failure to meet the minimum objective of a nationalism that by now was too well entrenched; a sovereign state.

The fourth plan brings us nearer to the end of the spectrum where Israeli preferences dominate, and goes back to the 'Allon Plan' of 1974. It is a variation of the Jordanian option, the main differences being that Gaza is excluded and Israeli forces are allowed to retain defensive positions at strategic positions within the new, 'sovereign' state of Jordan/Palestine.

The fifth plan is the most that the Likud bloc in Israel has ever been prepared to contemplate, and a version of which Menachem Begin put on the table during the Camp David negotiations in 1978. In this the Palestinians in the West Bank and Gaza get neither a mini-state nor autonomy within a federated Jordan. Instead, they get heavily qualified 'administrative autonomy' *within the state of Israel*: that is, something similar to the 'devolution' which has been periodically canvassed for Scotland and Wales within Britain. In contrast to the status of the Scots and the Welsh in the latter scheme, however, Likud has traditionally seen the West Bank and Gaza Arabs as nothing more than 'guests' within the Jewish state; hence they should look for their political–citizenship rights in Jordan, though they might alternatively be granted Israeli citizenship. In this regard, the nearer analogy is with South Africa in the period of grand apartheid, when blacks who had lived all their lives in 'white South Africa' were required to apply for citizenship in their 'true' tribal homelands, such as Bophutatswana, though they were allowed to remain as visitors in 'South Africa'.

The sixth plan is the platform of the most extreme Zionist parties and is, of course, the polar opposite of the first plan, Yasser Arafat's 'dream'. This is that Israel retains its present borders (which are roughly those of the whole of mandated Palestine), and the Arabs presently within them should settle on the East Bank of the River Jordan. Jordan would remain exactly as it is now, which is in effect the 'Transjordan' that adjoined the Palestine mandate. If the Jordanian option has proved unacceptable to the Palestinians, it is hardly surprising that they have never been prepared even to contemplate any of the last three.

Step-by-step versus a comprehensive solution

The Arab–Israeli conflict has witnessed not only dispute over the shape of a settlement but also controversy over the best diplomatic method by which approach to one might be made. This was articulated most fully in the United States in the mid-1970s, when a 'step-by-step' method was self-consciously employed by Henry Kissinger following the Yom Kippur War.

The step-by-step approach was, nominally at any rate, based on two assumptions: first, that the positions of the Arabs and the Israelis were so irreconcilable that any attempt to proceed to a comprehensive solution was completely unrealistic; and secondly, that this prospect was rendered even more forlorn by the immense depth of the distrust between them. On this view, therefore, the only hope was to promote, by means of superpower mediation, agreements on limited matters without obvious political significance, mainly to do with the disengagement of forces following the 1973 war. Moreover, rather than being conducted with all of Israel's Arab neighbours simultaneously, the negotiations would be conducted with them consecutively, starting with Egypt. The idea was that in this way, if limited agreements were made, and if they stuck, two advantages would follow: first, other Arab states, encouraged by successful precedents, would be drawn into the negotations; and secondly, the Arab–Israeli trust which was the essential pre-condition for proceeding to negotiation of the more controversial matters (return of the occupied territories and Palestinian national rights) would slowly be nurtured. In the process, the Arabs would gradually get used to the idea of Israel's existence. At the very least, the step-by-step approach would keep the lid on the conflict and prevent it bursting out into war again.

This approach was directly analogous to the functionalist approach to regional integration adopted by pan-Europeanists after the Second World War (see Chapter 15).

The problem with the step-by-step approach, of course, is that it requires not only consistent direction by a third party capable of exercising pressure for concessions on both sides, *but also time*. Though Kissinger made some progress in the mid-1970s, achieving disengagement agreements between certain Arab states and the Israelis, the Republican Administration in which he was Secretary of State left office at the beginning of 1977. Thus, while some tentative 'steps' towards a settlement of the Arab–Israeli conflict had certainly been taken by this time, the approach was not believed by the incoming Democrats to have shown sufficient promise to warrant its continuation. Their belief (which in the event did not prove entirely correct) was that the nettle of Palestinian rights had to be grasped because no Arab state would risk the charge of putting its selfish interests in peace with Israel before those of the Palestinians. The only way forward, in other words, was believed to be the ambitious one of seeking a 'comprehensive' solution: that is, one which embraced peace treaties between the Arab states and Israel based on territorial settlements *plus* gratification in some form (perhaps 'the Jordanian option' outlined in the previous section) of Palestinian national claims.

As we know, the comprehensivist approach to peace in the Middle East also failed, foundering on Israeli intransigence over the West Bank, and Democratic President, Jimmy Carter, had to fall back on the reviled step-by-step approach. This at any rate produced a peace treaty between Egypt and Israel that is still in place. In the early 1990s, however, the comprehensive approach came back into vogue because it seemed that the time was as ripe as it was ever likely to be for a comprehensive solution. This was a result of two developments: the collapse of the Soviet Union and the Gulf War.

The collapse of the Soviet Union deprived hard-line Arab opinion (for example, in Syria) of its most important source of extra-regional support, while at the same time causing an exodus of Soviet Jews to Israel. This at once led many Palestinians to conclude that they had better negotiate for the best terms possible before the West Bank was overrun by Jewish immigrants, and placed a huge economic burden on Jerusalem that made it more than ever dependent on American goodwill. As for the Gulf War, this suggested that Israel was now a strategic liability to the Americans in the region rather than (as it had previously boasted) a strategic asset, and also forced the United States to promise that an Arab–Israeli settlement would be high on its post-war agenda in order to hold together the anti-Saddam Arab coalition. Furthermore, the PLO backed the losing side (Saddam), thus giving more credibility in the region to the more 'moderate' kind of Palestinian with which the Shamir government in Jerusalem was prepared to negotiate. All of this added up to the Middle East Conference held in Madrid in November 1991, the like of which had not been seen since December 1973 in Geneva.

In the event, Madrid proved a disappointment, and it is clear that there is unlikely to be any serious progress in this perennial dispute until after the elections in both Israel and the United States in 1992. It is also possible that since the end of the cold war means that Arab–Israeli wars are no longer likely to threaten world war, the incentive of the United States to continue on its mine-strewn task of mediation may be greatly reduced. This will be the more likely as memories of the promises made during the Gulf War grow dimmer, and other crises demand attention.

The Arab–Israeli conflict contains many lessons for those involved in national struggles, and just as many for those involved in the job of preventing the fires that they ignite from spreading. Of the former, the most important is probably that, compared to rival national movements convinced by scripture of their right to the same land, imperial powers from distant homelands are a push-over. Of the latter, the most important is possibly that settlements *imposed* from the outside will not stick but that external pressure is both justified (prudentially as well as morally) and necessary.

Part III

Order

11

The 'Big Five' and the UN

A great power is a state that possesses a reputation for existing or latent military strength that may be equalled but not significantly surpassed by that of any other power. It is, in other words, a power of the first rank in terms of reputation for military strength, or military 'prestige'. Such powers have always taken the lead both in shaping and enforcing international law, as well as the less formal rules of the system of states such as those defining spheres of influence. They are therefore the central pillar of world order (which means a condition governed by rules) and, to the extent that they act in concert, the nearest thing that the states-system has to a 'government'. In the twentieth century this has been explicitly recognised by allowing (as if this could be prevented!) the great powers a privileged position in the international organisations charged with maintaining international peace and security, since 1945 the United Nations. Who are they? What interests pull them together? Has the operation against Iraq in 1991, in which three of the major powers, with the blessing of the UN Security Council, played such a prominent role, ushered in a 'new' world order? First, however, a little history.

The emergence of the 'Big Five'

At the end of the Second World War only three great powers remained: the United States, the Soviet Union and Britain. Not surprisingly, these states were the chief architects of the United

Nations, and gave themselves permanent, veto-wielding membership of its most important organ, the Security Council. However, two other states were also admitted to the Security Council on the same privileged terms: France, at the insistence of the British, and China, under pressure from the Americans. (Britain was anxious to restore French power after the war in order that France might assist with the occupation of Germany and act as a counter to the Soviet Union after the withdrawal of American forces from Europe, while the United States wanted to strengthen the position of China so that it would have a useful lieutenant in the Pacific.) Thus had the 'Big Three' of the war against the Axis powers been replaced by the 'Big Five' of the United Nations Organisation, though it was many years before it became common to refer to them in these terms. This was largely because they were obviously not all equally 'big'.

France and China were only 'courtesy' members of the Big Five in 1945; by 1949 this had become even more obviously true of China. In this year the Communists seized power in Peking and caused their domestic rivals (the Nationalist Kuomintang) to flee to the large Chinese island of Taiwan (Formosa), where they set up the 'Republic of China'. Appalled at the speed with which Communism was spreading in the Far East and determined to deny it the least semblance of respectability, the United States recognised the Formosa regime as the legitimate government of China and for two decades blocked attempts to install the (Communist) Peoples' Republic of China (PRC) on the Security Council. Hence the 'Chinese' seat was occupied by a government which had no legal authority on the mainland at all. (This absurd position was not rectified until October 1971.)

It was not long after the war, however, that Britain, too, was acknowledged by everyone – except, of course, the British – to have lost its standing as a great power or, as such a power was now known, a 'superpower'. As a result, for much the greater part of the post-war period America and the Soviet Union were the only genuine superpowers, marked off from all other contenders by the size and sophistication of their conventional as well as nuclear arsenals. In these circumstances, it would have been difficult to speak with any conviction of the 'Big Five'.

Circumstances now, however, are radically changed and thus the differences between the members of the Big Five are not so marked.

With the end of the cold war, huge stockpiles of nuclear weapons are no longer so important; in any case, Britain, France and the PRC have all been nuclear weapons states for decades. Russia has taken over the Soviet seat on the Security Council, and while still a major nuclear power is clearly greatly reduced in international status. By contrast, the China seat on the Security Council has now been occupied by mainland China for over twenty years, while Britain and France are now leading members of the immensely successful European Community. America – as the Gulf War demonstrated – is still out ahead in the military stakes but its economy is in deep trouble, and it was very anxious for financial support from other wealthy states at the time of that engagement. This is all very different from the late 1940s.

The common interests of the major powers

A states-system can tolerate internal opponents (for example, Iraq, Libya) provided its most powerful members are in agreement on certain fundamentals. What are the *perceived* common interests of the major powers?

Until the late 1980s, the Soviet Union and the United States acknowledged few shared interests. Nevertheless, even during the 'new cold war' of the Reagan–Brezhnev era the superpowers possessed sufficient common interests to make the states-system work. For example, they demonstrated a common interest in the solution of many relatively non-political problems, in fields such as transport and communications (including space exploration), and disease and pollution control (with particular attention, following the Chernobyl meltdown, to nuclear power stations). But, vastly more important, the superpowers shared an interest in *the avoidance of nuclear war*.

Awareness of this interest was suggested by the slogan of 'peaceful coexistence' adopted by the Soviet Union in the mid-1950s, and the support that each power gave to the Vienna Convention on Diplomatic Relations in 1961. It was confirmed by the postures struck by the superpowers following the intense fright of the Cuban missile crisis in 1962. These included the circumspection with which each treated the behaviour of the other in its acknowledged sphere of influence, the anxiety shown by both to restrain their clients in the world's most dangerous region (the Middle East), their joint hostility to the acquisition of nuclear weapons by third states, and their determination not to allow acute political differences either to overthrow existing arms control agreements or to interrupt for long their negotiations on new ones. The interest in avoiding nuclear war was so strong and its implications so pervasive, that this alone was sufficient to make the great powers – ideological rivals though they were – work together. In short, a constitutional order in world politics was underpinned by the concrete strength of nuclear fear.

Though strong, this was nevertheless a slender basis for world order, and might have been destroyed – as some American strategists hoped – by unequal breakthroughs in the science and technology of nuclear defence. What provided an infinitely more durable foundation for world order in the late 1980s was the transformation of the Soviet Union and Eastern Europe, and the 'New Thinking' in foreign policy announced by Mikhail Gorbachev. Acknowledging that 'class conflict' in world politics was a thing of the past, the new Soviet approach explicitly accepted that what unites inhabitants of 'our common planetary home' was now more important than what divides them. Hence the emphasis on the urgent need for superpower co-operation in finding solutions to the 'regional conflicts' which had hitherto wrought such local destruction, strained their exchequers, complicated their diplomacy, and threatened to drag them into direct military confrontation. Hence, too, the much greater stress on collaborative approaches to old international problems like terrorism, old ones which had become much more serious (like environmental pollution, drugs and Third World impoverishment), and entirely new ones like the AIDS epidemic. 'Interdependence' had finally become a Soviet cliché as well. And it had beneficial implications for Soviet–Chinese as well as Soviet–American relations.

In the course of jettisoning the ideological baggage of more than half a century, Mikhail Gorbachev also gave much greater emphasis in Soviet thinking to the United Nations, that temple of sovereign states held by Marxism–Leninism to be historically doomed. The Soviet Union had decided that it now wanted the UN to function as it was always supposed to function, and – after a period of intense hostility to the organisation – the United States seemed to be coming round to this view as well. It was against this background in the second half of the 1980s that the Big Five on the Security Council began to pull together. The formal disintegration of the Soviet Union at the end of 1991, and acquisition of its seat on the Security Council by a Russian government pleading for Western aid, has merely reinforced this trend.

Collective security

Increasingly inclined to caucus in secret from about 1985 onwards and then impose their view on the ten non-permanent members of the Security Council, the Big Five have begun to make a speciality out of arm-twisting belligerents in regional conflicts to the negotiating table. The first successful example of this was seen in the events leading up to the ceasefire in the terrible Iran–Iraq War, which was accepted by Iraq in July 1987 and by Iran a year later. Depending on the history of the conflict and the attitude of the parties to the UN, the Big Five's involvement may take the form of muscular support for mediation by the UN Secretary-General (as in the Iran–Iraq War) or the much more low-key support provided to the diplomatic efforts of one of its own number (as in the Angola–Namibia negotations, orchestrated by the United States in 1988). In such cases, and in others such as Cambodia and Yugoslavia, the Big Five have sought results by propaganda and economic pressure (including the threat of arms embargoes), and by providing ceasefire observers and fully fledged peacekeeping forces (see Chapter 13) where appropriate. Nevertheless, the arm-twisting in the Gulf in 1991 was of a quite different character, and it is this achievement that has really drawn attention to the role of the Security Council in the world's trouble spots and provoked talk of a 'new' world order. This, after all, was 'collective security' in action, in action for the first time in three decades and only the second time in history.

The doctrine of collective security assumes that insecurity is the major cause of war. As a result, it concludes that the best way to stop war is for each state to provide to *all* other states (irrespective of their importance, ideology, remoteness and so on) a legal guarantee of swift assistance in the event that they are a 'victim of aggression', a 'police action' that will be orchestrated by a permanent international body set up for the purpose. Thus relieved of anxiety about their security, states will have no need to take the unilateral steps to increase their military strength that initiate the spiral of fear which culminates in war; alliances can be foregone and armaments reduced to a level merely sufficient for members to discharge their responsibilities to the international body.

The obstacles to collective security

Unfortunately, conditions in the four decades following the end of the Second World War were extremely unfavourable to the operation of collective security. Among other factors, the division of the world into ideological (including religious) and regional camps made it almost inevitable that any 'aggression' would have significant support. The notion of the universally condemned 'lone aggressor', in other words, was simply unreal, as Britain found to its chagrin after Argentina lauched its 'aggression' on the Falkland Islands in 1982 and received considerable sympathy throughout Latin America. Even when Saddam Hussein launched his spectacular invasion of Kuwait in August 1990, he was supported by the PLO, while Jordan, Libya and Iran remained effectively neutral, and some key states (Syria, Egypt, Algeria and Morocco) were under strong popular pressure to throw in their lot with him. On the Security Council itself two members (Cuba and Yemen) voted against the key resolution (678) and China abstained. This illustrated the fact that although cold war divisions may have almost disappeared, plenty of others remain. Besides, most acts of 'aggression' today are much more ambiguous than the ones mentioned above, often involving covert support for the internal enemies of a regime. In such circumstances, 'aggression' is seldom easy to substantiate.

The enormous discrepancy in power between states is also a major obstacle to collective security, and the ending of the cold war has had no bearing on this. Thus, while a collective response to an aggression by a small, non-nuclear state which lacks the protection of an alliance with a major power is not unrealistic (as the Iraq case showed), a similar response to a limited aggression by a major nuclear power (say, the invasion of Afghanistan by the Soviet Union in 1979) certainly is. This is because it would probably prove fatal to the whole word if tried. (It is for this reason that the framers of the UN Charter provided the great powers with the right to veto any proposal that they considered inconsistent with their interests. Of course, should a great power launch a *major* war, there may well be no alternative to a collective response, whatever the risks.) Finally, the speed and destructive capacity of modern weapons is such that states can hardly be blamed for taking little comfort from promises of assistance *after* an attack. Though eventually rescued from the Iraqis, Kuwait's blazing oil fields make this point with considerable eloquence.

With collective security confronting such formidable obstacles, it is hardly surprising that except in Korea in the early 1950s it was left on the shelf, and the world fell back on national armies, alliances and all the other paraphernalia of the balance of power. What, then, made possible the collective security operation to drive Iraq out of Kuwait in 1991? And is this the shape of things to come?

Iraq and collective security

Not all members of the UN favoured the use of force against Iraq, as we have already noted. Furthermore, the Security Council *requested* support for the action; it did not *require* it. The forces ranged against Saddam did not in the event wear UN blue and were not referred to as a UN army; they were described instead as the 'Coalition' or 'Allied' forces. Nor were they even nominally directed by the Military Staff Committee of the Security Council, which, though moribund for decades, had never been disbanded; they were directed instead by the President of the United States as Commander-in-Chief of the US armed forces under the American constitution, advised in the first instance by the (American) Joint Chiefs of Staff. Nevertheless, there is little doubt that the American-led operation against Iraq was a near-classic collective security action.

In twelve separate resolutions, beginning with number 660 of 2 August 1990, the UN Security Council defined the crimes and identified the criminal. And in resolution 678 of 29 November 1990, it authorised member-states of the United Nations 'to use all necessary means to uphold and implement Security Council resolution 660 and to restore international peace and security in the area'. In short, the Security Council, led by the Big Five, *authorised* the action against Saddam and *sub-contracted the job* to the Americans and their friends (or at any rate Saddam's enemies, such as Syria). In any hue and cry there are always some more eager to join in than others.

What made this collective security action possible? Apart from the greatly improved relations between the Big Five already mentioned, the first and most important point to note is that Iraq was not a great power. Furthermore, it did not possess powerful regional allies; Saddam was loathed and distrusted by the leading Arab states (Egypt, Syria and Saudi Arabia) and hated by the Iranians, with whom he had still not settled issues that had provided the spark to the war of the first half of the 1980s. Hence the job was practical and was never likely to blow up the whole world. Secondly, Saddam's aggression against a UN member-state in good standing was utterly unambiguous; even if the world had wanted to avert its eyes, it would have found this impossible. (South Africa would probably have got away with racism if it had not elevated it to the status of doctrine.) Finally, Saddam's aggression was compounded by the harassment of diplomats in Kuwait, the ill-treatment of Kuwaiti citizens, and above all by the manipulation of hostages (including children) for propaganda purposes. This was not ordinary burglary; it was aggravated burglary.

Collective security in Kuwait worked: the final military operation was a resounding success; the Kuwaitis got their country back; and the aggressor was punished very heavily indeed. Libya is currently another weak and friendless state that has incurred the wrath of the Security Council (over involvement in the sabotage of the PanAm jet over Lockerbie) and in 1992 might just provide another case of collective security in action. (There is a view that such states should not be 'picked on' when others similarly delinquent are allowed to 'get away with it' because they do not provide such easy targets. Syria, which sided with the Coalition in the Gulf War and – unlike Libya – is a serious power in the Middle East, is usually mentioned in this context. This argument is illogical.) Is it likely that these cases have decisively revived the doctrine of collective security, and that more states will not only support it but come to rely on it to a greater degree? Are we on the verge of the 'New World Order' that has been announced by President Bush?

It has to be emphasised that the circumstances in which collective security was revived in the Gulf in 1991 remain fairly exceptional. Moreover, some aspects of the operation may not encourage future enthusiam for the doctrine, particularly if no reforms are introduced to its methods. It proved expensive to some countries with no direct interest in the affair, and resulted in some governments (especially in the Maghreb and the Middle East) being seriously out of step with their peoples. To some extent the victory also turned sour when the Coalition proved unable to prevent the disasters which befell the Iraqi Kurds and Shias in the immediate aftermath of the war; this also demonstrated in graphic fashion that interventions of this kind are rarely as simple as they may at first sight appear, either practically or morally. Because it was rather too obviously an American operation on behalf of an American friend, it also provoked the widespread suspicion that collective security was only something to be relied on if one had a lot of oil and was on good terms with the United States. And the extent to which the United States obtained UN blessing for an agenda in Iraq which had not surfaced in any Security Council resolution (such as the destruction of Saddam's military capability) may well make the UN more reluctant to subcontract collective security in the future. Above all, while it is true that the Kuwaitis got their country back, the existence of the UN and its doctrine of collective security did not deter the Iraqi aggression in the first place, and the counter-attack was not launched until five and a half months later, by which time the country had been well and truly plundered.

In the light of all this, it is perhaps not surprising that there is as yet little evidence that the world in general or the Middle East in particular are placing much faith in the New World Order; most states are doing what they have always done – keeping their powder dry (and their chemicals temperature controlled).

Should the Security Council be reformed?

There is a view, to which the British Conservative government appeared deeply wedded in 1991–2, that since the Security Council is at last working as it was supposed to do, this is hardly the time to start 'tampering' with its membership and procedures (its powers are regarded as a different matter). This is certainly a good argument against *radical* reform, but it is no argument against modest reform, since it begs the question as to whether or not the Security Council could not do better. Suggested reforms of the Security Council, which have been very much in the air as a result of the increase in importance of this body over the last decade, vary greatly in the support they receive. There are, for example, occasional mutterings about the need to rehabilitate the Military Staff Committee and reduce the secrecy that has increasingly enveloped the Security Council's key sessions. But no one with a genuine interest in conducting collective security operations swiftly and efficiently seriously believes that the chiefs of staff from five different military traditions can do this together, or that considerable secrecy is essential if Security Council deliberations are not to return to the sterile public debate of earlier years (Berridge, 1991, Chapter 1). As a result, these ideas seem to have little real support. Instead, those that do, concern the membership of the Security Council and its enforcement, or war-making, capacity.

It is important to note first the proposals that have surfaced since the Gulf War, which are designed to give the Security Council more teeth and its operations less of an *ad hoc* and, frankly, American flavour. These include giving the Council its own rapid-deployment force (composed of 'ear-marked' national contingents) and pre-positioning heavily armed forces (*not* 'peace-keeping forces', which are discussed in the following chapter) in areas of known tension, such as the Iraq–Kuwait border. If taken, such steps would greatly increase the ability of the Big Five, acting through the Security Council, to deter aggression (unless, of course, this is launched by one of their own number, in which case they would quite properly be able to veto use of these new UN forces against themselves in order to prevent a small war becoming a world war). A corollary of such developments would have to be a great strengthening of the impartial military advice available to the UN Secretariat. These are ambitious proposals, and it remains to be seen what will become of them. At the time of writing (April 1992) they are being investigated by a task force of the UN Secretariat in New York.

The issue of membership has become a live one because the possession of permanent seats on the Security Council reflects the distribution of power in 1944 rather than the 1990s (see Box 11.1). Thus it pre-dates the re-emergence of the ex-enemy states (Germany – now re-united as well – Japan and Italy) and the collapse of the European empires. Any 'new' world order in which the Security Council is to play a key role will thus be based on a narrow foundation unless its membership is changed. The issue here is one of giving the Security Council more *authority* without making it so large that it becomes unworkable. Germany and Japan would be happy to oblige by accepting permanent membership. After all, they are both among the biggest contributors to the UN's regular budget and – in highly significant moves – relaxed slightly post-war restrictions on the overseas deployment of their armed forces during and after the Gulf War.

Box 11.1 New permanent members for the Security Council?

The Security Council currently has fifteen members, of whom the following are permanent and veto-wielding:

	United States
	Russia
The 'Big Five'	Britain
	France
	China

(The ten non-permanent members are elected by the General Assembly for two-year terms in the light of the need for 'equitable geographical distribution').

In late 1990 the following proposals were all being actively discussed:

- United Germany should become the sixth permanent member (a *Soviet* suggestion)
- Britain and France should allow their two permanent seats to be replaced by one occupied by the European Community, and Japan should be given the one thus vacated (an *Italian* suggestion).
- Brazil and two or three other Third World Countries (India, Nigeria and perhaps Egypt) should be given permanent seats, though without veto powers (a *Brazilian* suggestion).

Though a highly desirable objective, increasing the Security Council's authority by modifying its membership is easier said than done. It might be achieved either by changing the composition of the Big Five or by adding new permanent members – with or without the veto. The Italian proposal is probably the best of the three being discussed presently (see Box 11.1). It would certainly result in a more accurate reflection of the world distribution of military and economic power, and also broaden the racial composition of the Big Five. Britain and France would not lose their influence on the Council altogether since they would remain influential within the EC delegation, which would also represent Germany, another prominent EC member. Supporters of further EC political integration should also be attracted by its proposal because it would put much greater pressure on the Community members to develop a common line in foreign policy (the liaison machinery for which has long been in place), as they have had to do on trade policy in the Uruguay Round of international trade negotiations. The Italian proposal gives no permanent seat to a Third World state, though it should be remembered that Third World *regions* (such as Africa and South America) *are* permanently represented in the remaining ten seats. The Brazilian suggestion (see Box 11.1) is also interesting because it draws attention to the fact that there is no necessary connection between a permanent seat and possessing a veto, always providing that any beneficiary of this arrangement is not a major military power. However, it will not be acceptable because it overlooks the huge economic power and military potential of Germany and Japan.

Having said all this, there seems no immediate prospect of change. The present arrangement is, it is true, at least working better than it has ever worked before, and their exclusion from permanent membership does not prevent the Germans and Japanese from collaborating *informally* with the Big Five. The British and the French are naturally disinclined to surrender the prestige which their own permanent seats provide, and can point with some justice to the great difficulties of getting political agreement among the twelve members of the EC, a number which might rise. Furthermore, Japanese opinion, while changing slowly, is still deeply divided over the desirability of playing a global role. It may well, therefore, be some years before there are changes to the permanent membership of the Security Council, and the 'New World Order' will be the poorer for it. Unhappily, changes of this sort tend to come only after major military conflicts have dramatically underlined shifts in the world distribution of power.

With changes in its permanent membership and the addition of the sort of military teeth which will give it more deterrent power both desirable but not in immediate prospect, the UN Security Council is nevertheless not in bad shape. The Big Five are working well together and most other members are prepared to follow their lead. In these circumstances, *ad hoc* arrangements for preserving world security can be made to work: where there is a will there is a way. It is also in these circumstances that old methods get a new lease of life. The most important of these in the context of world order is international peacekeeping. It is to this that we turn next.

12

Peacekeeping

'Peacekeeping', an important adjunct of diplomacy, pre-dated the creation of the United Nations, and the UN is still by no means the only body under whose authority the activity is conducted. Nevertheless, peacekeeping under the aegis of the UN is now the principal species of this key institution and it is, therefore, this which will be the chief focus of this chapter.

Ceasefire observation groups were sent by the UN to Palestine and Kashmir in the late 1940s but UN peacekeeping did not develop fully until the United Nations Emergency Force (UNEF I) was hurriedly created and dispatched to Egypt during the Suez crisis in 1956. A small number of additional forces of greatly varying size were created over the following decades and at the end of the 1980s and the early 1990s the creation of new forces really took off (see Box 12.1). In 1992 alone two very large peacekeeping operations were launched in Yugoslavia and Cambodia. What are the purposes of such forces? How are they made up? Under what rules do they operate? What conditions must obtain for them to be launched? How useful are they? Are they necessarily more effective than the non-UN 'multinational' forces which were introduced into the Middle East in the 1980s? These are the questions which this chapter will consider.

Peacekeeping and collective security

The first and most essential point to grasp about UN peacekeeping, however, is that it has got very little in common with 'collective security'. Peacekeeping was the pragmatic, second-best solution

Box 12.1 UN peacekeeping forces

In contrast to observer missions, UN peacekeeping forces are generally larger and have broader mandates. They are also armed, albeit lightly.

UN Emergency Force (UNEF I) Egypt, 1956–67. Maximum strength: 6,073.

Organisation des Nations Unies au Congo (ONUC) Congo Republic (ex-Belgian Congo), 1960– 4. Maximum strength: 19,828.

UN Force in Cyprus (UNFICYP) 1964– . Maximum strength: 6,411.

UN Emergency Force (UNEF II) Suez Canal sector and Sinai, 1973–9. Maximum strength: 6,973.

UN Interim Force in Lebanon (UNIFIL) 1978– . Maximum strength: 5,827.

UN Transition Assistance Group (UNTAG) Namibia, 1989–90. Military component: 4,650.

UN Protection Force in Yugoslavia (UNPROFOR) 1992– . Total projected strength: 14,000.

UN Transition Authority in Cambodia (UNTAC) 1992– . Total projected strength: 22,000.

invented in the mid-1950s by Dag Hammarskjöld, the most assertive of the UN's Secretaries-General, in response to the failure of collective security when faced with the obstacles described in the last chapter. In marked contrast to collective security, UN peacekeeping (which is not *explicitly* provided for in the UN Charter at all) does not proceed on the strong moral and legal idea of 'crimes' in which there are 'aggressors' and 'victims' but on the relativistic concept of 'conflicts' in which *all* are victims. Into such situations UN forces are not injected in order to give battle to the 'aggressor' but with instructions to maintain complete impartiality between the combatants and, most strikingly, *to use force only in self-defence*. In what sense, then, do UN peacekeepers purport to 'keep the peace'?

The mandates which have been given by the Security Council to the various peacekeeping forces that it has authorised have varied both in detail and (notoriously) in clarity, and have typically included the monitoring of a cease-fire or truce. Behind all of the major ones, however, has been the idea that their chief purpose was to interpose a neutral buffer between warring parties. (Even so, the force can only be deployed on the invitation of the lawful government in question.) Such a response, according to the theory, should at least contribute to the *containment* of their conflict and prevent the intervention of the great powers. At most it should allow time for a diplomatic settlement, which the peacekeepers themselves might help to implement.

Unlike a collective security operation, therefore, a UN peacekeeping operation is not conceived principally as a military mission at all, but rather as a *political* one. Like the priest who intervenes in a bar-room brawl, its hope is that by moral authority, minimal physical obstruction, and the provision of a face-saving excuse for the cessation of hostilities ('OK – if *you* ask us to'), it will have a calming influence and thus create an interval in which saner – or at any rate more pacific – voices might prevail. It is for this reason that Hammarskjöld preferred to regard the activity as part of what he called 'preventive diplomacy' and Michael Harbottle (1975), who was Chief of Staff to UNFICYP from 1966 until 1968, insists that it is best thought of as 'peaceable intervention' (p. 1).

The character of peacekeeping operations

Most of the distinguishing characteristics of UN peacekeeping operations flow logically from the lack of explicit reference to them in the UN Charter and their extremely limited role: These characteristics are as follows:

1. They are created on an entirely *ad hoc* basis. One reason for this is that the existence of any genuine intelligence, planning or operations staff in the UN Secretariat would be likely to arouse suspicions on the part of some member-states that the UN is exceeding its remit. (Extensive planning might also prove a waste of time since the UN never knows for certain where it will have to go or what resources it will be volunteered.)
2. Since the crisis provoked in the first half of the 1960s by the refusal of certain member-states, in particular France and the Soviet Union, to make financial contributions to ONUC, the financing of peacekeeping has had a large voluntary element.

3. While the commanders of both UN forces and their constituent units are subject to the formal authority of the UN, the units remain to a great extent under the effective control of their national governments.
4. Not being fighting formations, UN peacekeeping forces are generally small (see Box 12.1) and only lightly equipped. (ONUC was more than twice the size of any other force until the creation of UNTAC because of its exceptional and controversial brief to end the secession of Moise Tshombe in Katanga. UNTAC is so big because it has to *govern* as well as keep the peace in Cambodia until a freely elected government is in place.)
5. Finally, in order to minimise internal tensions and make impartiality more likely in conflicts with cold war overtones, contingents from the permanent members of the Security Council have generally been excluded. Instead, the forces have been traditionally composed of units from small and medium powers, especially those which – like India, Austria, Ireland, and the Nordic countries – have traditions of neutrality. Having said this, the United States has often provided back-up assistance, typically in the form of transport, while British forces in Cyprus (on hand in the Sovereign Base Areas) play an important role in UNFICYP, and troops from France, which has historical connections with Lebanon, have served in UNIFIL. Soviet bloc troops were employed for the first time in UN peacekeeping when in 1973 Poland contributed a contingent to UNEF II.

Conditions required for launching peacekeeping operations

UN peacekeepers can only be introduced when invited, and no side winning a war is likely to do this. Hence only when there is either a stalemate or total confusion – as in the Congo after the precipitate withdrawal of the Belgians and the mutiny of the *Force Publique* – is it possible for the creation of a UN force to be considered. Then the great powers have to calculate that their own interests are better served by deference to the UN. However, they do not instinctively arrive at this sort of conclusion even now; and they are not normally encouraged to do so by the parties themselves. Consider, for instance, the Angolan civil war, and Israel's repeatedly expressed preference for American rather than UN intervention in the Middle East. The combatants, together with the members of the Security Council or the General Assembly (depending on which has authorised the operation), also have to agree on the size, composition, mandate and commanding officer of the peacekeeping force. Finally, voluntary force contributions from member-states have to be forthcoming. Yet this is a requirement which cannot be taken for granted in view of their cost, the exceptional vexations of the duties which they may be called on to perform, and the political problems which tend to come in their train. (Ireland's relations with Israel were not under strain until Israeli-backed militia started murdering Irish members of UNIFIL.)

These are exacting conditions. It is thus not surprising that, despite the great number of armed conflicts that have occurred since the creation of the United Nations and are still occurring, until recently only a handful of them have witnessed the intervention of the 'Blue Berets'. But this, of course, is no argument against UN peacekeeping when the conditions are right. After the mid-1980s this fortunate conjuncture occurred on an increasing number of occasions. The main reasons for this, of course, were the end of the cold war and the increasing anxiety displayed by the Soviet Union for face-saving exits from the intractable regional conflicts that were draining its diminishing resources, its mounting pre-occupation with domestic reform, and its desire to use the UN to place a curb on American 'adventurism' in North Africa and the Middle East. With Mr Gorbachev paying off Soviet debts to UN peacekeeping operations, urging their wider use and generally co-operating to an unprecedented degree with the United States in various attempts to settle regional conflicts, from Afghanistan to Angola, it is not surprising that UN peacekeeping operations multiplied.

How effective is UN peacekeeping ?

There is a view that, owing to the legacy of Hammarskjöld's more or less pacifist conception of UN peacekeeping and the great practical difficulties under which its soldiers labour, this activity is completely ineffective. With one hand tied behind its back, this argument goes, UN peacekeeping only 'works' when it is not needed. When the chips are really down, as on the eve of the Middle East war in 1967, as in Cyprus on the occasion of the Turkish invasion in 1974, and as in Lebanon at the time of the second Israeli invasion in 1982, UN forces either withdraw or are contemptuously brushed aside.

This attitude ignores two significant considerations. In the first place it ignores the role of UNFICYP in breaking up the momentum of the Turkish advance into Cyprus and the invaluable work which UN forces have often done in reducing the mayhem caused by armed bands (especially in Cyprus and Lebanon) and mutinous troops (the Congo). Secondly, it mistakes the principal function of UN peacekeeping altogether; this function is not so much to prevent wars between states as *to consolidate their termination*. Without the face-saving facility of UN troops it would have been less easy to end the Suez War in 1956, or to separate the Israelis from the Egyptians in Sinai and from the Syrians on the Golan Heights in 1974. Though there was a subsequent increase in general Israeli hostility to the UN and a refusal to believe in UNIFIL's ability to prevent Palestinian infiltration into southern Lebanon and northern Israel, it would be surprising if the first Israeli withdrawal from Lebanon had not been made easier by the presence of UN forces. And UNTAG, after a difficult start, was clearly central to the peaceful transition of Namibia to independence in 1989–90.

One reason why the Blue Berets sometimes prove effective even when obviously outgunned is that the forces arrayed against them, while having no fear of 'the UN', may be apprehensive of the diplomatic consequences of killing, say, French, Irish, or Indian troops. Another reason is that, as the years have passed, a slightly more muscular interpretation has been given by the UN to the rule that its soldiers will use force only in self-defence. In September 1964 this was broadened to include attempts to disarm them or to remove them from positions which they occupied, and in March 1978 it was made even more permissive. On this occasion, the Secretary-General, Kurt Waldheim, announced that as far as UNIFIL was concerned, 'self-defence would include resistence to attempts by forceful means to prevent it from discharging its duties under the mandate of the Security Council' (Verrier, 1981, p. 130). As Verrier remarks, the vagueness of this formulation 'in effect [gave] a pretty wide latitude to the men on the spot to decide what their duties were' (pp. 130–1).

Both of the above points were well illustrated by an incident in early 1985 involving on the one hand the Israelis and on the other the French contingent in UNIFIL, which flew over each of its barracks in southern Lebanon a large *drapeau tricolore* alongside a handkerchief-size UN flag. On direct orders from Paris, the French informed the Israelis that they would not be permitted to conduct a punitive raid on the village of Marrake, which the Israelis believed housed PLO sympathisers. When this advice was ignored, the French paratroopers laid their national flag across the road outside the village and announced that they would kill the first Israelis to drive over it. The Israelis retreated (*The Times*, 28 February 1985). (After violent exchanges with Lebanese militia, the French battalion in UNIFIL was subsequently withdrawn; this was probably just as well.)

A further criticism of UN peacekeeping is that by 'containing' conflicts it takes the pressure off the parties (and, in some cases, their superpower backers) to find a political settlement. But this assumes that a political settlement is always obtainable. In fact, in conflicts such as those between the Arabs and the Israelis the forces are so evenly balanced and the issues so intractable that, at least in the foreseeable future, there is no 'problem' capable of a *political* 'solution' at all (see Chapter 10). Instead there is a *dilemma*, and with a dilemma all that one can do is try to contain it and thereby reduce the grief which it causes. Ultimately, since people eventually forget, or acquire more important things to worry about, time may throw up a solution. It is precisely to buy time that we have UN soldiers.

Besides, many intractable conflicts have ramifications which are wider than their nominal geographical frontiers. Thus, while leaving the parties to their own devices might well produce a quicker (though not necessarily durable) solution, it may in the process drag in other states. Here a case in point, where UN forces have been successfully operating for nearly three decades, is the Cyprus conflict, one of the major issues in the perennially tense relations between Turkey and Greece. American diplomacy in relation to its two potentially warring NATO allies has without doubt played the major role in preventing the Cyprus affair from producing the collapse of the alliance's south-eastern flank, but there is little doubt that UNFICYP has played its part in helping to keep tempers on the island at least relatively cool.

With the development in the late 1980s of an unprecedented Big Five consensus behind the need for more – and more varied – peacekeeping operations, attention has naturally focused on how their effectiveness might be increased. An obvious priority here is the need for more money, including a general fund to give the Secretary-General the ability to react quickly in emergencies. (At the beginning of 1992 the *existing* peacekeeping forces were still owed $638m by member-states of the UN, while the bill for UNPROFOR, which began to arrive in Croatia in March 1992 was originally set at £375m a year.) There is also a need for a bigger staff at UN headquarters, a better logistical network, the addition to operations of aerial surveillance, and better stand-by and training provision for the Blue Berets. Much interest, however, has concentrated on the suggestion, strongly supported by the Soviet Union in that state's final years, that peacekeeping forces should henceforward contain contingents from the Big Five themselves.

There are clear advantages to this idea. Peacekeeping forces including soldiers from the Big Five would have vastly more authority and would be likely to retain enthusiastic Security Council support. Financing would also be much less of a problem. On the other hand, apart from being more attractive targets for hostage-taking, such forces might be more inclined to throw their weight around. The problem with this (which is the general problem of whether or not 'peacekeeping' forces should be allowed to become more aggressive), is that they may then become part of the problem rather than part of the solution. As Brian Urquhart has rightly observed, it is the non-threatening character of UN peacekeepers that enables those wishing to stop fighting to defer to them without loss of face: 'the use of force, unless very carefully considered, will tend to destroy this characteristic and, along with it, the necessary co-operation of at least one of the parties to the conflict' (Urquhart, 1990, p. 202).

Nevertheless, if peacekeeping forces are to become marginally more assertive (without becoming collective security operations on the model of the action against Iraq), it is perhaps as well that they should contain contingents from the Big Five in some circumstances, though not be dominated by them. Indeed, this is what seems to be happening now, though American and Chinese troops remain conspicuous by their absence. Soldiers from France as well as Australia were prominent in the UN Advance Mission in Cambodia (UNAMIC) in late 1991, and are also due to play a role in UNPROFOR. British and Russian Federation troops are also slated for UNPROFOR, which, however, is also due to contain contingents from twenty-two other countries. With a Big Five presence in a UN peacekeeping force, the *show* of force is more likely to prove adequate. In any event, it is highly unlikely that the Israelis will ever agree to the insertion into the West Bank and Gaza of UN forces that do not contain superpower soldiers.

Non-UN peacekeeping

Peacekeeping – even of the armed, large-scale variety – is not an activity carried out by the UN alone and pre-dates its creation. Any state or group of states will have a chance of conducting peacekeeping sucessfully provided the intervention is acceptable to the main parties to the conflict in question.

Small observer missions have for a long time been established on the authority of associations like the British Commonwealth and regional organisations such as the Organisation of American States (OAS) and the Organisation of African Unity (OAU). The European Community itself became involved in 1991 in this sort of activity, in parts of the former state of Yugoslavia. And in the previous year there were hopes in some quarters – in the event stillborn – that the much broader CSCE (see Chapter 2) would provide the basis for the creation of European peacekeeping forces directed by a 'European Security Council'.

The most significant cases of non-UN peacekeeping since the founding of the UN, however, are the three forces created in the Middle East because of local hostility (chiefly from Israel) to UN intervention. The 'Multinational Force and Observers' (MFO) operating in Sinai (see Box 12.2) has been very successful, and the 'Multinational Force' (MNF I) in Beirut, a 2,000-strong force made up of troops from the United States, France and Italy, fulfilled its own instructions (to cover the evacuation by sea of PLO 'fighters' under the guns of the Israel Defence Force in 1982) and was then wound up. Why, then, did the third non-UN peacekeeping force,

MNF II, end in humiliating failure and call into question the very conception of this sort of operation?

Box 12.2 The multinational force and observers (MFO)

In the Egypt–Israel Peace Treaty of 1979 it was assumed that UNEF II would oversee the implementation of the Treaty's provisions on the Israeli withdrawal from Sinai and the substantial demilitarisation of the desert peninsular. However, as a result of Arab hostility to the Camp David 'peace process', this was blocked by the Soviet Union and in April 1982 MFO came into being as an American-sponsored substitute for the United Nations force. The United States, Colombia and Fiji each contributed an infantry battalion, and various kinds of small scale support have been provided by Britain, France, Italy, Netherlands, Norway, New Zealand, Canada, Australia and Uruguay. The United States has made the largest financial contribution to the MFO. The force was about 2,700-strong until 1988 but has declined somewhat since then.

MNF II, which had a maximum strength of 5,200 troops drawn from the United States, France, Italy and Britain, assembled in Beirut in the latter half of 1982 and early 1983. Its mandate was to interpose itself between the Israel Defence Force and the Muslim Lebanese militias in Beirut and assist the Lebanese government to restore its authority in the city. Unfortunately, after a smooth start, the operation fell to pieces during 1983 (with considerable loss of life on all sides) and in early 1984 the various contingents were withdrawn. The main reason for this was that the task of supporting the narrowly based (Christian-dominated) Lebanese government made MNF II a partisan in Lebanon's internal affairs in the eyes of the government's Muslim enemies and their friends abroad, a situation analogous to that in which ONUC had found itself in the Congo in the early 1960s. However, the situation in the Lebanon was compounded by the composition of MNF II, since France (the ex-colonial power) had long been associated with the protection of the Lebanese Christians and the United States was aligned with Israel, which was itself allied to the Lebanese Christians.

The experience of MNF II does not prove that peacekeeping forces should not be used on any 'law and order' missions, nor that non-UN forces engaged on such operations are always doomed to failure. However, it does suggest that the employment in this role of peacekeeping forces constituted on *any* basis is inappropriate when the recognised government has a sectarian character. Having said this, it remains likely that a UN force would have had a slightly better chance than MNF in holding the ring in Beirut.

13

UN Organs and Agencies

Origins and structure

Many a technical and economic problem is quite beyond solution by the autonomous actions of separate states. But if *inter*national action is necessary, how is it to be organised? By private, non-governmental organisations? By collaborative efforts on the part of the governments of the world's states? Or by bodies operating under the aegis of the United Nations?

The UN Charter provides that organisation with a generous, not to say formidable, remit in this respect. Article 55 reads (in part):

> With a view to the creation of conditions of stability and well-being which are necessary for peaceful and friendly relations amongst nations . . . the United Nations shall promote . . . solutions of international economic, social, health, and related problems; and international cultural and educational co-operation.

But not just 'promote'. Article 57 asserts that:

> The various specialized agencies, established by intergovernmental agreement and having wide international responsibilities, as defined in their basic instruments, in economic, social, cultural, educational, health, and related fields, *shall be brought into relationship with the United Nations*. [our emphasis]

Well before the creation of the United Nations – in the half-century before the First World War – international bodies of various kinds had been established in an unco-ordinated way to meet particular international needs. The Red Cross was founded in 1863 for collaborative humanitarian work; many interest-groups established international linkages, such as the International Federation of Trade Unions in 1901; and by 1914 over thirty bodies for technical co-operation had been set up: for example, the International Telegraphic Union (1865), the Universal Postal Union (1874), the International Health Office (1907).

When the League of Nations was established after the First World War the British saw an opportunity to bring some tidiness to this *ad hoc* proliferation of bodies. They therefore inserted into the League Covenant Article 24, which included the requirement that:

> There shall be placed under the direction of the League all international bureaux already established by general treaties. . . . All such bureaux and all commissions for the regulation of matters of international interest hereafter constituted shall be placed under the direction of the League.

Clearly Article 57 of the UN Charter is directly descended from this League of Nations article. The UN also inherited several such bodies still in working order. Some, like the Universal Postal Union (UPU), passed on from the previous century; others, like the International Labour Organisation (ILO), were created by the League or adapted from its work.

Yet the untidiness remains. Sometimes the collaboration of UN-associated bodies is called a system, sometimes a 'family', sometimes a network. The original inheritance from the pre-1945 period has been added to by immediate post-war creations and subsequent reactions to needs such as the establishment of the Industrial Development Organisation (UNIDO) as recently as 1986. However, the General Assembly (via its Economic and Social Council), which has nominal responsibility for this area of work, exercises minimal authority over the most important bodies, known as the Specialised Agencies (see Figure 13.1). By allowing virtual autonomy to the agencies, they sometimes overlap in their activities, and arguments have erupted concerning their basic philosophies and priorities.

There are now over forty organs undertaking specialist work of a technical, social or economic kind within the UN system. It is obviously impossible to mention them all. However, Figure 13.1. provides a list for guidance and a rough classification.

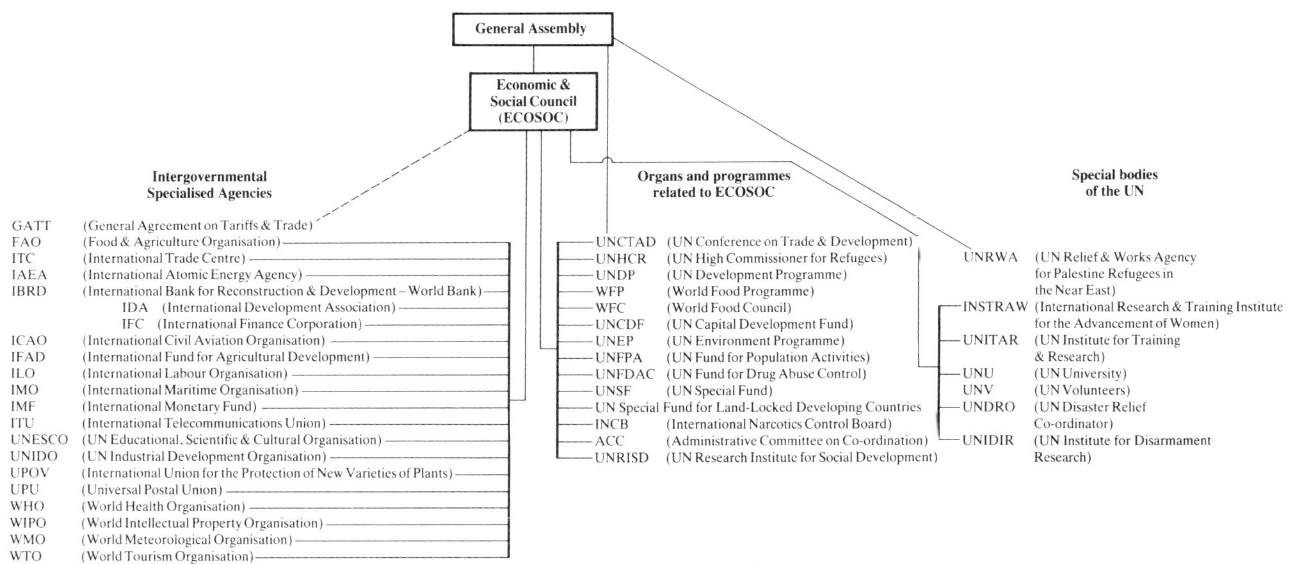

Figure 13.1 The structure of the UN specialised agencies and other organs

Work

One of the major criticisms of the UN system is that agencies, organs, programmes and bodies have proliferated in such an unsystematised way that the use of the word 'system' to describe it is an unhappy misnomer. In order to outline the activities of the network classification by function is more helpful than reference to the constitutional status as shown in Figure 13.1. Douglas Williams (1987, pp. 29–30) has provided a convenient clustering. (The present chapter relies heavily upon his book.) His list is composed of the Big Five (UNESCO, FAO, WHO, ILO, UNIDO); the 'economic' institutions (IMF, World Bank institutions, GATT, IFAD); the technical organisations (for example, ITU, WMO, IAEA); and the organs and programmes related to ECOSOC (to which we may add the Special Bodies).

To start with the 'Big Five'. These are 'big' in the sense of the size of the staff they employ and the scale of the practical work they have undertaken. Little need be said about UNIDO, which has only recently been created: it is 'big' in potential rather than achievement. The other four have been part of the UN system since its early days.

As its name reveals UNESCO's remit covers education, science and culture. Education, which absorbs the largest portion of its budget, has embraced two main concerns. One is a programme to promote basic literacy. It is estimated that UNESCO has enabled over 15 million people without access to other educational facilities to learn to read and write. The other educational concern is to use the schools to promote international understanding. The extension of the meaning of this term to include education for peace, disarmament and the promotion of human rights provoked fears of political indoctrination and contributed to the decision of the United States and the United Kingdom to withdraw from membership (see p. 180). The scientific projects of UNESCO have been less contentious. Invaluable collaborative research has been undertaken, most notably in the International Hydrological Programme, the International Geological Correlation Programme and the International Programme on Man and the Biosphere. Thirdly, UNESCO is dedicated to preserving the human cultural heritage. The British educationist Dr Richard Hoggart has told how he was influenced to work for UNESCO by the comment of a Malian that 'When an old man dies in one of our villages a whole library disappears' (quoted Hoggart, 1978, p. 17).

The purpose of the FAO is to raise nutritional levels in the poorer countries by improving agricultural productivity and distribution systems. This involves research and practical help in the field related to crop production, animal husbandry and irrigation. FAO also concerns itself with fisheries and forestry. Two offshoots of the organisation have been the Freedom From Hunger Campaign (FFHC) and the World Food Programme (WFP). The first of these, launched in 1960, has sought to raise both public consciousness about and funds for the food problems of the poorer lands. WFP was set up two years later to use the supply of food as a form of aid to raise living standards and as a method of disaster relief in times of emergency. Ships, lorries and produce are provided by many states on a voluntary basis to support this work.

WHO's objective is 'the attainment by all citizens of the World of a level of health that will permit them to lead a socially and economically productive life'. Its constitution asserts the relevance of this aim to the overall purposes of the UN by stating that: 'The health of all peoples is fundamental to the attainment of peace and security and is dependent on the fullest co-operation of individuals and States.' The programmes it has devised in pursuit of this objective have been some of the most successful of all the UN Agencies' work. WHO operates in three major contexts: running its own services; assisting individual countries' health services; and undertaking research and providing data. It has concentrated on four main kinds of activity. One is the provision of primary health care. WHO has set up clinics to advise on such topics as family planning and child nutrition. It has helped train medical and para-medical staff and water and sanitation engineers. Secondly, it has produced a determined policy to immunise the world's young people against childhood infections. Thirdly, WHO has been controlling the incidence of many tropical diseases and (one of its proudest achievements) has virtually eliminated smallpox. Fourthly, WHO's work in improving the health of millions of people world-wide is underpinned by research and training in the fields of medicine and technology.

Finally, in this survey of the Big Five, the ILO. We shall see below that its constitution makes it one of the most overtly political of the specialised agencies (see p. 178). Moreover, the composition of its institutions is unique. Both its General Conference and Governing Body have tripartite memberships from governments, employers and workers (on a 2–1–1 ratio). The main function of ILO is to recommend minimum standards for wages, hours of work and ages for employment, to draft regulations for safety and insurance and to ensure trade union rights. It publishes these guidelines in the form of Conventions, which it invites member-states to ratify. The organisation has also been concerned to reduce the incidence of unemployment and has helped mount training schemes.

Let us now turn to the economic institutions of the UN family. In the shadow of the Second World War the contribution of monetary and trading competitiveness to the political instability of the 1930s was very fresh in people's minds. The IMF was therefore created 'To promote international monetary co-operation. . . . To facilitate the expansion and balanced growth of international trade. . . . To promote exchange stability. . . . To give confidence to members.' The resources of the Fund derive largely from quotas of gold and convertible currency that the members pay in. The amount of any borrowings to stabilise a country's exchange rate or reduce a deficit in its balance of payments is related to these quotas. However, the provision of this assistance is often made conditional upon specified changes in the suppliant government's fiscal and economic policies. These have sometimes involved savage deflationary measures; and the consequent social suffering and protest have led to bitter criticism of the IMF's operations.

The World Bank – 'for Reconstruction and Development' – was originally founded to help in the rehabilitation of the European countries shattered by the Second World War. In more recent years, inevitably, its activities have largely been concentrated on the underdeveloped countries. The Bank both provides its own funds for development purposes and also encourages private investment . The IBRD has two subsidiary institutions. One is the IDA for the provision of loans to particularly poor countries on extremely favourable terms. The other is the IFC, the aim of which is to stimulate private sector development projects.

The danger of trade wars leading to fighting wars was an article of faith of some nineteenth-century free-traders such as Richard Cobden. The protectionism of the 1930s did indeed heighten international tension. The creation of GATT (General Agreement on Tariffs and Trade) was an attempt to preclude a repetition of this experience. Negotiations within GATT have succeeded in liberalising world trade amongst the countries of the industrialised Western world particularly. These agreements were reached in multilateral negotiations known as 'rounds'. The most conspicuous achievements were made by the Kennedy Round (1964 –7) and the Tokyo Round (1973–9). The Uruguay Round, which started in 1986, has been inhibited, amongst other problems, by the reluctance of the EC to abandon the protection of its farmers.

IFAD (International Fund for Agricultural Development) is the most junior of the economic agencies, having been established in 1977. It is financed mainly by OECD and OPEC countries (that is, the capitalist industrialised and the oil-rich states). Its purpose is to provide funding for the improvement of agricultural production in poor countries.

Of the technical agencies little need be said. Quite evidently our technologically interdependent world could not function without the facilities and standards provided by these bodies.

Finally, a few comments about some of the miscellaneous bodies. The work of UNEP is discussed in Chapter 9. UNDP provides funding for some Specialised Agency programmes. UNICEF has undertaken some splendid work, but since much of it has related to child health it has come into conflict with WHO because of overlapping programmes. These kinds of friction and duplication of activity have been some of the causes of the criticism that has been levelled at the UN family. The familial relationships have not always been entirely harmonious.

Interpretations and problems

Is the fundamental purpose of the UN organs and agencies the provision of technical assistance to ameliorate the lot of mankind? Or is there a deeper purpose behind their existence, namely to dampen down the causes of discontent and thereby enhance the prospects of peace? These are not insignificant questions to be lightly dismissed. The purpose of the UN is, in the words of the preamble to the Charter, 'to save succeeding generations from the scourge of war'. If, therefore, the organs and agencies do not directly contribute to that purpose, perhaps they should revert to the pre-1919 condition of being unrelated to any overarching institution. There is, indeed, a body of opinion that holds the view that the technical and humanitarian work would be more efficiently undertaken if it were separated from the unwieldy and querulous UN system. The contrary belief is that the *political* task of maintaining universal peace *is* inseparable from the *socio-economic* task of providing universal well-being.

The theory of 'functionalism' goes even further than this proposition by asserting that collaboration in technical (or functional) operations is a more effective means of moving towards a peaceful world than direct political action to defuse conflicts. Experience of co-operation will lead to more co-operation. As the functional international bodies become increasingly effective in satisfying social needs, so the will and the ability of states to cease collaboration and fight are diminished. This idea was influentially expounded in Britain from 1943 onwards by the Romanian scholar David Mitrany. However, the enthusiasm with which the theory of functionalism was once held has considerably waned: the operation of the UN functional bodies has not led to any enhancement in the political process of world pacification. On the contrary, differing interpretations concerning their proper roles have led to some bitter disputes.

One of the central problems has been the query over the justification for the specialised agencies in particular to engage in overtly political activity. In the case of some agencies their work necessarily involves trying to affect the policies of state governments – always justified as a means to securing peace. The clearest examples of political activity are the ILO and UNESCO, as revealed by their constitutions. The ILO document declares that: 'A universal and lasting peace can be established only if it is based upon social justice.' It complains about the failure of some nations 'to adopt humane conditions of labour' and of conditions 'involving such injustice, hardship and privation to large numbers of people as to produce unrest so great that the peace and harmony of the world are imperilled'. The UNESCO constitution starts with the ringing affirmation: 'That since wars begin in the minds of men, it is in the minds of men that the defences of peace must be constructed.' It continues by asserting the need 'to further universal respect for justice, for the rule of law and for human rights . . . without distinction of race, sex, language or religion'.

These documents were written against the backgrounds respectively of the grim employment conditions even in the advanced states of North America and Western Europe at the beginning of the century and of Nazi indoctrination and persecution policies. By the 1960s the global scene had changed. The world was now riven by the East–West ideological conflict of the cold war (see Chapter 1) and the North–South tensions deriving from the poverty of former colonies (see Chapter 9). As a result, differences emerged concerning the proper functions and priorities of the specialised agencies. In terms of voting power the underdeveloped Third World and the Communist world together could always outnumber the Western industrialised world. Yet it was the latter, and most conspicuously the United States, that provided the bulk of the funding.

US administrations became increasingly irritable at the criticisms they endured in various UN bodies and particularly at what they considered to be the 'politicisation' of some agencies. In 1975 the US Secretary of State Dr Kissinger announced his government's intention of withdrawing from the ILO (it resumed membership in 1980). He wrote that:

> In recent years the ILO has become increasingly and excessively involved in political issues which are quite beyond the competence and mandate of the Organisation. . . . Questions involving relations between States and proclamations of economic principles should be left to the United Nations and other Agencies where their consideration is relevant to those Organisations' responsibilities.
> (quoted, Williams, 1987, p. 55)

These accusations of improper political activity are, moreover, not only of historical interest. They revealed deep disagreements about the ways the system should operate and remain particularly acute in the context of UNESCO, from whose membership both the United States and the United Kingdom have withdrawn. Although the quarrel about UNESCO has been fiercer than those in which other agencies have been embroiled, the case provides an illuminating exemplification of the problems of the UN agency system. A little detail about the disagreements may therefore prove helpful.

Throughout its life UNESCO has been dogged by controversy. Poland, Hungary and Czechoslovakia withdrew from membership in 1953 on the grounds that it had become 'a docile instrument of the Cold War'. Portugal withdrew in 1971 because of criticisms of her determination to cling to colonial possessions in Africa. In the early 1960s the United States, the United Kingdom and France criticised budgetary allocations. Then, in 1984 the United States withdrew. The major reason given for this action was the pursuit of policies contrary to the Constitution of the organisation and in particular an 'ideological emphasis' and a tendency to serve 'the political purposes of member states rather than the international vocation of Unesco' (Letter from Secretary of State George Schultz to UNESCO Director-General, 28 December 1983, quoted, Maddison, 1985, p. 6).

A year later Britain followed the American example, as did Singapore. Britain's complaints, repeating the charges brought by the United States, were manifold, though three stood out. One concerned financial and administrative mismanagement, including the alleged incompetent autocracy of the Director-General and the overweighting of expenditure on headquarters to the detriment of work in the field. The second related to the attempt by Third World countries to create a 'New World Information and Communication Order'. They claimed they wanted to control reporting because of Western media distortions; Britain stood by the principle of the freedom of the press. The third worry was politicisation, exemplified especially by anti-Israeli attitudes.

Many commentators and experts in Britain, Europe and the Commonwealth (including the UK National Commission for UNESCO) opposed Britain's withdrawal. The main argument was that, although the criticisms had some validity, Britain could provide a signal service by remaining in the organisation to push through reforms. Dr Richard Hoggart was UNESCO Assistant Director-General, 1970–5, and well aware of the organisation's faults. He wrote at the time of Britain's withdrawal that most Western countries 'have been inept at keeping Unesco on a reasonably right track. Britain's judgement is still respected by other nations. . . . The decision to give notice this year combines lameness, belatedness, impulsiveness and irresponsibility' (CEWC, 1985, p. 11).

Reforms, which were continued with even greater commitment by a new Director-General after 1987, have yet to convince the United States and the United Kingdom that they should resume membership. Even so, the official stance of both states is that they will return when they judge that the organisation has sufficiently mended its ways. By 1990, indeed, the hostility of these two important powers to the UN system generally had somewhat abated. President Reagan and Mrs Thatcher, for whom the UN family was a special anathema, were no longer in power. Furthermore, the Soviet Union, under Gorbachev's leadership, had discontinued its provocative policy of distorting technical issues for political ends.

So how may we sum up the work of the UN specialist organs and specialised agencies? In the first place, their abolition is virtually unthinkable. The highly technical agencies are indispensable and all hold and collect invaluable data. We have surveyed the range of work in the second section of this chapter: it is a record of useful achievements. However, in taking stock one must recognise that circumstances change: what was a priority in one decade is not necessarily pressing in another. In the foreseeable future we must therefore judge the efficacy of the network as a whole by the way that it deals not just with the continuing vexed question of North–South economic imbalance, but with problems of relatively new salience. These include relief for refugees and victims of natural disasters and the defence and preservation of the planet's ecosystem.

Apart from the internal problems of inefficient bureaucracy and overlapping of programmes, the difficulties the system faces derive from the ambivalent attitudes of the member-states. They neither wish for the system's demise nor are sufficiently altruistic to commit themselves to truly internationalist policies. When the work of the agencies and organs is hamstrung by particularly selfish nationalist interests one is reminded of the couplet in Arthur Clough's 'Latest Decalogue':

> Thou shalt not kill; but need'st not strive
> Officiously to keep alive.

Yet the will of the system itself to stay alive is still strong.

14

The European Community

How the EC evolved

The idea of forming a political union amongst the states of Europe is by no means recent. From the early fourteenth century numerous politicians and philosophers drafted schemes with a view to bringing collaboration and peace to the continent. The horrifying experience of the Second World War intensified and broadened interest in this basic notion. In 1948 a Congress of enthusiasts for a united Europe was convened in The Hague. This led, in the following year, to the creation of the Council of Europe. This body has since undertaken some valuable work, particularly in setting and enforcing standards in the field of human rights (see Chapter 7). However, in its early years it seemed to those who wanted to make speedy progress that the Council was a disappointingly ineffectual organisation.

In the 1940s many advocates of European unity envisaged the creation of a fully federal United States of Europe. But there was an alternative strategy, a strategy called 'neo-functionalism'. This was a development of the functionalist theory we have already outlined (see p. 178). Practical co-operation, mainly in a number of economic spheres, would be easier to achieve than outright political unification; it would also produce most of the desired results of peaceful collaboration instead of warlike conflict.

By 1950 pressures from the United States for the West European states to proceed in harmony with their economic reconstruction together with problems in the French and German coal and steel industries provided the motive force for the launching of the

Community enterprise. The organising genius was Jean Monnet. He was a French economic administrator dedicated to the ideal of persuading people to work in unison for the solution of problems. Monnet and a few colleagues produced a plan for a coal and steel 'pool', initially between France and Germany, but to include other states willing to collaborate. The French Foreign Minister, Robert Schuman, secured the agreement of the German Chancellor, Adenauer, and of his own cabinet. The scheme was called the Schuman Plan. Within months Monnet and his co-authors had converted the plan into a treaty. This was signed in Paris in 1951 by the representatives of six nations: Belgium, the Federal Republic of Germany, France, Italy, Luxemburg and the Netherlands. The European Coal and Steel Community (ECSC) thus came into being.

The signatories, it should be noted, dedicated themselves to ambitious developments from this beginning. They declared themselves: 'Resolved to substitute for age-old rivalries the merging of their essential interests; to create, by establishing an economic community, the basis for a broader and deeper community amongst peoples long divided by bloody conflicts' (Preamble to the Treaty of Paris).

Saddened by Britain's refusal to join but heartened by the initial successes of the ECSC in operation, the believers in European unity tried to proceed to a pooling of military resources in a European Defence Community (EDC). But the French National Assembly rejected the plan. Nevertheless, despite this setback, the European idea was soon relaunched (*relance européenne*). In due course two more treaties were signed by the Six – in Rome in 1957 – to create the European Economic Community (EEC) and the European Atomic Energy Community (Euratom).

By virtue of its wide co-ordinating powers the EEC, or Common Market, became the most important of the three Communities. The breadth of its remit inevitably meant that its work of harmonising economic and social regulations was slow-paced. But the wider objective of laying 'the foundations of an ever closer union amongst the peoples of Europe' (Preamble to the Treaty of Rome establishing the EEC) was hindered by the policies of de Gaulle. He was President of France, 1958–69. A haughtily proud nationalist, he refused to surrender any further powers to the Communities. The integration process should confine itself, he declared, to a '*Europe des patries*'. Also, when Britain eventually decided to seek membership in 1960, he vetoed the application.

Two developments in the 1960s have proved to be controversial. One was the start of the Common Agricultural Policy (CAP). Its objective was to create an assured food supply for the people of the Community. But the payment of guaranteed prices to farmers became extremely costly, inefficient and a cause of complaint from producers outside the EEC. The other development was the start of a series of Conventions, initially signed at Yaoundé, subsequently at Lomé, to give preferential treatment to some of Europe's former colonies (ACP countries – African, Caribbean and Pacific). However, they have complained in recent years about unfairness in the arrangements. (One may note that also in the 1960s – in 1965 – the institutions of the three Communities were merged so that one normally now refers to the 'European Community' (EC) in the singular.)

The 1970s and 1980s saw a doubling in membership of the Community. Britain, Denmark and Ireland joined in 1973; Greece, in 1981; and Portugal and Spain, in 1986. Not only, of course, did the Community expand, but it changed its character with the accession of three Mediterranean countries.

Another spurt of activity to tighten the bonds of European union came in the period 1985–91. In 1985 the Commission (see p. 186) proposed that full economic union should be achieved by 1992. This aim was embodied in the Single European Act (SEA), which came into force in 1987. Interestingly, the SEA speaks of the objective of 'making concrete progress towards European unity', whereas the Treaty of Rome had used the vaguer word 'union'. The prime function of the Act is to provide the legal framework for common economic procedures and regulations and complete freedom of movement of people, goods and money throughout the Community. But it also sets the enterprise of European unity in a broad international context:

> Aware of the responsibility incumbent upon Europe to aim at speaking ever increasingly with one voice and to act with consistency and solidarity in order more effectively to protect its common interests and independence, in particular to display the principles of democracy and compliance with the law and with human rights to which they are attached.
>
> (Preamble to the Single European Act)

Before the terms of the SEA were finally implemented two further sets of agreements were reached at a summit meeting in Maastricht. This occurred in 1991 in order to make progress on both European Monetary Union (EMU) and European Political Union (EPU). During the negotiations Britain put herself at odds with the other eleven members on several issues. Nevertheless, a number of decisions were made.

1. On the question of progress towards EMU the Maastricht meeting agreed to the introduction of a single currency by 1999 at the latest, to be managed by a European central bank. An opt-out clause was devised especially for Britain.
2. On the matter of the 'deepening' of integration, again in deference to Britain, the word 'federalism' was dropped as the Community's objective in favour of the phrase 'ever closer union'. Even so: (a) decision-making by majority voting was extended to education, public health, the environment and energy; and (b) tentative moves were made for the closer co-ordination of members' foreign and defence policies (for the latter, WEU (see p. 27–8) would be the institutional context).

However, soon after the signing of the agreements at Maastricht a cooling of the federalist ardour could be detected in many of the member-states. Indeed, at the time of going to press the treaty has not yet been ratified by the member-states' parliaments.

How the EC works

(Note: This section takes no account of the proposals made in the Treaty of Maastricht.)

The institutional structure of the European Community is an amalgam of flexible compromises. There is a compromise between retained national power and centralised Community power; but the ratios can be adjusted without changing the structure. There is a compromise in the allocation of power as between the various EC institutions; and again these may be adjusted at will. Thus the Community does not work in exactly the same way as in its early years; and, by the same token, is likely to continue to adapt in the future.

Let us therefore outline the spheres of competence of the various institutions. (Figure 14.1 will help you to understand their inter-relationships.)

First, the European Commission. This is the body which has the most effective supranational powers and therefore gives the EC its particularly 'Community' character (see p. 194). It consists of seventeen members appointed for four years. Their chairman has the title of President and often represents the Community as a whole at international meetings. The Commissioners are required to act in the interests of the Community as a whole and are expressly forbidden to take instructions from any national government.

The Commission has three main functions. One is to ensure that the Community operates properly and that decisions are effectively put into practice. It has powers to investigate any suspected malpractices and to impose fines if EC rules are broken, for example by a business company. Another function is to make detailed proposals to the Council of Ministers for achieving the purposes of the Community. The third function is to act as an executive authority. It shares with national governments the responsibility for actually implementing decisions. The Single European Act extends the Commission's powers in this respect.

The Council of Ministers is composed of one minister from each member-state. They meet in Brussels to make the main political decisions. The post of President of the Council is held by the representative of each state in turn for a period of six months. The particular minister designated to attend depends on the topic to be discussed: for instance, ministers of agriculture attend for items relating to farming.

The foreign ministers meet for what is called Political Co-operation (or EPC). This is an attempt to co-ordinate the policies of the member-states in response to events in the rest of the world.

The Council of Ministers is assisted by a Committee of Permanent Representatives (COREPER) and has its own secretariat.

The Council makes decisions on the proposals sent to it by the Commission. The Council has been reluctant to proceed except by unanimous decision. However, the SEA increases the number of topics in which a majority vote is allowed (see p. 184).

Community laws are made by the following procedure:-

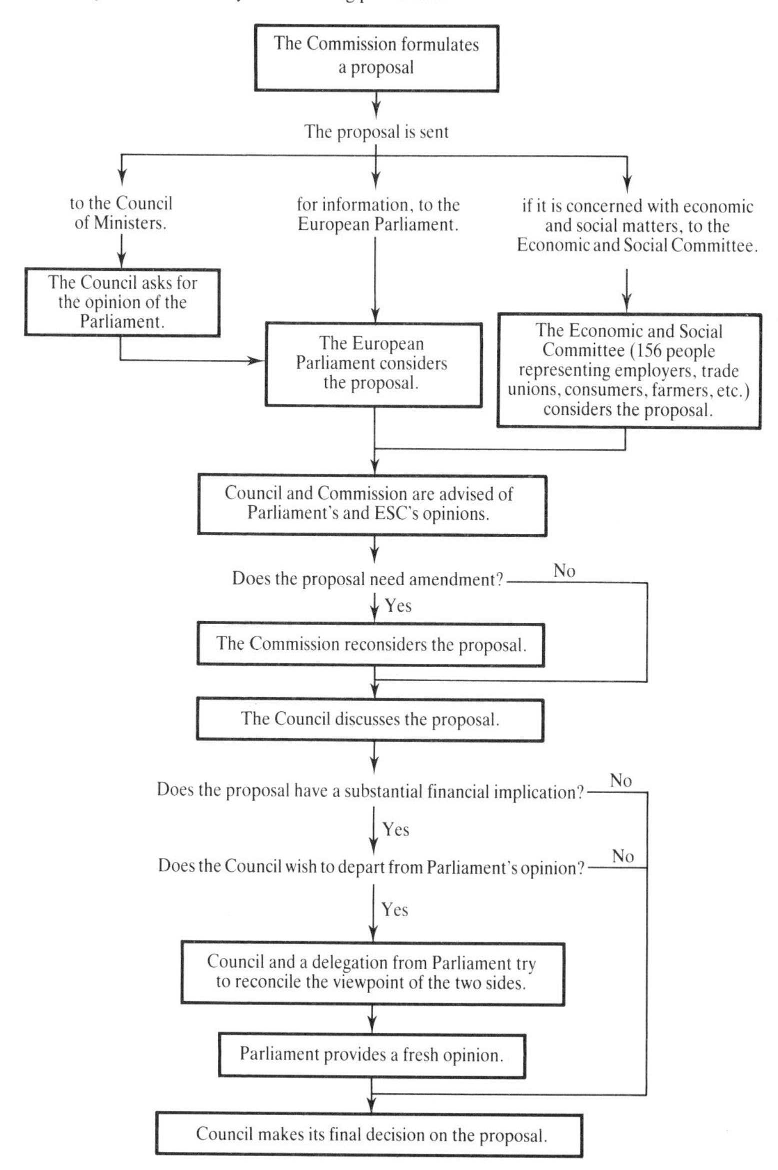

Figure **14.1**(a) The interrelationship of EC institutions

The Community budget is agreed by the following procedure:-

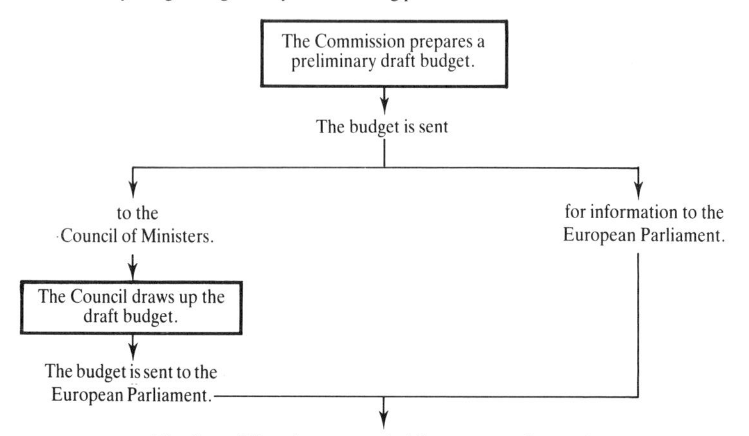

The Council fixes the amount of 'obligatory expenditure', that is 'expenditure necessarily resulting from the Treaty or from acts adopted in accordance therewith'. Most of this money goes towards agricultural spending. Parliament, within certain limits, has the last word on all other expenditure.

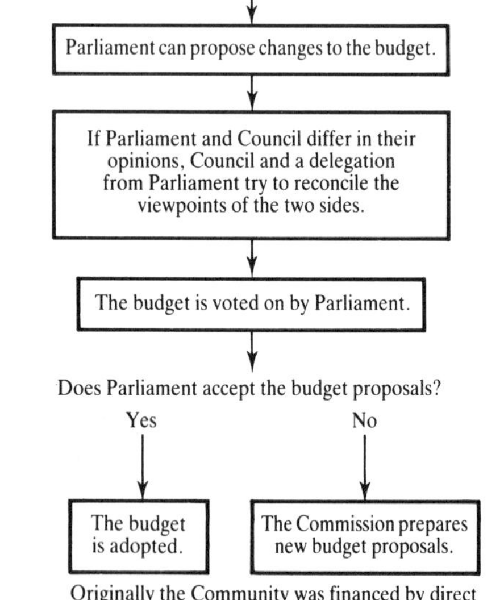

Originally the Community was financed by direct contributions from member-states. The Community is now financed by its 'own resources' consisting of customs duties and levies and up to a 1% rate of VAT (*not* 1% of VAT revenue).

Figure **14.1**(b) The interrelationship of EC institutions

In 1975 the heads of state or government together with the President of the Commission started to meet in 'summit conferences'. These meetings are now held two or three times a year and are called the 'European Council' (not to be confused with the Council of Europe (p. 182) or the Council of Ministers). The European Council has an important influence on the overall policy of the Community.

Next, the European Parliament. Members (MEPs) are chosen in elections held in the member-states every five years. In the meetings of the Parliament, however, they occupy blocks of seats not according to nationality but according to political groupings (for example, the British Labour MEPs and German SPD MEPs sit together in the Socialist Group).

The European Parliament has a number of functions. First, through consultative processes it can affect the work of the Commission and Council. The SEA increases its authority in relation to these other two bodies. Secondly, the budget must be approved by the Parliament. Threat of non-approval can be used to force the Council to amend the budget. Thirdly, it can initiate ideas for consideration by the Commission. And fourthly, as an ultimate sanction, the Parliament can (by a two-thirds majority vote) require the whole Commission to resign. It has never exercised this power.

Finally, in this survey of EC institutions, a few words about some specialist bodies. The Court of Justice gives judgments about and interpretations of Community law. The Economic and Social Committee is an advisory group of various interests such as employers, trade unions and consumers. There are also other specialist advisory bodies for professional and commercial matters. A Court of Auditors oversees the EC's financial management.

Now the primary purpose of this complex institutional edifice is to harmonise, co-ordinate and regulate the economy of the area covered by the EC member-states. And so, although the subject-matter of this book is international politics, at least a brief sketch of the economic work of the EC is essential.

From its very start the EC has been committed to dismantling the tariff barriers between the member-states so as to create a large free-trade area. In this way there has been established a domestic market for the production and distribution of goods comparable with the United States. However, the poorer, less economically efficient regions might be even less able to cope with this wider competition than they have been in their national contexts. Therefore, a portion of the EC budget is allocated to a regional fund to help renovation and development. The bulk of funds available (for many years as much as two-thirds) are, however, expended on the price-support mechanism of the CAP (see p. 184).

Much of the economic work has necessarily been in the form of producing detailed regulations for standardising economic activity throughout the EC. These directives cover innumerable areas of production and distribution such as quality-control, safety measures, control of fishing-rights, and reduction of pollution.

All economic activity involves money – for investment, wages, purchase. Clearly a complete Common Market is difficult to achieve if each member-state has an exchange rate which fluctuates not only in relation to outside currencies like the dollar and yen, but also in relation to the other currencies within the Community. Consequently, the European Monetary System (EMS) has been devised to peg the exchange rates within narrow confines of variation. But this is only a partial monetary standardisation. The EMS is supplemented by the planned Economic and Monetary Union (EMU) system of a central bank and progress towards the general use of the common currency, the European Currency Unit (ECU).

All these devices for economic union inevitably impinge upon the freedom of the member-states independently to control their own destinies. They therefore underlie the political controversies that have yet to be resolved concerning the ultimate nature of the Community.

Political problems to be resolved

The history of the European Community is a story of continuous evolution. Political changes have depended and will depend on the resolution of different views about what is politically possible and desirable. The differences of opinion relate particularly to the relationship of the member-states to the Community; and the relationship of the various Community institutions amongst themselves. There are six such issues that we need to discuss.

The *first issue* is membership. Since 1986 twelve states have been members, including an expanded Germany when East and West

Germany united in 1990. By 1991 five more applications had been submitted – from Austria, Cyprus, Malta, Sweden and Turkey. (See Figure 14.2.) Interest has been expressed too by Finland, Iceland, Norway and Switzerland. Several ex-Communist states – Czechoslovakia, Hungary and Poland (not to mention some former members of the USSR) – would also like to join. The possible expansion of the Community raises two important questions.

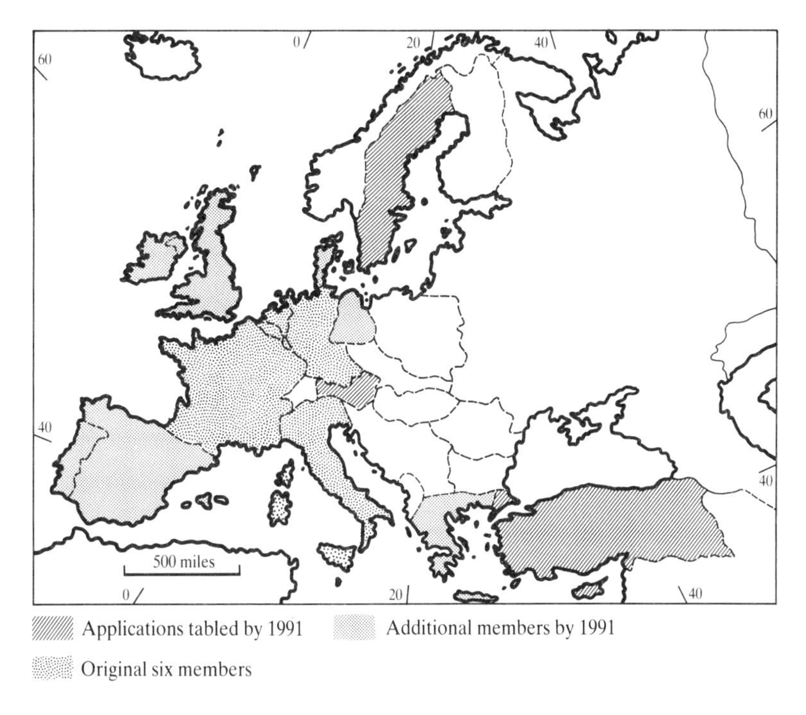

Figure **14.2** The European Community

1. One concerns the management of such a large group of states – perhaps as many as twenty, two dozen or even, ultimately, thirty. We shall see later (p. 193) that there is already some discontent with the way the Community institutions work. Could they cope with very many more members? One view is that the only way to handle a greatly expanded Community is to increase the powers of its central bodies at the expense of the state governments; in other words, to make it a fully fledged federation.

2. The second question raised by the prospect of more members is whether they could all genuinely abide by the common principles of the Community. On this score, the above lists of applicant and interested states raise several queries, as follows:

- The former Communist states would need to have properly developed capitalist economic systems because the Community is run on these lines.
- All would need to have reasonably clean bills of health regarding their reputations for democracy and respect for human rights – we have seen how these qualities are highlighted in the Single European Act (p. 184). Turkey's application has caused doubts to be raised already on this score (and it is in any case being blocked by Greece in an attempt to prise the Turkish army out of Cyprus).
- A less clear-cut case concerns a country's policy on defence. If the Community wishes to develop a common defence policy, would the traditionally neutral states – Austria, Sweden and most particularly Switzerland – be comfortable in participating in the military aspects of the Community? It is, of course, an easier step to contemplate since the end of the cold war.

This brings us to the *second issue* – the question of whether the Community should pursue common defence and foreign policies. The matter of defence has already been considered in Chapter 2.

An attempt has been made, especially since 1981, to co-ordinate the foreign policies of the member-states. This process is called European Political Co-operation (EPC), and has worked reasonably well in some areas such as policy towards South Africa. The Gulf War (see p. 71), however, highlighted the difficulties of maintaining a united front. For example, Britain aligned herself closely with the very firm US policy against Saddam; France clearly believed a more flexible attitude would have been desirable; while Germany stood by the letter of her constitution and refused to commit armed forces to the conflict. Even so, both the Single European Act and the Maastricht agreement on Political Union emphasise the need to strengthen EPC.

The *third issue* is the basic constitutional issue of how decisions are made. If decisions in the Council of Ministers can be arrived at only by unanimous vote, then one state, however small, can exercise a veto. A single state can prevent a proposal from being put into effect, however beneficial it might be to the Community as a whole. On the other hand, if the serious objections of one country are overridden, would this not represent an intolerable disregard of that country's interests?

In practice, the Council of Ministers can in some instances make decisions by 'qualified majority'. In total the twelve members of the Council have seventy-six votes. These are made up as follows:

France, Germany, Italy, United Kingdom	10 each
Spain	8
Belgium, Greece, Netherlands	5 each
Denmark, Ireland	3 each
Luxemburg	2

A qualified majority is fifty-four. The Single European Act extends the use of the system to a wider range of circumstances than hitherto.

But should not the Council of Ministers, in carrying out its executive function, be under constant and effective scrutiny? And should not the Commission also be similarly monitored? This is the *fourth issue.* In a democratic system this critical function is performed by a representative assembly. However, the European Parliament has too few powers to force the Council or Commission to change their minds on anything except the budget. (The dismissal of the whole Commission (see p. 189) is too massive a weapon for the Parliament ever to have used it.) National parliaments also have the power to ask the Commission to rethink proposed regulations. But few MPs have the time with all their other business to give full attention to the enormous amount of documentation which emanates from Brussels.

This lack of effective monitoring has been called 'the democratic deficit'. How, then, to make it good? MEPs themselves want their powers to be increased, to act towards the Commissioners in the same way as national parliaments carefully watch over the actions of government ministers. However, national parliaments (especially the British) fear that if this happens, they will lose their right to criticise the Commission in defence of their own countries' interests.

The *fifth issue* concerns the role of the ultimate guarantor of democracy, the individual citizen. When references are made to the population of the Community as a whole, the term 'European citizens' is sometimes used. In what sense, we may ask, are inhabitants of the member-states truly 'citizens' of the Community? A citizen is someone who has that legal status in relation, normally, to a state. And by virtue of that status the citizen has certain rights and duties. Furthermore, a citizen has a feeling of belonging to that state. Using this rough definition we may ask how far European citizenship exists.

A conscious effort has, in fact, been made to ensure that, at least in some primitive sense, European citizenship is a status that has effective meaning. Both the Commission and the Parliament have expressed the wish to transform the technocrats' Europe into a citizens' Europe.

What has been accomplished? Symbols of European identity have been produced – a Community flag and a Community passport, for example. All Community citizens have the right to vote for an MEP. And a Charter of Basic Social Rights has been drafted. However, if a true dual national/Community citizenship is to exist, the status of 'Community citizen' needs to be considerably enhanced.

Any effective moves to achieve this will inevitably again raise the issue of federalism. This is the *sixth issue*. To understand the problem we need to clarify our definitions. Three terms must be distinguished: 'federation', 'confederation' and 'Community'.

'Federation' is a system in which the central, federal government has considerable powers over taxation, defence and foreign policy, for instance. The constituent states, however, have a large measure of sovereign control over matters like police and education. 'Confederation' is a much looser arrangement. Germany from 1815 to 1871 was a confederation. The former USSR has recently moved in that direction. In confederations the central government has very few and weak powers over member-states, which really remain very independent. In many ways the European Community at the moment is more like a confederation than a federation. For example, the power which the authorities in Brussels have over Britain cannot really be compared with the power which the authorities in Washington have over Massachusetts. And yet the system is more than a confederation. There are now very many regulations which apply thoughout the Community. This is why the separate word 'Community' is used.

A number of enthusiasts wish to proceed to the creation of a federal United States of Europe. These include many MEPs and in 1984 the Parliament produced a Draft Treaty for European Union.

Among national politicians, however, there have been wide differences of opinion on the matter.

Three facets of this sixth issue need some commentary.

1. The first is the question of national identity. Some commentators, notably Mrs Thatcher when she was prime minister and the 'Bruges Group' of British MPs, believe that if some form of political unity comes about, national character will be lost. The result, in Mrs Thatcher's words, will be the replacement of Britons, Italians, Germans and so forth by 'identikit Europeans' (see p. 108). Opponents of this point of view believe that it is crucial to distinguish between *political* integration and *cultural* integration. It is possible to retain a national cultural identity while adopting a European political identity.
2. The second facet concerns sovereignty. This concept asserts that a state has complete authority both inside its own boundaries and to conduct its external relations. Clearly, in a federation the ultimate authority lies with the central, federal government. The opponents of a United States of Europe deplore the prospect of such a loss of sovereignty. In contrast, the advocates of European federalism point to the fact that in an interdependent world, such as we live in today, no state is truly master of itself. Sovereignty is an obsolete concept. Moreover, what the Community is undertaking is a 'pooling' rather than a surrender of sovereignty. In other words, by banding together the states of Europe are stronger than they would be singly to protect themselves against dangerous outside forces, most particularly economic.
3. The third facet is the geographical level at which political decisions should properly be made. Here the principle of 'subsidiarity' comes into play to allay some fears. The idea is that the Community, even as a federal state, should be thought of as a pyramid of authorities – local, provincial, state, Community. Once this is accepted then every effort must be made to ensure that decisions are taken at the lowest possible level. Therefore, a federal government in Brussels would not interfere in matters that are the proper responsibility of, say, the United Kingdom or Scotland or Aberdeen.

Throughoout the centuries a number political forms have been tried in Europe: city-states, nation-states and empires; unitary states, confederations and federations. The European Community has been virtually unique both in focusing its work on economic matters and in the gradual evolution of its political structure. For all its faults there are many more states in Europe queueing to join; and it has many admirers in other parts of the world where there are flickers of hope that similar systems for peaceful collaboration might be constructed in the twenty-first century.

15

International Law

Origins and problems

In the mid-fifth century BC, during the Sabine wars, the Romans adopted one of their enemy's gods and foisted upon him the responsibility for oaths, good faith and treaties. Since aggressive wars were unacceptable to the gods the priests who attended to these new rites had the task of proving that all Rome's wars were defensive. We thus see that one of the earliest attempts at international law related to warfare and was clouded by an aura of cynicism in its application. In many people's minds these are still two of the main characteristics of international law.

But if international law has existed for at least two and a half millennia, is it not likely that it will have developed principles and codes covering a wide range of international relations? And if those principles and codes were constantly abused by lack of good faith, would not the task of developing international law (still being actively pursued) long since have been abandoned as a fruitless enterprise? The purpose of this section of the chapter is twofold. First we aim to show very briefly how international law has in fact evolved over the centuries. Secondly, we shall discuss how far international law is law in any true sense.

Present-day international law is substantially European in origin. Such an observation must, however, be modified by the recognition that other civilisations have developed their own systems: ancient India is a prime example. Moreover, in the case of Islam, the system is still vigorous and not totally consonent with European-generated law.

The Romans established the distinction between three kinds of law: *ius civile* (in modern terminology, domestic or municipal law); *ius naturale* (natural law, or universal principles of rational justice); and *ius gentium*. This last started as laws which related to the non-citizen peoples of the Empire and came by the sixteenth century to mean the 'law of nations' or between states. In its evolution international law has taken cognisance of all three kinds of law, though the *ius gentium* tradition has clearly been paramount.

It was in the seventeenth century that interest in international law became particularly widespread in Europe. It was the age of the early great codifications and arguments by notable jurists. Most famous of all was the Dutchman Grotius. In the words of the late James Fawcett:

> By the middle of the seventeenth century then we find laws of war established; accepted rules of practice of diplomacy; the establishment of the freedom of the seas; treaty-making developed into an art designed for many uses, with forms that have not been substantially changed; principles being progessively accepted through treaties to govern trade and commerce between countries; and the first attempts to tackle the issues created by contact between different cultures.
>
> (Fawcett, 1968, p. 18)

It is a formidable list and reveals how diverse were the concerns of international law more than three centuries ago. And even before the very term 'international law' had been invented – it was coined by Jeremy Bentham in 1780.

Since the seventeenth century other topics have been added to the canon of international law. These have included the principle of neutrality, the technique of arbitration in disputes, the constitutional law of international institutions, the codes of human rights and the creation of international courts. Most recently the whole area of the use of resources and the protection of the environment has come within the purview of international law. The result of the constant accretion of customs, conventions, treaties and judgments over the centuries is that international law is today exceedingly complex and pervasive.

The basic unit in municipal law is the individual; the unit in international law is the state. The consolidation of international law has paralleled the consolidation of the state. In this process there have been four major landmarks. The first was the recognition of state sovereignty in the Westphalia peace treaties of 1648. The second was the principle of the legal equality of states, expounded by Vattel a century later. The third landmark is the emergence of nationalism at the time of the French Revolution, giving the concept of the state a popular and emotional content. Fourthly, and as an extension of this, was the principle of national self-determination, enshrined in the peace settlements after the First World War (see Chapter 8).

But if the basic unit for English law is nearly 50 million people, how can international law with only about 180 sovereign states operate along lines that are at all comparable? In order to respond to this question we need to look at three matters: the sources of international law, the debate about its characteristics and an assessment of its major achievements.

As we have already indicated, international law has been built up from a massive range of diverse writings and practices. These are called 'sources'. They are listed in the Statute of the International Court of Justice as follows:

> (a) international conventions, whether general or particular, establishing rules expressly recognised by the contrasting States;
> (b) international custom, as evidence of a general practice accepted as law;
> (c) the general principles of law recognised by civilized nations;
> (d) . . . judicial decisions and the teachings of the most highly qualified publicists of the various nations.
>
> (Article 38.1, see Brownlie, 1990, p. 3)

But does all this add up to true law? Take the following argument. Laws are enactments by a recognised legislative authority, they are enforced by courts and the police and those who break the law are punished. These institutional structures and procedures are lacking in any international context. Therefore, the rules of international conduct are not so much laws as guidelines for moral inter-state behaviour. Moreover, the purpose of law is the preservation of order and the settlement of disputes by peaceful means. The persistence of war alongside the supposed evolution of international law further undermines the pretensions of these customs, conventions and rulings to the status of law.

The whole of this case can be effectively countered. The source of law is not especially important. England is a prime example of a municipal law which is an accumulation of custom, royal decrees and charters and local by-laws as well as parliamentary statutes. In fact, the bulk of present-day international law comprises formally signed treaties and conventions couched in carefully framed legal language. Moreover, like all laws, international law is a framework of rules and institutions to be used whenever the will to use them is sufficiently strong. If there is a breakdown of law and order inside a country, we do not deny the existence of the domestic law; rather we recognise the unwillingness of significant numbers of the populace to obey it. Similarly with international law: insofar as history is littered with examples of states acting in disorderly and illegal ways, this behaviour is evidence of a lack of political will to obey the law, not an absence of law itself.

But we can be even more positive. There is considerable evidence that international law is recognised and obeyed. At the basic level of diplomatic activity, as the English jurist Pollock pointed out, a legal framework is assumed:

> the framers of State papers concerning foreign policy . . . appeal not to the general feeling of moral rightness, *but to precedents, to treaties, and to opinions of specialists.* They assume the existence amongst statesmen and publicists of a series of legal as distinguished from moral obligations in the affairs of nations.
>
> (quoted, Starke, 1947, p. 7).

Part of the problem of achieving a balanced perception is that breaches of the law attract more attention than its observance. In all the multifarious day-to-day transactions between states and their representatives international law is in fact being constantly applied and obeyed. One has only to think of inter-state trade, for example, conducted by adherence to codes of maritime navigation, commercial treaties and trading conventions.

True, there is no centrally administered global police force. However, self-interest and fear of penalties do often act as powerful inhibitions against breaching international law. Most statesmen wish to be held in good repute and to be seen to be acting in accord with international law. For those who judge that loss of reputation is a small price to pay for the gains from breaking an agreement or using violence there is always the fear of the victims responding in kind. Or if the crime is particularly heinous, international economic sanctions (as in the case of South Africa, see p. 84) or war (as in the case of Iraq, see p. 71) can inflict penalties.

Those who break the law, whether a burglar or a violator of frontiers, believe they have a chance of escaping punishment. In international relations such confidence is often kept in rein by the balance of power system. If a potential aggressor state knows that a potential countervailing coalition is more powerful, it will hesitate to act contrary to international law.

What, then, in sum have been the major achievements of international law seen in historical perspective? We may discern a number of ways in which it has made international relations more civilised and harmonious than they would otherwise have been.

Most basically international law has established the principle of the expectation of orderly international conduct. Secondly, it has created a set of rules and procedures for the peaceful conduct of inter-state affairs in normal peace-time conditions. Even, and thirdly, in times of war the savagery of combat has often been mitigated by the honouring of some rules. Fourthly, the principle of the freedom of the seas has enabled trade to flourish. And most recently, international laws relating to human rights and the environment have undermined the traditional notion in two crucial spheres that the internal affairs of a state are its own concern.

We have already suggested that international law has been a pervasive influence. Other chapters (notably Chapters 3, 4, 7, 9, 12 and 14) deal with particular applications of international law. In the rest of this chapter we shall examine its function in relation to the state and the legal nature of treaties.

The state

The state is the basic unit (a 'person' in legal terms) of international law. Consequently, international law has much to say about the state. It provides a definition: 'The State as a person of international law should possess the following qualifications: (a) a permanent population; (b) a defined territory; (c) government; and (d) capacity to enter into relations with other States' (Montevideo Convention on Rights and Duties of States, Article 1 (1933), quoted Brownlie, 1990, p. 72).

A little commentary on each of these criteria will be useful. The requirements of a permanent population and a defined territory mean that a state must be a settled identifiable community. On the other hand, 'defined territory' must be understood loosely. The existence of ill-defined or disputed borders does not preclude the status of statehood. This must be obvious when one considers how many disputed boundaries there are in the world. The most important case, however, was the recognition of Israel as a state in 1948 when the UN-defined boundaries were still to be settled by war. Thirdly, for a territory to be a state it must have some form of organised government and legal system.

It is the fourth criterion that requires most commentary, namely effective evidence that the territory is independent, not subordinate to another state and is capable of autonomous actions. Thus the British Dominions such as Australia and Canada only gradually achieved statehood as Britain devolved powers to them. It is notable how micro-states such as the Pacific islands of Kiribati and Tuvalu have sloughed off colonial dependency and become recognised as states despite their tiny size. We may notice also the legal distinction between a confederation and a federation. The component parts of a confederation are states in the heyes of international law; those of a federation are not. To put this distinction another way: in a confederation the component states are sovereign; in a federation the overarching state is sovereign.

Sovereignty is a slippery concept and requires some comment. First, sovereignty has a domestic facet. It means that a state has complete jurisdiction over its own 'permanent population' and 'defined territory'. It also means that it must respect the internal sovereignty of all other states. Secondly, it means that it is independent: externally it is not effectively controlled by another state or organisation. Thirdly, a sovereign state cannot be bound by treaties or international regulations except by its own express agreement. Fourthly, a sovereign state, by virtue of its own discretionary power, can surrender portions of its own sovereignty. The exercise of this discretion in the creation and development of the European Community has produced heated arguments, particularly in the United Kingdom, about the desirability of this erosion of national sovereignty (see p. 195).

New states have been created in recent history by the processes of secession, unification and decolonisation. But a mere declaration of sovereign statehood by the new political entity is not sufficient to guarantee that status. There is also the matter of recognition by the international community.

Recognition may be accorded to a state or a government *de jure* or *de facto*. The former is the full accolade of official recognition; the latter, the grudging acceptance that the state or government does exist in fact. There is little difference in practice between the two formulas.

It is rare for a state to be totally rejected by the international community. One example was Rhodesia after the Unilateral Declaration of Independence by Ian Smith's government in 1965. The very next day the UN Security Council called on all states to withhold recognition of the 'illegal racist minority regime'. An even clearer case was the establishment of the 'Turkish Republic of North Cyprus' (declared in 1983). One state only has recognised it – Turkey! The cold war created political problems for a number of states regarding the enjoyment of full recognition in the sense of membership of the UN. The most anomalous case was the holding of the Chinese seat (including permanent membership of the Security Council) by the Nationalist government of Taiwan until 1971. Not until 1991 were North and South Korea admitted.

An interesting development took place in 1991 in response to the collapse of the Soviet and Yugoslav states. The United States and EC states added to the Montevideo Convention extra criteria for those republics seeking recognition to achieve. These included the following conditions: respect for the UN Charter and Helsinki Declaration; guaranteed minority rights; acceptance that borders can be changed only by peaceful negotiation; and commitment to existing arms agreements, including nuclear non-proliferation. It will be interesting to observe whether any of these demands eventually become generally codified.

A state has jurisdiction over its territory. This includes not just its land and inland waters, but also territorial sea around its coast (unless, of course it is landlocked) and the airspace above its land and territorial sea.

The land over which a state has jurisdiction is defined by historic right, effective occupation or treaty. International law has a preference for clear boundaries – a physical feature such as a river or a line of longitude or latitude. Even so, the exact boundaries are often the cause of inter-state disputes. Sometimes, in ill-mapped territory, there is genuine uncertainty. Most frequently in recent years the quarrels have been political and not legal – related to ethnic distribution (see Chapter 8).

Two of the longest frontiers in the world are of interest. That between the United States and Canada is demilitarised by virtue of a treaty concluded between the United States and Great Britain in 1818. However, the nineteenth-century treaties between Russia and China have been constantly repudiated by the latter since 1949. The Chinese have argued that the territory ceded in their 'Great Northwest' by the Treaties of Chuguchak and Ili and in their 'Great Northeast' by the Treaties of Aigun and Peking should be restored. They base their case on the 'unequal treaties' imposed by a bullying tsarist government (see p. 207).

A state exercises jurisdiction not just over its land but also over its adjacent territorial sea. The breadth of this stretch of water has been the subject of considerable dispute and variation since the seventeenth century. By the nineteenth century most states accepted a three-mile limit. It was not, however, firmly established in international law. The matter was made tidy by the Law of the Sea Convention of 1982. This agreement provides that 'every state has the right to establish the breadth of its territorial sea up to a limit not exceeding 12 nautical miles' (Article 3, quoted Brownlie, 1990, p. 189). The Convention reiterates an earlier definition that sovereignty over the territorial sea includes the sea bed and its subsoil. It also provides for certain rights over the continental shelf if this exists beyond the twelve-mile limit. These are described as 'sovereign rights for the purpose of exploring it and exploiting its natural resources' (Article 77, quoted Brownlie, 1990, p. 218).

The airspace above land territory, internal waters and the territorial sea is also part of the territory of the state. Although the development of aerial transport has led to rapid codification of the law of the air, two interesting problems have been raised in recent years.

One concerns the sanctions that a state may legitimately exact for unauthorised trespass of its airspace. Legal opinion is that the destruction of the intruder is not legitimate. However, the Soviet Union did shoot down an American U-2 reconnaissance aircraft in 1960 and a Korean airliner in 1983. The first incident was perhaps a justifiable act of defence; the second, a tragic instance of overreaction. The second matter of interest is the failure of international law to define the vertical limit of airspace, or how high is the sky. The Treaty on Principles governing the Activities of States in the Exploration and Use of Outer Space, Including the Moon and

Other Celestial Bodies was signed in 1967. Article 2 specifies that outer space 'is not subject to national appropriation by claim of sovereignty' (quoted Brownlie, 1990, p. 268). But it fails to lay down a precise definition of outer space.

We may add as something of a footnote to this section a significant exception to the rule that a state has complete jursidiction within its territory. Accredited diplomats from a foreign state and the property of their legations have certain privileges and immunities. These are defined in the Vienna Convention on Diplomatic Relations of 1961 (see p. 47).

It will have been obvious from the foregoing material that the standing of the state in international law depends to a certain extent on treaties. We now therefore need to analyse this form of international agreement and source of international law.

Treaties

An extraordinary number of different words have been used to describe what we generally term a 'treaty'. That is only part of the confusion surrounding the drafting, implementation and interpretation of the thousands of international agreements or treaties, which Fawcett has called 'the staff of international life' (p. 96). In order to codify and simplify this area of international activity the United Nations established an International Law Commission, which has produced the following definition of a treaty:

> any international agreement in written form, whether embodied in a single instrument or in two or more instruments and whatever its particular designation (treaty, convention, protocol, covenant, charter, statute, act, declaration, concordat, exchange of notes, agreed minute, memorandum of agreement, *modus vivendi* or any other appellation), concluded between two or more States or other subjects of international law and governed by international law.
>
> (quoted, Brownlie, 1990, p. 605)

This work of the ILC was consolidated by the Vienna Convention on the Law of Treaties, which came into force in 1980.

Treaties may be concluded between two parties (bilateral) or more (multilateral). Most frequently the parties to the agreement are states, though they can be 'other subjects' such as organisations (for example, the UN). Commercial companies cannot conclude treaties. Nor, normally, can component states of federations. The main exception to this has been the Soviet Union, which, from 1944, allowed each of the constituent republics as a hypothetical constitutional right to conduct its own foreign policy and conclude treaties. This constitutional amendment helped to justify the separate representation of the Ukraine and Byelorussia in the UN.

Although treaties are sometimes renounced or become obsolete as a result of changing conditions, the general assumption of international law is that, once signed, a treaty remains binding. This well-established principle is summed up in the Latin tag *Pacta sunt servanda* – treaties must be obeyed. It is often the case, however, that a certain vagueness of wording is incorporated into the text so that the operation of a treaty can be modified and adapted according to circumstances.

Some authorities have identified a number of different functions that treaties are designed to perform, though a rigid classification has not found general favour. A treaty may be in the form of a contract between the signatories. In trading arrangements the most-favoured nation (MFN) concession is of this kind. This is an agreement by one state (A) not to impose trading restrictions on the other party (B) of any greater severity than those imposed by state A on its most liberally treated trading partner (C).

Other treaties with similar contractual obligations have the intention of being applied to the whole community of nations. For example, the Convention of Constantinople of 1888 made the Suez Canal a recognised international waterway; and even after its nationalisation in 1956, the Egyptian government maintained that the status held good.

A third purpose of treaties is to create an international organisation – as the Treaty of Rome, for instance, created the European Economic Community in 1957.

Finally, some treaties have the prime function of creating or codifying general international law. A great deal of work has been undertaken since the Second World War, for example, to codify the multifarious aspects of the law of the sea. The result has been the Law of the Sea Conventions of 1958 and 1982. Another very important area of 'law-making' treaties concerns the conduct of war: for example, the Hague Conventions of 1899 and 1907 on neutrality and the Geneva Protocol of 1925 on prohibited weapons.

The ceremony of signing a treaty, although the symbolic culmination of sometimes years of diplomatic negotiation and legal drafting, is not truly the completion of the treaty-making process. For instance, the US Constitution states that the President 'shall have power, by and with the consent of the Senate, to make treaties, provided two thirds of the Senators present concur' (Article II(2)). True, presidents have found ways of circumventing this requirement for ratification; nevertheless, some important treaties have been blocked because of Senate hostility, most notably the Treaty of Versailles after the First World War and more recently SALT II (see p. 39).

All international agreements entered into by the executive branch of the US government (when ratified, if so required) automatically become part of US law. This is the constitutional position in a number of other states. Alternatively, as in Britain, separate domestic legislation is required. For example, Britain signed the Treaty of Accession to the European Communities in January 1972; but this had to be followed by the European Communities Act, which was given the Royal Assent and therefore passed into UK law in October of that year in readiness for the start of British membership the following January. The term 'accession' requires a brief comment. Some treaties are designed in such a way as to allow or even positively encourage other states in addition to the original signatories to join the agreement whenever they so wish. An important example of this practice is the nuclear Non-Proliferation Treaty of 1968 (see p. 39).

The final authoritative seal on a treaty is its formal registration with the UN: 'Every treaty and every international agreement entered into by any Member of the United Nations . . . shall as soon as possible be registered with the Secretariat and published by it' (Article 102(1)). No party to a treaty can invoke the assistance of the UN in the event of a breach of an agreement if the text has not been so registered.

And complaints about treaties certainly are made. One of the most interesting reasons is the claim that some treaties are 'unequal'. This is a doctrine that has been used by Communist states and some former colonial territories. The arguments derive from the claimed injustice of treaty provisions exacted by exploiting bourgeois states and oppressive imperial powers respectively. We have already seen how China has used the argument against Russia (p. 204). However, it is a concept that is by no means universally recognised.

Despite the constant wrangling of states, most of them most of the time find it convenient, even essential, to have treaty relationships. Treaties provide comforting amicable connections. Let us, however, not forget the advice E.H. Carr gave over half a century ago:

> Respect for law and treaties will be maintained only in so far as the law recognises effective political machinery through which it can itself be modified and superseded. There must be a clear recognition of that play of political forces which is antecedent to all law.
>
> (Carr, 1939, p. 245)

Bibliography

Baldwin, D.A. (1985), *Economic Statecraft*, Princeton University Press: Princeton, NJ.

Ball, G. (1976), *Diplomacy for a Crowded World*, Little, Brown: Boston, and Bodley Head: London.

Barnaby, F. (ed.) (1988), *The Gaia Peace Atlas*, Pan: London.

Berridge, G.R. (1991), *Return to the UN: UN diplomacy in regional conflicts*, Macmillan: London.

Brandt Commission (1980), *North–South: A programme for survival*, Pan: London.

Brownlie, I. (1990), *Principles of Public International Law*, 4th edn, Clarendon Press: Oxford.

Bruntland Commission (1987), *Our Common Future*, Oxford University Press: Oxford.

Bull, H. (1977), *The Anarchical Society*, Macmillan: London.

Carr, E.H. (1939), *The Twenty Years' Crisis 1919–1939*, Macmillan: London.

Carter, J. (1982), *Keeping Faith: Memoirs of a President*, Collins: London.

CEWC, (1985), *Britain and UNESCO*, Council for Education in World Citizenship: London.

European Communities (1987), *Treaties Establishing the European Communities*, Office for Official Publications of the European Communities: Luxemburg.

Fawcett, J.E.S. (1968), *The Law of Nations*, Allen Lane The Penguin Press: London.

Forsyth, F. (1977), *The Making of an African Legend: The Biafra story*, Penguin: Harmondsworth.

Freedman, L. (ed.) (1990), *Europe Transformed: Documents on the end of the cold war*, Tri-Service: London.

Fukuyama, F. (1989), 'The end of history?', *The National Interest*.

Gorbachev, M. (1986), *Political Report of the CPSU Central Committee to the 27th Party Congress*, Novosti: Moscow.

Gorbachev, M. (1987), *Perestroika*, Collins: London.

Gromyko, A. (1989) *Memories*, Hutchinson: London.
Halliday, F. (1974), *Arabia Without Sultans*, Penguin: Harmondsworth.
Harbottle, M. (1975 rev. edn.), *The Blue Berets*, Cooper: London.
Hiro, D. (1988), *Islamic Fundamentalism*, Paladin: London.
Hoggart, R. (1978), *An Idea and its Servants: UNESCO from within*, Chatto & Windus: London.
Hufbauer, G.C. and J.J. Schott (1985), *Economic Sanctions Reconsidered: History and current policy*, Institute for International Economics: Washington, DC.
Humana, C. (1983), *World Human Rights Guide*, Hutchinson: London.
Kaldor, M. (1982), *The Baroque Arsenal*, Deutsch: London.
Kennedy, P. (1988), *The Rise and Fall of the Great Powers*, Fontana: London.
Kissinger, H.A. (1979), *The White House Years*, Little, Brown: Boston, and Weidenfeld & Nicolson and Michael Joseph: London.
Kohn, N. (1955), *Nationalism*, Van Nostrand, New York.
Little, R. and M. Smith (1991), *Perspectives on World Politics*, Routledge: London.
Luard, E. (1981), *Human Rights and Foreign Policy*, Pergamon: Oxford.
Macartney, C.A. (1934), *National States and National Minorities*, Oxford University Press: Oxford.
Maddison, J. (1985), *UNESCO and Britain: The end of a special relationship*?, Museum & Archives Development Associates: Royston, Herts.
Mayall, J. (1984), 'The sanctions problem in international economic relations: reflections in the light of experience', *International Affairs*, vol. 60, no. 4.
Mill, J.S. (1861, 1910 edn.), *Considerations on Representative Government*, Dent: London.
Morley, J. (1903), *The Life of William Ewart Gladstone*, vol. II, Macmillan: London.
NATO (1981), *The North Atlantic Treaty Organisation: Facts and figures*, NATO: Brussels.
NATO Review, August 1990, December 1990, February 1991.
Nicolson, H. (1969, 3rd edn.), *Diplomacy*, Oxford University Press: London, Oxford and New York.
Nyerere, J.K. (1974), *Man and Development*, Oxford University Press: Dar-es-Salaam.
Prins, G. (ed.) (1983), *Defended to Death*, Penguin: Harmondsworth.
Renwick, R. (1981), *Economic Sanctions*, Harvard University Center for International Affairs: Cambridge, MA.
Roberts, A. (1991), 'A new age in international relations?', *International Affairs*, vol. 67, no. 3.
Rogers, P. (1991), 'Myth of a clean war buried in the sand', *Guardian*, 19 September.
Ryssdal, R. (1989), '30th anniversary of the European Court of Human Rights', *Forum*, 2/89, Council of Europe: Strasbourg.
Sampson, A. (1977), *The Arms Bazaar*, Hodder & Stoughton: London.

Schreiber, A.P. (1973), 'Economic coercion as an instrument of foreign policy: US economic measures against Cuba and the Dominican Republic', *World Politics*, vol. 25, no. 3.

Smith, A.D. (1991), *National Identity*, Penguin: Harmondsworth.

Starke, J.G. (1947), *An Introduction to International Law*, Butterworth: London.

Tocqueville, A. de (1956, ed. R.D. Heffner), *Democracy in America*, Mentor: New York.

Uldricks, T.J. (1979), *Diplomacy and Ideology: The origins of Soviet foreign relations, 1917–1930*, Sage: Beverly Hills and London.

Urquhart, B. (1990), 'Beyond the "sheriff's posse" ', *Survival*, May/June.

Verrier, A. (1981), *International Peacekeeping: United Nations forces in a troubled world*, Penguin: Harmondsworth.

Wight, M. (1979), *Power Politics*, Penguin: Harmondsworth.

Williams, D. (1987), *The Specialized Agencies and the United Nations*, Hurst: London.

Zielonka, J. (1991), 'Europe's security: a great confusion', *International Affairs*, vol. 67, no. 1.

Index

Previous books by Derek Heater

Political Ideas in the Modern World (Harrap, London, 1st edn 1960, 4th edn 1971)
Contemporary Political Ideas (Longman, London, 1st edn 1974, 2nd edn 1983)

Britain and the Outside World (Longman, London, 1976)

Our World Today (Oxford University Press, Oxford, 1st edn 1985, 2nd edn 1990)

Citizenship: The civic ideal in world history, politics and education (Longman, London, 1990)

The Idea of European Unity (University Press, Leicester 1992)

Previous books by G. R. Berridge

Economic Power in Anglo-South African Diplomacy (Macmillan, London, 1981)

Diplomacy at the UN, ed. with A. Jennings (Macmillan, London and St Martin's Press, New York, 1985)

The Politics of the South Africa Run: European shipping and Pretoria (The Clarendon Press, Oxford, 1987)

Return to the UN: UN diplomacy in regional conflicts (Macmillan, London, 1991)

International Politics: States, power and conflict since 1945 (Harvester, Hemel Hempstead, 1st edn 1987, 2nd edn 1992)

South Africa, the Colonial Powers and 'African Defence': The rise and fall of the white entente, 1948–60 (Macmillan, London, 1992)